SAVANNAH SPECTRES
AND OTHER STRANGE TALES

Margaret DeBolt

For Frank, who is keeping an open mind

SAVANNAH SPECTRES AND OTHER STRANGE TALES

By Margaret Wayt DeBolt

The Donning Company/Publishers
Norfolk/Virginia Beach

Distributed by
Schiffer Publishing Ltd.
77 Lower Valley Road, Atglen, PA 19310

Distribution by Schiffer Publishing, Ltd.
77 Lower Valley Road
Atglen, PA 19310
Please write for a free catalog.
This book may be purchased from the publisher.
Please include $2.95 postage.
Try your bookstore first.

We are interested in hearing from authors
with book ideas on related subjects.

The Donning Company/Publishers
184 Business Park Drive, Suite 106
Virginia Beach, Virginia 23462

Library of Congress Cataloging in Publication Data

DeBolt, Margaret Wayt, 1930–
         Savannah spectres.

         1. Ghosts—Georgia—Savannah Region. I. Title.
BF1472.U6D42   1983   133.1'09758'724   82-23455
ISBN 0-89865-201-4 (pbk.)

Printed in the United States of America

Contents

Introduction

In Search of Spectres

"Ghosts are strange beings which other people have seen," I might have quipped when I began this work several years ago. Like the writer who said, "I do not believe in ghosts, but I am afraid of them," I put such things in the category of legend and superstition, charming escapism from the grimmer horror stories of modern life.

Early in my residence in Savannah I realized that the area, and indeed all of Dixie, seemed to have more than its share of what the Scotsman called "things that go bump in the night." From restored townhouses on the historic squares, when a gentle presence might come with the lease, to newer homes on the sites of old plantations and battlefields, each has its story. So do the forts, house museums and restored waterfront of Georgia's first city, which has survived pirates, wars, two military occupations, fires, epidemics, and tourist popularity after decades of genteel "too poor to paint, too proud to whitewash" poverty.

"Are there really ghosts in the South?" asks author Mary Allice Kellogg, who also answers: "You bet your sweet magnolia there are! The antebellum South isn't dead—it's merely wandering, rising, hovering and drifting from plantation to plantation, searching for lost loves and old enemies. And in the process, it's scaring the bejesus out of a lot of normally sensible folk."

In his book *The Phantoms of Dixie*, ghost hunter Hans Holzer, who has visited Savannah, theorizes that the area has more than its share of such stories because "Dixie is not a place: it's a state of mind. . . . The slower, more tradition-bound atmosphere of the Southern states tends to encourage a preoccupation with the occult. The personal attitude of many Southerners in the unseen differs sharply from that of the Northerner. . . . In the South, one takes these things in stride, especially when the story being told is romantic, and interesting. And Southerners are great story tellers."

Holzer believes that another influence is the region's old houses,

1

"built by families of long standing and great repute. . .a continuous emotional tie with the past." The Anglo-Saxon Celtic heritage seems to play a part, for the early settlers brought with them a healthy respect for such experiences. To this in the Low Country was added the African heritage of voodoo and Gullah, the unique black culture which thrived for over 200 years at isolated coastal islands.

This work was begun with the innocent aim of compiling a short collection of Savannah's plentiful stories. It was undertaken more in the spirit of dealing with legends and folklore than eyewitness experience. Some had already been written on the subject, but I knew that much more was available.

At the time, I had never felt a presence of the sort the stories describe. A few unusual experiences, however, lingered in the back of my mind. They were vivid because they were not legend, but had happened to real, average people that I knew.

Such experiences would have seemed too fragmented to mention if I had not in the meantime met Stephen, the friend who is both a historian and a psychic. As a result of our first conversation, this work took a different and much deeper approach to what I had at first seen as a summer's project. What would it be like, I wondered, to visit some of the area's most famous houses with a psychic sensitive, recording his impressions and talking with the people who live there now?

Stephen was frankly ambivalent about the proposal. Since he considers his gifts God-given and very real, he feels they should not be taken lightly. In particular, he warned me, any effort on his part to use them for his own benefit, or "on cue," had never been successful.

Too, he works professionally in the museum curatorial field. While his unique ability has occasionally helped him by allowing him to visualize a room or a piece of furniture in an earlier setting, which he then verifies through research, he did not desire a general advertisement of his talents. As he put it, "I don't do Halloween talk shows."

At the same time, he was intrigued by the offer. If it could be done, he told me, in the spirit of deeper inquiry into the most essential matters of life, it would be worthwhile.

Whenever possible, our method of investigation was to visit a site and get Stephen's first impressions before hearing the story of the location. Where this was not possible, in cases where the stories were already well known, such as the Pirates' House and the one on St. Julian Street where an exorcism was once performed, we could only strive for objectivity.

In some cases, legendary tales seemed affirmed, as in our visit to the Pirates' House with sensitives Lorraine and Ed Warren, internationally known "ghost hunters." In others, past mysteries seemed to be explained, such as the little old lady in a long dress who used to be seen in the garden of the Owens-Thomas House.

No attempt was made to "catch a ghost" with a tape recorder, thermometer, or high-speed camera, except for one which Stephen sometimes carried for his own records. For one thing, I suspect any self-respecting presence would have as much contempt for such devices as for the conventions of our time and apparent reality. I had also been warned by other reporters of occult topics that such equipment has a maddening way of not working at times, for whatever reasons you care to imagine.

Every effort was made to get as much information as possible about the persons and places visited, using a reporter's instincts as to the sincerity and stability of subjects interviewed. The seeming normality of those with the most startling tales was one revelation of our search.

In some instances, however, we avoided or downplayed interviews because of suspected emotional problems which we did not want to encourage. Those who seemed too much to want a presence in their homes were also suspect, perhaps unfairly.

Where requested, we have protected the identity and privacy of the person interviewed. One can only offer a past reputation as a journalist in stating that such interviews took place. Writing fiction would have been simpler.

The American Heritage Dictionary of the English Language defines the word spectre as "a ghost, phantom, apparition. A mental image, phantasm. A forboding." That will do, although some of our contacts prefer the word presence, which they feel is more indicative of the sensation of energy or being present, if sometimes unseen.

When this inquiry began with a series of articles for *Savannah Magazine*, some of my colleagues found the topic too vague for serious study. Others worried that I was not only encouraging a dangerous influence, but might even be flirting with supernatural forces of evil.

Some might question whether a book such as this is a valid project in a world where research into such things as dreams and extrasensory perception (ESP) and in-depth study of paranormal happenings are being carried out in sophisticated university laboratories.

My answer is that much of what we were told would never have come to light in such a situation—the inexplicable "everyday" experiences of very normal people. Persons sharing such stories had

3

little motive except an honest interest in the subject. They were not compensated for even their time, and in most cases they asked to be anonymous.

The comments made by Stephen at sites visited or in answers to questions some of the persons asked about their experiences, are also included. They have been, however, somewhat edited and compressed in order to avoid repetition, where they were given in general conversation over a period of time. In the process, which took not only a summer, but several years, my own ideas changed considerably.

"Matter can neither be created nor destroyed," says my husband, Frank, a sensible scientist and engineer. If this thought is applied to the spirit which animates the body, the thing called a soul, it seems also likely that spark must go on in some form after death, and not be simply extinguished forever.

"The deeper I get into this subject, the less I know for sure," says Naomi Hintze, gothic novelist and co-author of *The Psychic Realm: What Can We Believe?* So we found it, as each case seemed to take us deeper into the unknown rather than closer to any answers.

What we have been told is offered for the instruction of those who may be able to use it as a stepping stone toward further knowledge. As a footnote to the rich cultural heritage of the area, some folklore and very old stories are included. So are other relevant anecdotes from people interviewed, and some stories of houses I had visited before meeting Stephen.

In the process, I never saw a spectre—but I've talked with plenty of Middle America, Norman Rockwellish people who swear they have. I had one ESP experience which probably saved a good friend's life, and I've walked through rooms with chills you wouldn't believe.

I also saw a locked door open. But more about that later.

I would like to thank the many who helped with and encouraged this work, including many who shared painful and even embarrassing memories. Some of this material previously appeared as a series in *Savannah Magazine*, with former editor and publisher Dr. Ilse and Marshall Earl as supportive friends.

I am grateful to the area artists who allowed the use of their drawings of historic houses, and to my good friend Yon Swanson of Tybee Beach, who contributed several original drawings. For the help of friends and family, and the patience of Bob and Donna Friedman of Donning Publishers, who have waited a long time for this book, I am especially thankful.

—Margaret Wayt DeBolt

The Door Opens

"Well, have you seen any ghosts yet?" friends would occasionally ask me during my work on this book. When I would reply, "No, but I've seen a locked door open," the conversation would generally turn to another subject. What had happened was too complicated to easily explain. Besides, it had been in broad daylight, and with three other people present, on the November afternoon when I first met Stephen.

The door, which I later took to be symbolic, belongs to Claire, a friend who is an artist and lives in a small white concrete house near White Bluff Road. We had first met earlier by telephone during a call-in show conducted that Halloween by "Easy Ed" Hartley, a radio personality who has since relocated to Columbia, South Carolina. Claire and I had been invited to be on his show because we had both written articles on Savannah ghost stories that month for different publications.

I found her contribution to the show, especially her accounts of personal experiences, so interesting that I asked her if I could discuss them with her later in more detail. She readily agreed, suggesting a Sunday afternoon at her home. Claire also mentioned that she had a friend named Stephen, a young man whom she knew was quite psychic, but who generally avoided discussing the subject with anyone else. As a favor to her, she added, he might consent to join us.

Ringing Claire's doorbell that first afternoon, I found her to be a small, attractive woman of obvious breeding, education, and intelligence, who welcomed me warmly to her comfortable home and studio. Examples of her art, from autumn New England and winter snow scenes to her more recent Thunderbolt shrimp boats and Savannah townhouses, were in evidence, representative of the years which she had spent in the north before moving to Savannah.

Stephen, who was already there when I arrived, was equally compatible. He was a tall, slender, polite young man, reserved at

5

first, but articulate on the subject which we had gathered to discuss as the conversation flourished. It was clearly one on which he had done a great deal of reading and thinking, as had Claire. The two also had their interest in art in common, and a love of music, having both sung in the choir of St. John's Episcopal Church in Savannah.

What ensued as we three sat together that afternoon was one of those magical and relaxing times of total rapport. Meeting for the first time we were like old friends, comparing our years of similar likes and dislikes, favorite authors, and common experiences. Feelings of *deja vu*, ESP, and precognitive dreams were confided, some for the first time.

Some of the time was spent in discussing an acquaintance of theirs who had died not long before, a talented and sensitive artist named Harlan, who had also had a strong interest in the psychic, and they had shared a dramatic precognitive experience with him.

Stephen remarked that he had also sensed the presence of this man several times soon after his death, but had resisted the feeling. He feared the older man wanted to influence his work and continue to paint through him. "Harlan was very fond of painting sea shells," he said. "It worried me when I found myself suddenly doing them for the first time in my life, and the painting itself better than anything I had done before. It was too much like an attempt at possession. I saw him several times in my apartment after he died, and so did my Sheltie, Christopher Robin."

At that point, Stephen had to interrupt his story of Harlan to drive a few blocks and pick up his mother, Etolia, who had called asking if she could join us. When he returned with her, and followed her through Claire's front door, he closed it firmly behind him. It opened again.

"Close that door, Stephen," Claire prompted from the kitchen, where she was preparing a platter of iced tea and fresh ginger cookies. He did so, and we all sat down in the living room. The conversation resumed, and Claire passed the cookies. The door opened again behind us. With some impatience, Claire went to close it. She locked it this time with a resounding click.

She sat down and sipped her tea as Stephen resumed his story about Harlan. To our amazement, the door opened again.

"Why, hello," Claire surprised me by saying pleasantly in that direction. "Come in, and make yourself at home." Then she crossed to the door and locked it, this time putting the night chain across the top.

"Are you having trouble with your door, Claire?" Stephen asked as she sat down again in her green armchair.

6

"Not that I know about," she replied. "I don't understand it. You were just out, and you know there is no wind. . . . It's never done this before."

That time, the door stayed closed until we were ready to leave several hours later. The next week, Claire told me that on a very windy day, she had deliberately left the door unlocked to see if it would open again. It did not.

"I only had one other experience with that door," she told me much later. "You know I throw my junk mail in the fireplace in cool weather, and burn it every night. One day I came in from outside, sorting the mail, and threw a few pieces on the grate. Just as I did so, the door opened. A voice seemed to say, not out loud but in my mind, 'Look in the fireplace.'

"I did, and found, between two large pieces of advertising, a check I had been waiting for! To think, I nearly burned it, as I was about to light it all off.

"'Thank you,' I said to the quiet room, and thought of your first Sunday here."

The Man with a Knife

The precognitive incident which we had been discussing as the door came open, concerned a vision in which Stephen had not only seen Harlan's home on West Gordon Street before he had actually been there, but also a violent scene which was about to occur in it.

"The strange thing about it," Claire began the story again after our interruptions, "was that I knew Harlan better than Stephen did. We had our art in common, and the fact that we had both lived in New Jersey. But Stephen had this vision, in which he saw the townhouse and a blond woman screaming, and a man with a cap pulled down over his eyes, and a knife in his hand. This was taking place on the ground floor. The man had come in an unlocked door, and that is the way he ran out, and was gone through the garden and over the fence.

"I was a little amused at the way Stephen told it to me," she recalled, "since Harlan was a confirmed bachelor! I just couldn't see a young woman living there. 'Are you sure it was Harlan's place?' I insisted. Stephen went on to describe the furnishings as he had seen them, such as the blue and white vase on the old yellow chest in the den, with some dried ferns in it, and some old wooden weights hanging from the ceiling. 'Tell him to keep that downstairs door locked,' he repeated. All this had suddenly come to him in a moment, while we were talking on the phone about Harlan.

"Well," Claire continued, "I couldn't wait to get over there to check out the things Stephen had described! I had been there briefly, but had never paid that much attention. There they were, even to some leopard print cushions he had also mentioned! I still didn't understand the premonition. But I passed the warning along in a general way: I didn't want to scare him too much.

"Well, a little later, would you believe, a young blond woman named Kitty asked him if she could live in the downstairs of the house on the ground floor just until she could find a place! He said yes; he lived upstairs.

"Not long after that, one evening he heard her screaming. He came tearing down the stairs just in time to see a young man with a knife, and a cap pulled over his eyes, go flying out the back door, through the garden, and over the fence! He had been hiding in the bath downstairs, after sneaking in a door she had carelessly left open a few minutes before. When he saw Harlan, he decided to run. So, it all came true."

"I only saw Harlan about eight times, five while he was alive," said Stephen. "The other three were in my apartment on Jones Street. One time my dog saw him first, and he growled. I could see his reflection in the dog's eyes, before I turned to where he had materialized. Another time, I was sleeping and the dog barked. I saw Harlan standing by the door to my room, which was closed. The room had suddenly become freezing cold. Then, he disappeared.

"At the time, I had a small cribbage board of his up on the third shelf of my etagere. I put it in the closet. A few days later I came into my apartment, and saw that it was back on the third shelf.

"At that time, the thought was in my mind that he was there and wanting to paint through me. As I told you, when I sat down to work, it was suddenly sea shells, better than I had done anything before. I didn't want to go that route! When he materialized, I could also hear him saying in my mind, 'Let's paint. Move that piano out, and set up the easel.' The piano stayed.

"One time, he materialized by the aquarium, and stayed about three minutes, then gradually faded.

"About this time," Stephen continued, "I was at a party downtown one night, and some people were working a Ouija board. I think they are dangerous, nothing to play with, so I stayed in the other room away from the whole thing. Suddenly, someone who knew nothing of all this, came to the door and said, 'Hey, we have someone on the board who says he wants to talk to Stephen. Says his name is Harlan.'

"That was the end of the party for me! I was out that door, and gone! After that, he must have realized it was futile.

"Another strange thing," Stephen concluded. "At the time of his death, the alarm clock in my apartment stopped. It has not run since, though it was a fairly new clock."

"I have always thought there was something very strange about our whole relationship with Harlan," added Claire. "You know I do believe in reincarnation, and that we go on working out relationships with one another in different lives. It has come to me that Harlan and I were married in 17th-century England, and Stephen was our son.

He also feels strongly about that period, as he will tell you.

"I don't think we did too well as parents then, and maybe we were getting a second chance."

Reflections on a Mixed Blessing

As I talked with Stephen on that first afternoon at Claire's about his psychic abilities, he told me that like her, he had been aware of them since childhood. "As a boy," he said, "I would sometimes see people quite clearly, and when I got closer to them, they would just disappear. Later, those same people would actually come to visit! It took me awhile to figure that one out!

"I remember once we were driving over to South Carolina. I pointed out an old black man I saw climbing a fence. The others in the car all asked, 'What man?'"

According to Stephen, his sensitivity has taken the form at different times of precognitive dreams, premonitions of coming events, sensitivity to a presence, and experiences suggestive of reincarnation. He is also what psychic Lorraine Warren calls a light trance medium, capable of being seemingly transported at times to the past, while in a certain location.

He stressed that while he had experienced all these at one time or another, they could come and go without warning, and were affected by weather and medication. "Cool, dry days are the most conductive," he explained. "There are times in the fall when I feel I am getting so much information at once, that I can hardly stand it!

"On the other hand," he said, "it is often difficult for a psychic person to get guidance about their own situation. Sometimes what you feel is not what you want to believe, as when you would like to trust a certain person, yet something seems to hold you back. You tend to hope, but be wary.

"Such a psychic person is rather difficult to surprise," he added with a smile. "I generally know what I'm getting for Christmas. But, the premonitions are not always pleasant. There is no worse feeling than to know you are going to have an accident, and being powerless to prevent it! Once when this happened to me, I walked around with a sick feeling for three days, trying to be extra careful but not getting

11

so anxious that it would affect my judgment.

"The accident, when I finally had it, was at night at the corner of Washington and Abercorn Streets. I stopped for a light, and was hit hard, from behind. Knocked across the intersection. At the same time, a car going very fast ran the red light from the other direction. If I had not stopped, I would probably have been killed.

"Sometimes I instinctively know if the time is right for me to do something. This may seem like procrastination to some, but until you get that positive feeling, it's like taking a psychic wave-off, in aviation language. You have to listen to your feelings, and be able to act on them."

After going through a period of actively wanting to develop his psychic potential, and realizing he was able to go further than he necessarily wanted to go, Stephen said that he had gone to an attitude of taking impressions as they came, but not actively seeking them. "It is nothing to play with," he repeated his earlier comment about a dislike of Ouija boards. He added that he did believe there were really disembodied spirits, often evil or confused, which were attracted to such things, and to seances. "These are sometimes called 'drop-ins,'" he explained. "No, thank you!

"I believe in the struggle for good against evil in this world, and that the power for good must ultimately be the stronger," he said. "I do wear a cross as protection against the powers of evil, which I think are very real, and I would suggest that you do so, too, if you really want to visit some 'haunted' houses. You don't want to take 'anyone' home with you."

I remarked that Sybil Leek, the English practitioner of witch-craft, who, like Hans Holzer, has visited Savannah, says that a cross is only powerful against demons from the Christian ethic. "I would disagree with that," he replied. "You have to believe that the power of a Christian cross is stronger than any evil, or you wouldn't wear one."

As we discussed various fortune telling methods, such as crystal balls and tea leaves, which he had never used, he remarked, "I believe those are actually just props to help a person concentrate, to center their attention," a statement which Emily Trammer was later to confirm of her use of cards to predict the future. "I do believe that anything seen in these things may be available if the situation is right. If this is unfavorable, it is good to be warned.

"On the other hand, I don't necessarily believe that it must happen. I do believe that we can with our own actions, sometimes change or avoid certain things. Otherwise, I would believe in the Calvinist doctrine of predestination, which I find very depressing.

"I do believe," Stephen continued, "that certain objects can be imbued with evil. For instance, I wouldn't have the Hope diamond!

"I also believe that certain houses have impressions of good or evil imprinted in their atmosphere. Sometimes they also have active or passive presences. For instance, a friend wanted me to go with him to look at a white stucco house on Liberty Street here which was available for renovation. I have never felt worse vibrations of cruelty in my life! We went up to the second floor. I had the continual impression that a male presence, a big, husky man, was there, and that he wanted to push me through a broken place in the old railing.

"Going down the stairs, which were very old, with a comparatively low railing, I had the feeling of being forced over toward the long drop to the front hall. I hugged the wall all the way down, and ruined a good white summer sports coat in the process! My friend took my advice and did not buy the house. Later, a man moved in that had been accused of murder, but acquitted. I've often wondered what the presence and he thought of one another! I understand that workmen there have also reported strange footsteps and other activity on the second floor.

"Another example of this is a house downtown on East Liberty Street, a two-story house built of Belgian block. It is said that a couple once lived there with their son, a priest. One day they are supposed to have come home and found him hanging in the stairwell, where he had hanged himself.

"Later, this same house was used for storage by a company next door. People working there didn't want to go in it because of its cold, depressing atmosphere. I understand they could also sense the presence of a man, and hear him rocking in the stairwell."

In a happier context, Stephen recalled that he had grown up in the area near 36th Street and Bonaventure Road, which had once been an old plantation. One day, he found a very old, long-handled cooking spoon in the back yard under some bushes. "I picked it up," he said, "and suddenly I was picturing an antebellum house, the swish of petticoats, the scent of roses...sometimes, either through visiting a house or picking up an object from that time, we can sense what has gone before."

As we discussed presences, Stephen said that for him they could be detected by the altered quality of the atmosphere in some houses. He explained that this might take the form of a chilled feeling, which has led to the theory that the presence is drawing from the available heat in the room, for the energy to materialize. He then went on to say that a great range of energy is involved, from very low level presences, which seem to repeat a certain experience or motion over

13

and over, to the more active ones which appear to make decisions and act on their own, and may even be aware of others now in "their" homes.

More intensive forms of energy are thought to result in poltergeists, the German "noisy spirits," or psychic kinetic energy, which moves objects and frequently causes real disturbances. "A ghost won't stay with a poltergeist," he added. Often, an adolescent child, sometimes one who is physically or mentally handicapped, is found in the house where this type of activity occurs. This suggests that their budding and repressed sexual energies may be involved in the activity in some way.

"There is so much we don't know yet," said Stephen. "For instance, in cases where people say they heard a terrible crash and yet find nothing out of place, it would appear that for some reason the psychic energy there has built up, until it is released all at once in that way."

As we spoke of presences, Stephen said that it appeared that sometimes it is an earth-bound spirit, lost and confused, which does not realize yet that the person involved has died. "This seems to happen most often with a head injury," he said, "this not knowing to go on....Sometimes other spirits come back to help them, or a psychic living person tries to get the point across, that they should go on.

"At other times you have a very protective ghost, looking over a certain loved spot, or one who feels that his or her job here is not done yet.

"Sometimes I wonder how many of the people I think I see walking the streets of Savannah, are really there," he continued. "For instance, I saw what I know was a presence on York Street, near the Federal Building, just last week.

"An older man I had known, a man in his late 70's, had died of cancer not long before. I had not been able to attend the funeral, though I had meant to go. Well, I was walking along the street, and suddenly I saw three men coming toward me, each walking separately along a pretty busy street. I recognized the center one as this man. He was wearing grey slacks and a sweater, as he often did.

"When he was about ten feet away, before I could speak to him, he just disappeared. The other two were real enough, and each passed by as I just stood there! It wasn't as though I had been expecting him, or we had been especially close, though I saw him at church, and we often spoke. He was just walking along the street, and then he was gone. As a matter of fact, he looked so natural, it wasn't until later that I realized he was dead."

Stephen added that he believed he had inherited his psychic abilities from his mother, Etolia, and from her father. "There is definitely a psychic connection between us, too," he went on. "This may not be too unusual, but the experience we had one night during a bad wind storm, illustrates what I mean."

"Oh, that," said his mother. "First I woke to the sound of a falling tree limb, and I looked out the window. I saw that a power line was down across the back yard, arcing and emitting sparks in a dangerous fashion. 'I've got to call my neighbor, and the power company, and waken Stephen,' I thought almost simultaneously. As I dialed the telephone, he appeared sleepily in the doorway.

"'What do you want?' he asked. He had the distinct impression, he said, that I had been in his room, shaking him awake, when I had in reality just thought of doing so."

A MATTER OF DREAMS

"For the most part," Etolia continued, "my premonitions have taken the form of dreams." She added that in one of these, she dreamed of a former employer on the night he died. The manner in which she would learn of the death, by a minister at the door, was also revealed just as it was to happen.

On another occasion, she dreamed that Stephen's dog was sleeping on her bed. At the sound of her late father's very distinctive whistle, the dog jumped up and ran into another room. A few days later, it died after finding some poisoned meat.

"In one of my most vivid dreams," she added, "I saw a wide marble staircase in what was obviously the hall of a very elegant mansion. Stacks of books were piled all over the steps, and I was walking up the steps carrying more. I couldn't imagine what the books were doing in such a grand setting.

"Then I decided to go back to college, at what was then Armstrong Junior College in the old Armstrong mansion on Gaston Street. As I walked through the wide hall and up the stairs with my books, I realized it was the place I'd seen before, books and all!"

The Restless Past:
Old Shadows in a New House

One of Savannah's most unusual houses in terms of what a family has experienced there, is not an antebellum mansion, or a restored townhouse on a historic square. It is, instead, a pleasant but conventional one-story home in suburbia, not far from Oglethorpe Mall on the southside of the city. The family has asked not to be identified.

The woman to whom these extraordinary events occurred is a friendly, stable young business woman, deeply religious, with a devoted husband and four lively children. It is only after one has talked with her for awhile that the feeling of uneasiness begins at the events which she so calmly describes, and the chill, and the small hairs rising on the back of one's neck. . . .

"First of all there was the location, the land," she told Stephen and I when we visited her one Sunday afternoon.

At the time she first saw it, she said, she and her growing family were living in another nearby development, some ten years ago. It was in a house "like all the others on the street," which bored and depressed her, but one which she had no real hope of leaving until the children were grown.

"One day I was in the car, driving over to see my mother, who lives not far from here," our hostess explained. "Somehow, and I still have no conscious memory of how, I found myself driving down this street. I had never been here before, but I seemed to know where I was going. There were only a few houses here then. I found I was stopping in front of this lot, then vacant and overgrown. I said to myself, 'That's where I'm going to build my house!'

"Well, of course, when I went home and told my husband, he thought I was crazy. Sensibly, he pointed out to me that it was financially just impossible. At my urging, he did agree to drive by and look at the location. On that trip, I located a 'for sale' sign in the underbrush, and contacted the owner. It turned out to be a man in

Atlanta who really wanted to sell the land, and he accepted our offer, much to my husband's surprise.

"After that, things fell into place. Friends and relatives helped, we sold the other house, breaks came our way in terms of material and equipment. It all seemed too good to be true. At last, we moved in, not long after our fourth child was born."

Almost from the beginning, she went on, strange things happened in the house, such as noises and appearances and disappearances of material objects. "At first I didn't connect it to the house, or the supernatural! I was a good Baptist, had taught Sunday School, sang in the choir. The thought of ghosts and hauntings was against everything I believed, or so it seemed.

"Instead, I blamed myself. I began to think I was losing my mind! When I tried to discuss these things with my husband, he said it was only my imagination, that I was alone in the house too much with the baby. Finally, in desperation, I made an appointment to discuss the situation with my minister.

"Fortunately for me," she continued, "he understood completely! He told me there was more to this life than what we can touch and see. When I told him I was afraid, he said gently, 'Are you afraid of God? Remember these experiences are a part of life, though we may not understand them now.'

"So much had happened," she added. "It was hard to explain it at first to anyone. But what a relief to talk about it!

"We had noticed that the disturbances in the house, loud noises and such, that kept us awake, seemed to occur most at the time of the new moon. The full moon would also bring some, but not as much.

"On this particular night, I had gotten up to check on the baby. I couldn't sleep anyway, with these weird creakings and so forth in the house. I came back, laid down on my bed, and tried to relax. Suddenly, I had the strange feeling that I was floating! I couldn't seem to help myself. I was still in my room, but now it was another period of time. I saw three people, dressed in the clothing of about 200 years ago.

"First, there was a man whom I sensed was a servant. He was just there, waiting. He had on a brown leather jerkin or vest, and a white shirt with loose, full sleeves. His hair was long, and tied back with a black ribbon.

"The second person was a blond woman, whose hair was done up in a kind of pompadour style. She was holding an old-fashioned lantern. I sensed there was a strong bond of affection between her and the third woman, who appeared to be getting ready to go somewhere. She was wearing a drab, coat-style dress with a small pattern, a plain dark dress you'd describe as one for traveling. Her hair, too, was long and piled up on her head, with one long curl down on her shoulder.

"The blond woman was saying, in a concerned voice, 'How long do you think you will be gone?'

"The second was answering very calmly, 'As long as the Lord prepares a place for me, I'll be there.'

"Then the first woman held the lantern up closer, as the second buttoned her sleeves . . . several little tiny buttons were on each wrist, I remember. I nearly fainted when the lantern lit up her face. It was me! It was my face, my long, thin hands, my dark hair. But something was wrong; I couldn't place what was different."

As she told the story to her pastor, he gently pointed out what the change had been. She was probably speaking in an eighteenth century, British accent, and she was without the glasses she now wears constantly.

"Why, no wonder the other woman was holding the lantern so close," she exclaimed at the revelation. "You know I can't see a thing without my glasses!"

There were other times, she told her pastor, when she seemed to hear the blond woman's voice in her room, calling to her at night. "Try not to be afraid," he had counseled her. "Remember that the power of God is stronger than any evil. If it is a soul in distress, you may be able to help. Next time, say to the voice, 'What, in the name of Jesus Christ, can I do to help you?'"

"Me! Talk to a spirit! I wouldn't dare!" she had exclaimed.

But when the voice came again in her room a few nights later, she forced herself to take his advice. She sensed that it was indeed the blond woman, standing by her bed. Gathering all her courage, she replied as she had been instructed.

"At first I felt foolish, lying there in bed talking out loud," she recalled. "But then the words calmed me. Suddenly, I wasn't afraid any more.

"That time there was no answer. Then the voice came again, just as it had the first time. A little stronger now, I made the same reply."

"Please bury a Bible in your back yard," was the surprising answer.

When the woman repeated this to her pastor the next day, he advised her to comply immediately with the request. That afternoon, a Saturday, she wrapped a Bible in plastic, and carefully buried it under the azaleas, just outside their bedroom wall.

"Well, that night was the worst we had in the house," she recalled. "You never heard such a racket. Banging, banging noises outside that wall all night long! It was impossible to sleep. All we could do, my husband and I, was to pray. And we did.

"But I had made up my mind that I loved that house. I had gone through a lot to live there. In spite of the problems, I felt that it was where I belonged. I was not going to give up, and run away now."

The next morning the sleepy couple and their children went off to church services. When they returned, three large dogs were lying over the spot in the yard where the Bible was buried.

"Now, I'm an animal lover," she interjected. "These were dogs from the neighborhood that we knew, just as we knew the children. They had all been in our yard before. Yet, on that day when we walked out to pet them, they bared their teeth and growled, ferociously! I couldn't believe it.

"I turned and went into the house. During the afternoon, I'd look out; the dogs would still be there. Eventually, the owners came looking for them. Same thing. They also refused food and water, and the children went home without them. So far as I know, they laid over that newly-dug hole for three days, growling and snarling at anyone who came near.

"When they finally left, my husband said, 'Are you going to dig the Bible back up now?'

"'Never, unless I'm told to! The voice only said bury it; nothing was said about taking it back!'

"Strangely enough," our hostess continued, "that was the first of three incidents here concerning Bibles.

"Soon after these things started, when we first moved in, I had decided to do some research on the property. I went to the Georgia Historical Society, and a very helpful woman said, 'Oh, that's the old Holloman plantation. We have a colonial map of that area,' and off she went with some keys. She said it was in a locked case.

"Well, then she opened the case, the map was gone! Believe me, she was quite put out. Old maps are not supposed to just disappear from under lock and key. But to me, it was in keeping with everything else that had happened.

"We were able to find out that the original plantation was part of an early land grant that had stretched at one time from the Wilmington River to White Bluff Road. There are still some huge old oaks here, and there is supposed to be an old cemetery in the area. No one knows where now, especially with the map missing.

"Someone told us that there was a Holloman Edition of the Bible, and so there is! We thought it might be nice to have one because of the family plantation connection, and we ordered it from a Bible book store. It looked nice enough, but was just a regular

Bible, so far as we could see.

"About that time, my husband surprised me with a hall table I'd been wanting for a long time. I put the Bible on it temporarily, though I planned to replace it with something else later.

"The next night we were getting ready for a dinner party, and my mother had sent a huge yellow bouquet of lovely silk flowers, beautifully arranged. I was busy getting ready for my guests when it arrived. I placed it on the center of my new table, and the Bible nearby, and went back to the kitchen.

"Suddenly there was a kind of "whooshing" sound like the wind, except that the doors and windows were all closed. I heard objects flying, and our oldest son was in the doorway. His face was absolutely chalky. 'Mom,' he finally said, 'I think you'd better come look. And before you do, remember, I didn't even touch it!'

"Well, I followed him back into the hall area. There was the Bible, back in the center of the new table, and there were flowers all over the floor! The place looked like it had been struck by the proverbial whirlwind!

"Since then, the Holloman Bible has been on that table. My sister says it looks like a shrine. I say, 'That's fine with me! I need all the help I can get!'

"The third Bible of my story belonged to my grandmother, who was then in a nursing home in South Georgia. Now, to put it mildly, she was not a very agreeable woman, especially in her last years. I was one of the very few in the family who could get along with her. For instance, when her brother gave her a large-print Bible, she asked for a pencil. In a shaky hand, she wrote in the front, that on her death, it was to go to me. Maybe she thought I needed it the most . . . but more about that later.

"Anyway, one night just at this time, I was alone in the house, working in a sewing room we'd fixed for me out in the garage. Suddenly I looked up, and saw this pretty little girl in a frilly white dress run from the laundry room into the garage, and around my work table. She reached for a pretty ball of satin ribbon I had there.

"I wondered whose child it could be, out alone at that time of the night," the woman continued. "I'd heard no one come in from the outside. Then I looked again, and she had simply vanished.

"But a moment later there she was again, trying to get on my daughter's bicycle. Then, she was gone. I knew what it must be. I could hardly move; my scissors refused to work in my hands. Then I saw her a third time, trying to get on another bicycle! That did it! I threw down my scissors, and ran into the house. Impulsively, I called my mother. She was crying.

20

"She told me that Grandmother was dying, and she was on her way to her. Then she wanted to know why I had called her at that hour.

"'Oh, it seems a foolish thing to bother you with now,' I said, but she persisted. 'Well,' I said hesitantly, 'do you believe in ghosts?'

"'Maybe,' Mother surprised me by answering. 'Why?'

"'Because I've just seen one in my garage!' I burst out. Then I went on to describe the child. She had been a lively little thing, quite young, maybe three. She was dressed in a longish white dress, like the early 1900s. It had a bottom ruffle, and blue ribbons running through the lace insertion at the sleeves and yoke. She had long, blond curly hair.

"There was a silence at the other end of the line. Then my mother said in a shaky voice, 'You have just described my little sister, and the dress in which she was buried.'

"Let me say," added the narrator, "I had never seen a picture of the child, or heard of the dress. She had died, very young, of some childhood disease; no picture of her was ever taken. But Mother did remember the little dress Grandmother had made for her.

"That child appeared to us two more times, always during a crisis situation. You see, Grandmother didn't die then, after all. Each time she would rally, and then get worse, we would see the child. She especially liked our bicycles!

"Then one night I was awakened by the most terrible sound I've ever heard. It was a heavy rasping, a choking, a gasping for breath. 'Oh, help me,' it would say, over and over. My husband could hear it, too.

"We got up, and checked all over the house and yard, but could find nothing that would make such a noise. Then, a horrible howling started on our back patio! It wasn't just a bark; it was deeper, more scary, like a wolf in those movies where they are howling at night out in the snow....It had an element of evil in it. I was terrified.

"We walked to the back of the house together, and looked out on our patio. There sat the largest black dog we'd ever seen, howling his head off. It was a great, deep, mournful sound. We'd never seen him before, and we weren't about to go out for a closer look!

"Then a cat we had never seen before, a black one, shot across our patio and disappeared.

"We went back to bed, and finally the wild, weird baying noise stopped. But the raspy 'Help me,' went on intermittently most of the night, or so it seemed. I even tried to speak to it, but there was no answer.

"Next morning," she continued, "we learned that Grandmother

had passed away during the night. She had cancer of the throat, and died a painful, gasping death. We were told that she sometimes called out for me. Of course, I already knew that.

"When I went with Mother to the nursing home for her things, I asked about the Bible. But it had disappeared! We finally located it on another floor; the patient who had it said she didn't know how it had gotten there. But I brought it home, and put it in my closet."

At this point, one might assume that the little girl in white was a family ghost, appearing during a time of crisis. But she also appeared to a neighbor with whom our hostess had shared on one occasion her feeling of being in another time zone while at the house.

"One of the first times I saw him was when we had just moved in, and were clearing the yard," the woman said of her neighbor. "I saw a tiny snake disappear under some lumber we had out back. It was probably harmless, but I can't stand snakes! Just then I saw this man out in his yard, with a hoe.

"I called to him, and asked him if he would kill the snake for me. 'Sure,' he replied, and easily jumped the little fence we had just put up between the two properties.

"Well, as he hit the ground, the expression on his face changed completely! He looked at me as though he hardly knew me, and was a little afraid. He did kill the snake, though. To ease a suddenly awkward situation, I tried to say lightly, 'Now I'm going to notice if it lives until sundown, as they are supposed to do.'

"'Oh, it will,' he said in a strange, grim voice. 'Nothing around here ever dies.' Then he gave me another odd look, backed away from me, and jumped the fence back into his own yard. Then he practically threw down the hoe, he was so anxious to get into the house. And he never looked back.

"'What a strange man!' I said to myself. 'I'm sorry I even bothered him.'

"But in time," she went on, "we did get to know one another well enough to compare notes about that day. He told me that as he jumped the fence, he had the darndest feeling of being in another time period, of being someone else! He had looked down, and seen his Bermudas, and thought, 'Why, that woman can see my legs! I'm so ashamed!'

"Then he had killed the snake. He was as much surprised as me at what he said then, that nothing around here ever dies. He has no idea what caused him to say that! It was only after he jumped back across the fence into his own yard that he began to feel normal. We wondered if the fence, like a barrier, was symbolic.

"We shared one more incident," she continued. "My family

22

and I were away over Thanksgiving that year. When we got back he said, 'I really hate to see you go anywhere. Then your "spooks" come to see me!'

"He explained that his son had been quite ill one night, and he was lying on the bed beside the child until he was sure he was asleep. He was stifling an impulse to cough, not feeling very well himself.

"Suddenly, he said, he was aware there was a child in the room, the little girl dressed in white that I had seen earlier in my garage! He felt the bed move as she climbed on it over the foot, and started crawling towards him. 'Don't cough, Daddy,' she said sweetly, as she put a little hand across his face.

"Well, he sat up quickly in bed, scared to death, and she was gone! He heard one quick rap down the hall at the bathroom door, as though she had lightly tapped it with her knuckles, in passing. Then he heard the chimes swinging on the front door, as she left.

"Oh, and another child has been seen at our house," the story continued, "only she was a brunette! She was seen by a whole van load of children from our church, who had stopped by to see why our children were not at Sunday School. Again, we were out of town.

"The pastor said that they rang the bell, and there was no answer, but they knew that someone was at home. A pretty little girl, one with long dark hair, a child they'd never seen before, came and looked out at them for a minute through the front curtains in the living room.

"Of course, there was no way such a child could have gotten in during our absence, or any other sign one had been there. But they had seen her, and wondered who she was.

"The big mistake we made in the beginning was to try to keep what was going on here, from the children," the woman said thoughtfully. "They, especially my daughter, were afraid they were the only ones seeing and sensing things. They were much more frightened than if we'd discussed it openly from the first. But the time came when we had to sit down and talk with them, reassure them. They came to accept it all as part of living here, and were generally not bothered.

"For instance, one evening we had company, and we sent the kids out to play in the garage. In a few minutes they came running back in, greatly excited, saying 'something strange,' was in the garage. It was like a shadow, a haze. You could distinctly see it, hovering in one corner. Of course, we had no explanation for them. They all played in the house, and our guests went home very early!"

Manifestations at that time included strange noises, and a garage door from the laundy room that would not stay closed. There was even a small, light-colored cocker spaniel that was glimpsed in the house and garage from time to time, with no logical way of getting in or out without being seen.

"The children finally decided that it, too, had been part of the old plantation," she added with a smile.

Then there was the night when she checked her youngest child in his bed, just in time to see "a hazy something," as she said, slide across and under it. It took all her courage to get down on her knees and look under the low bed, where "a kind of low cloud" hovered for awhile.

On another occasion, the couple was awakened by strange noises. As the father walked down the hall, the door to his youngest child's room slammed behind him, though there was nothing to create a sudden breeze. At the same time, under the door, he could see that a light had come on.

"At the time, the child was in his crib, on the other side of the room from the light switch," the mother recalled. "My husband said that it took all his nerve to open that door! He didn't know what he would find.

"When he finally did so, the room was just as he had left it, except that the ceiling light was on, and our little boy was sitting up in his crib. He was two at the time, just beginning to talk. 'Monster, Daddy!' he said sleepily. That was all he could tell us. He must have learned the word from a TV show, but we had never heard him use it before. It could have meant ghost, or anything he didn't understand. But at least, that was all that happened that night.

"Anyway, we decided it was only fair to have a talk with the maid about all this," she continued. "I'd been putting it off, afraid she would leave. But when I finally tried to find the words, she only looked relieved. 'Oh, you mean the ghosts,' she said with a smile.

"'I don't let them bother me any!' she told me. 'I knew about them the first time I found out the garage door wouldn't stay closed! I'd put the dog out there, close it, and in a few minutes, he'd be back in the house! But it's all right. You're good people. No bad ghosts are going to stay around here!'"

About this time another incident occurred which our hostess, in retrospect, felt was a turning point in their living in the house. "Along with everything else, we started having the TV go on in the middle of the night! Of course, we checked for electronic malfunction and so fourth; there was none. It had never done this before; it was a relatively new set. Suddenly, about two every morning, I'd be awakened to the late, late show in the empty den!

"One night, I'd had it! I was desperately tired, when I heard the

24

set go on. I dragged myself down the hall, irritated and half asleep. Somehow, the old fear had been replaced by anger. I snapped the set off, and spoke loudly to whoever or whatever was in the room.

"'Look,' I said, 'I know you're here! Now I don't mind sharing my house with you, so long as you behave yourself. I don't even mind your watching the TV! But it is our set, and this is our house! In the future, you will watch it only when we do!'

"Surprisingly enough, the rest of the night was peaceful. There were no more problems with the set. 'I guess it was just a matter of telling them who was the boss,' my husband said with great relief.

"Sometimes," the story continued, "when things started to get a little tense, something really funny would happen to restore our balance. One night, for instance, my other grandmother came to visit. She was asleep in one of the children's rooms, and he was in a sleeping bag out in the den.

"It so happened that the same weekend my parents were out of town, and my younger brother came over here to sleep. This was not unusual; he has his own key. He was always the one in the family who said he didn't believe in ghosts, and he had laughed at our stories.

"Well, he came slipping down the hall late that night, after we were asleep. He saw the boy asleep out in the den, and decided to go in his room for the night.

"Trying to be very quiet, he slipped into the room without turning on the light, sat down on the bed, and started to undress in the dark. Just then Grandmother sat up in the bed, in her long, white nightgown, and with her long white hair down her back!

"He thought it was a ghost, and started to scream. She thought there was a strange man undressing in her room, and she screamed even louder! You never heard such a racket! They both came tumbling out of the bed, and went racing out the door, neither stopping to flip on the light!

"At that point, my poor husband came tearing down the hall in his pajamas, turning on the lights as he went. My brother stood there blinking at poor Grandmother. 'She scared the Devil out of me,' was all he could say. 'I thought it was your ghost!'

"Unfortunately," the story continued, "poor Grandmother died not long after that. Then she, too, reappeared in that same room, to my son. He said that at 3:15 one morning, he was awakened by the feeling of other people in the room. It was Grandmother and three other older ladies, that he did not know. All he could say later was, 'Their eyes, their eyes!' It seemed they had been strange, horrible, and glowing, as they looked at him. He said they had stood there by his bed for about fifteen minutes, as he laid there, too terrified to move or speak.

"They had a specific message for him, which concerned some building going on at the church. They were getting ready to start digging the foundation for an annex. What they were saying was, 'They must not dig there! They must not sink pilings in that ground!' At last, they were gone. But he was upset over the incident for several days, and slept with the hall light on."

"What did you do?" Stephen and I both asked at once.

"Nothing! By then, the minister we had known so well was gone. My son was afraid everyone would think he was crazy if he told the congregation he'd just been talking to his dead grandmother! By that time, too, the church was committed to the project. So the work continued, but it was just one difficulty after another. Everything that could go wrong, did! It was finally completed, but much behind schedule and beyond budget. They were right about that!"

Many of the manifestations in the house seemed to center around the young daughter's bedroom. "My sister came over here to sleep one night when my husband was out of town," said our hostess. "She was kept awake, she said, by the murmur of indistinct voices, too low to hear, that seemed to go on for hours. Once, there was a rapping on the wall by her bed.

"Then she finally dozed off, and woke to find what she said was a woman in a long dress, with a lantern, walking about the room! At that point, two in the morning, she came into my room and said, 'I'm sorry, but either I'm going to sleep with you, or I'm going home!' With that, she got into my bed!

"She slept after that, but I didn't. All at once I could see a light like a candle, shining in my dresser mirror. It burned there until morning.

"When my sister got up to dress, the clothing which she had so neatly laid out over the back of the chair in the first room, was all wadded up and stuffed in the back of the clothes closet! I loaned her some of mine to wear home, for she said she wouldn't touch hers until she had washed it all. She has not spent a night here since!

"Another time, a gold maple leaf charm from Canada vanished from the bracelet of a niece sleeping in that room. Just vanished, period. She had it the night before, as it was a new charm, and she was very proud of it. When she woke up in the morning, the bracelet was there, but the charm was gone.

"On another occasion, my husband and I were awakened by strange noises in the house. After he had investigated, and found nothing, he came back and laid down. 'It's over by you, now,' I tried to tell him as calmly as I could. A misty white shape had materialized on his side of the bed.

"'Hell, no, it ain't!' he yelled back at me, as he grabbed up his pillow and one blanket, like a child's security blanket, and went out to sleep in the den!

"Not long after that, one of my neighbors was up with illness during the night, and stood at her window looking over into our backyard. The next day she said to me, 'Who on earth was that woman walking around in your yard last night in the long dress, and where did she get that wonderful antique lantern?'

"About that same time," our hostess continued, "I had volunteered to allow our neighborhood association to have a meeting here. The first to arrive was a man from down the street, while I was in the kitchen. I invited him in, and he sat down to wait for the rest. I went back to the kitchen for a minute. The next time I walked into the living room he said pleasantly, 'I didn't know you had your parents with you.'

"'They are not,' I said, fearing what was coming. 'Why do you ask?'

"'Well, two nice-looking older people just came in that front door, nodded and smiled, and went off down the hall,' he told me.

"Well, we walked down the hall, and looked in all the rooms. Of course, we were the only ones there. 'Look,' I said as we got back to the living room. 'Maybe there is something I should tell you about this house.'

"'Oh, no,' he exclaimed. 'This is the one I've been hearing about!' With that, he was gone—and he hasn't been back since."

After we had talked a little more about the house, Stephen asked our new friend if she had ever had any other psychic experiences. She replied that she had, in the form of precognitive dreams.

In one of these, she had seen a garage, and a house trailer beside it. A woman came out of the side door of the garage, and sat in a nearby lawn chair, shelling peas. Then she got up after a few minutes, walked into the house trailer, and lay down across the bed.

The next day, the dream was confirmed when word came that our hostess's aunt had died in South Carolina. Just as in the dream, she had been in her garage, and then gone outside, complaining of a headache. After a few minutes she had gone into her house trailer, and laid down across the bed. In a few more minutes, she was dead.

In another dream, our hostess had been with a multitude of people, as though waiting for something. Suddenly she had started digging hastily into the ground with her bare hands, ruining her fingernails as she patted and molded a large heap of dirt in the dry soil. When asked what she was doing, she had replied, "I'm making a place for the Lord to stand."

Sure enough, in a few minutes, Jesus Christ had appeared. Approaching her, he had climbed on her little mound, and began to speak. In the dream, he had then rewarded her for her faith by telling her that he was giving her sister back to her, "because her place is not with me."

Soon after that, the woman had received a telephone call from her sister in Baltimore. The sister, she added, had surprised the family earlier by converting to Catholicism, and going off to become a nun. She had then changed her mind about her vocation, just short of taking her final vows, and she was coming home. "I had no idea this was on her mind," the woman added. "We had accepted the fact, and thought she was happy there."

She went on to say that a dramatic ESP experience had concerned the same sister. She had come back to Savannah to resume her nursing career, and been injured in a terrible automobile accident. Her long hospital recovery included heavy medication for pain. When released, she insisted on staying alone in her little house in an isolated spot on the southside of Savannah.

On this particular day, our narrator told us, she was preparing to go see her sister. She had stopped first at the grocery story with her toddler, to do some shopping. Suddenly, upon calling her sister's number and getting a busy signal, she was seized by such an impulse to hurry to her house that she decided to do so immediately. Ignoring her shopping list, she took time only to pick up a box of ice cream bars and some cookies, neither favorite foods of the sister.

Then, child on hip and clutching the package, she ran to her car, and drove as quickly as possible to her sister's. There was no answer at the door, which was locked, though there was a car in the driveway.

Leaving her son in the yard with the package of ice cream bars and cookies, she had managed to break in through a back window. There she had found her sister, delirious with pain, and the telephone off the hook from a confused call for help. The little house was spattered with blood from a confused suicide attempt of which she later had no recollection. She was bleeding badly, with razor cuts on both wrists.

The horrified sister called for help, and managed to render first aid from directions given her by the emergency squad over the telephone, until help arrived.

"As for the cookies and ice cream, my impulse to get them was a godsend," she finished the story. "I don't know any other way I could have kept my little boy occupied while I was climbing in the window and dealing with the situation. He was still sitting in the driveway eating ice cream when the ambulance arrived!"

Finishing the narrative, she asked Stephen for his reactions to the house.

"I think you described it best when you said that you felt you were in another time period," he said slowly. "There is something about this particular area at times which makes me feel that if I closed my eyes, I would open them in another era.

"We don't know all there is to know yet about the nature of time and space, or our relationship to the past. It could well be that the house was built, since it is such a beautiful location, on the site of another house here a long time ago. Perhaps it was there that some of the things occurred which you saw with the three people in your room. You could have been brought here through ties from another lifetime, as indicated by seeing yourself in what you called old-fashioned clothing."

"I never thought about it until I came here," the woman replied, "but now I am beginning to believe in reincarnation. I also feel very drawn to the Georgia mountains. I get the impression there of having been an Indian woman . . . of riding behind a brave, on a horse. Just that one image, but it is very clear."

"There is one theory that not only are people reincarnated, but they also come back with others they have known before," Stephen went on. "The experience with your neighbor sensing the atmosphere of this place would indicate that he, as well as you, were drawn back here. Even more unusual is the fact of his seeing the child, a part of your past family, in his home! That would certainly indicate a deeper relationship between you."

"I wish you could have talked with him," our hostess answered. "But unfortunately, he and his wife have been divorced, and I understand he has left the area." She added that she had never had any particular feeling of rapport with the wife, or the wife with the locale.

As we had walked about the house earlier, that August afternoon, I had noticed the my feet became quite chilled in the area of the daughter's bedroom. It was a strange feeling, as though I were walking through unpleasantly cold, "heavy" air, that ended about my ankles. I was wearing the same shoes I wore on many other such expeditions that summer. I checked for air conditioning vents which might be blowing directly on the floor, but found none, nor was this effect apparent in the central cooling system, turned patriotically high to conserve energy, in the rest of the house.

"It may be only my imagination," I finally said, confessing my feelings, "but I'm not usually the sensitive one." Our hostess smiled.

"Well, I haven't heard that complaint in here before! But nothing surprises me any more."

As we walked into the family room, she pointed out to Stephen that part of the den, around the fireplace, was decorated with old stones from the Savannah River front which had first been brought to Georgia as ballast for English trading ships over 200 years ago. "Do you think that's where my colonial presences come from?" she asked half-seriously.

He shook his head. "Not of the type you're getting. It seems more likely that it has to do with the land itself. You may also be on the site of a family cemetery. You said there was one in the area."

"Whatever it is, I think we understand each other now," she concluded. "This is our home, and has really been quite peaceful lately. Whatever is here, we will accept, and only wish it—them—peace. As a result of this attitude, things have become a lot more restful here."

"I have no doubt of that," Stephen replied. "You know, fear seems to interact with these vibrations, and give them energy for more manifestations, and the tension can build from there."

Walking about the yard, he said that he sensed the strongest and most peculiar vibrations in one corner of the lawn, just outside the bedroom walls. It had also seemed much cooler there, though it was in the sun, and the day was quite warm.

Later in the car, after we had thanked our hostess and told her goodbye, Stephen said to me, "I think we were very close to a materialization there. Frankly, I was glad to leave."

"Do you think we ought to go back there again when there is a new moon, and wait for midnight?"

"You've got to be kidding. Look, if they've accepted the situation, and are happy there, let's leave it at that."

"I really enjoyed meeting her," I commented. "I'm sure she was sincere."

"Oh, no doubt of that. And remember, other people saw things, and had strange experiences, too. Remember the woman walking about the yard with the lantern, and the old couple."

Stephen was quiet on the drive home, deep in thought, while everything I had heard seemed to tumble through my mind like the confused jumble of a puzzle. We considered the theory again that the house might indeed have been built on the site of an old family cemetery.

"Cemeteries are usually peaceful places," Stephen mused,

"unless they are disturbed by the living.

"Or are no longer marked, and have a new bulding on them? Perhaps that's why they wanted a Bible, to reconsecrate the land. Or maybe the cemetery was where the church wanted to build its annex! Perhaps something so terrible, involving the three people she saw, happened at the house, that only a Bible could bring the area peace."

"We'll probably never know, will we?"

My strongest feelings concerned the two women our hostess had described. They might, as she had suggested, be indicative of reincarnation; or perhaps an emotional event had so charged the atmosphere, that persons living there later on were open to psychic influence. But the vibrations had seemed personal, directed towards her.

The manner of the one woman seen dressing, and the question about how long she would be gone, reflected an emergency situation, not a planned visit. In those days, one thing which would cause a woman to travel was the need for nursing care, for a relative or neighboring family. Savannah has seen many epidemics. The Bethesda Orphans House, opened in 1740 and now Bethesda Home for Boys, was only a few miles away. It had certainly seen its share of crisis. Or had it been a larger, even more traumatic event?

The thought occurred that the house would have been in the area directly involved in the sad aftermath of the Siege of Savannah, in 1779. After the bloody battle, casualties were housed in emergency make-shift hospitals at nearby plantations, such as Greenwich and Bonaventure. I thought, too, of the woman saying that when she was called upon to tend her sister's self-inflicted wounds, she had suddenly felt calm and competent. Later, she had been complimented on her skill by the medical technicians, who had assumed she was a trained nurse.

"Two things strike me about the woman we met, and what she told us," I said to Stephen as we arrived at his house. "First of all, she is a religious person, in the best sense of the word. The woman that she saw, said she would be staying as long as the Lord prepared a place for her. In the dream, she said she was making a place for the Lord to stand. There's a continuity there . . . maybe a reference to her psychic ability.

"The second thing is that she has obviously had a strong relationship with her sister in this life. Her sister also senses vibrations in the house, though hers seem more evil, and she has also seen the woman with the lantern. The women that she saw, you remember, seemed to have a strong bond between them. Maybe they, too, were sisters. I get the feeling that the woman with the lantern was waiting for the other to return, and for some reason, probably tragic, she did not."

"Until now."

Seance at the Pirates' House

"Come, stow this talk. He's dead, and he doesn't walk, that I know; leastways, he won't walk by day, you may lay to that."
—Robert Louis Stevenson, *Treasure Island.*

The rambling, two-story old frame house on Savannah's East Broad Street, its worn wooden shutters painted a faded 'ha'nt' blue to repel unwelcome spirits, has long been a place of legend. Here it is said that Stevenson's Captain Flint, "the thirstiest buccaneer that ever sailed," died one night calling, "Darby M'Graw....Fetch aft the rum, Darby!"

What Stevenson, who may have visited Savannah on his way to California in pursuit of another sea captain's wife, and eventually to Samoa, does say in the book is that "Blackbeard was a child, to Flint!" Flint's ship was the storied Walrus, often "a-muck with red blood, and fit to sink with gold....They were the roughest crew afloat, was Flint's; the Devil himself would have feared to go to sea with them." And he adds that Flint, "a boosy old seaman with a blue mug, died of rum at Savannah.

"Dead...ay, sure enough he's dead and gone below, but if ever a sperrit walked, it would be Flint's. Dear heart, but he died bad, did Flint!

"...Now he raged, and now he hollered for rum, and now he sang. 'Fifteen men,' were his only song, mates, and I tell you true, I never rightly liked to hear it since. It was main hot, and the windy was open, and I hear that old song comin' out, as clear as clear, and the death-haul on the man already."

What is fact about the Pirates' House, now a famous restaurant, is that it is an old building with a long tradition of strange noises and lights at night on its top floor, in the old front part, where they say seamen once stayed. It is whispered that no employee, even easy-going owner and manager Herb Traub, ever ventured up there alone

The Pirates' House in Savannah, from an original © copyright drawing by Pamela Lee.

at night.

The Pirates' House is in the middle of a historic area, the ten acres originally set aside at the time of the founding of Georgia in 1733 as Trustees' Garden, in honor of the colony's backers in London. Modeled after the Chelsea Botannical Garden, it was the first experimental plot in America. Here samples of fruit trees, flax, hemp, spices, indigo, and above all grape vines and mulberry trees were cultivated, in order to find valuable crops for the new land. The mulberry trees of the hoped-for silk industry were eventually frozen, but plantings of cotton plants and peach trees thrived with attending success.

The Herb House, said to be the oldest building in Georgia, was built in 1734 to house the royal gardener, his tool room, office, and stable. The garden area was turned into a residential one by John Reynolds, the first governor of the colony, in 1748, and acquired by the Savannah Gas Company one hundred years later. The Herb House is now a part of the Pirates' House complex, adding to its mystique of history.

Behind the house and along the river side of the bluff stand the brick walls of old Fort Wayne, built to protect the area in 1759 as

Fort Savannah, and then renamed for the Revolutionary War hero "Mad" Anthony Wayne, who once had a plantation a few miles up the river. Captured by the British during the Revolutionary War, it was rebuilt and garrisoned during the War of 1812. Later abandoned, the old fortification deteriorated, and became a popular spot for early morning duels. The place was known as the Old Fort section, a bawdy, brawling neighborhood of poor immigrant families and itinerent seamen.

The entire Trustees' Garden region has been given new life in the past few years as a fashionable and attractive residential and commercial area. It is one of Savannah's several urban success stories.

The Pirates' House was built on a bluff overlooking the Savannah River at what Georgia's founder James Oglethorpe described in laying out the city as "a healthy situation, about ten miles from the sea. The river here forms a half moon, along the south side of which the banks are about forty feet high, and on the top flat, which they call a bluff. . . . Ships that draw twelve feet of water, can ride within ten yards of the bank."

Built on high ground, the Pirates' House has what is unusual for Low Country houses, a bricked cellar. Rumors tell of an underground passage, portions of which may still be seen, linking the house with the river. It was said to be a haven for smugglers. Drugged, unconscious men, including one unfortunate Savannah policeman with the dreaded beat of "Foley's Alley," were shanghaied here, and awoke to find themselves on outbound sailing vessels.

Pirate legends of the area abound. In the late eighteenth century, one Savannah citizen complained of French privateers in the harbor, where "their sailors paraded the streets in bodies, night and day, armed with cutlasses, daggers and swords."

Records of the famous pirate brothers, Jean and Pierre Lafitte, allies of General Andrew Jackson at the 1815 Battle of New Orleans, indicate that they called at the docks of Charleston and Savannah. Pierre was aboard the schooner Nancy Eleanor when she left Charleston harbor one dark night in 1821, "in a clandestine manner, supposedly bound on a piratical expedition," according to the Charleston newspaper.

It is said that Jean married a Savannah girl, Mary Morton, perhaps from the Old Fort area, and "was redeemed through the love of a noble woman," It is known that the brothers' ship, *Jupiter*, stopped at Savannah in 1817 to take aboard a Greek sailor named Captain Nicholas, the same friend who was with Jean when he died in the Yucatan in 1826.

When I took a psychic from Virginia Beach to the Pirates' House while working on this book, her reaction was one of chills and depression from the cellar stairway, "the smell of old blood, the feeling that something very evil happened to some young men here."

While visiting there, Stephen had said that he had the feeling, as he has in so many refurbished buildings, of new images superimposed on old.... "It makes me depressed and a little sad," he said. "Somehow, looking at my arm, I really expected to see a thick, hairy wrist, a blue seaman's jacket with old braid and buttons, and a large hand holding a foaming tankard of ale."

Leaving the building, Stephen said to me, "I also think there is going to be a fire there, but it won't be serious. It will not be in the old part, where we were."

"Maybe I should tell Herb," I answered, but never did so. I sensed that for all his generosity and good-natured acceptance of the Captain Flint story, he was not really a believer in the supernatural.

Not long after that, we heard that there had been a slight fire in the Pirates' House in the new part, the kitchen. Fortunately, it was easily controlled and did little damage.

Ghost hunters Ed and Lorraine Warren during a press conference prior to their visit to the Pirates' House in Savannah. Photo courtesy of Armstrong State College.

A Visit to Coldbrook:
Can this Plantation be Saved?

West of Savannah, trucks and commercial traffic rumble out of town over the arching bridges and viaducts of Bay Street extension, a highway which parallels the Savannah River along a singularly unattractive terrain which stretches from the city to the busy western port section. Beyond it, over the denuded landscape, giant factories such as Union Bag paper mill make their contribution to the twentieth century, flanking the equally bleak landscape around the Savannah airport.

Little is left now to remind the traveler that this same region was once the location of some of the state's earliest and most elegant plantations, with their wide-verandaed houses at the end of tree-lined avenues, their vegetable gardens and rice fields, and their lush lawns fronting on the river. This was the area of Mulberry Grove, home of the Revolutionary War hero General Nathaniel Greene, where George Washington once stopped to see Greene's pretty young widow, Kitty, with whom he had danced at Valley Forge, and where Eli Whitney invented the cotton gin.

Nearby are what were once Brampton, Drakie, Coleraine, and the famous Hermitage, where Savannah grey bricks were manu-factured, and whose plantation house and buildings were later acquired by industrialist Henry Ford. They and others exist now as little more than names on historic land grants, or battered highway markers. Part of that era died in the fires of burning plantation homes like Mulberry Grove, which lit the path of General William Sherman's army to Savannah in 1864, and the rest in the acrid fumes of modern industry, and the attendant destruction of the land and much which was here at one time.

Few who pass that way know that a small section of that past still survives today, in a weathered country house not far from the industrial corridor. Stephen and I had first heard of Coldbrook Plantation from our friend Milt Rahn, a West Chatham County businessman and realtor with a passion for history and interesting people, and a quick interest in the unusual. Milt knows the area well, since he is a descendant of the Austrian Lutheran Salzburgers who came to Georgia for religious freedom only a year after James Oglethorpe founded the colony at Savannah in 1733.

The Salzburgers were sent further up the Savannah River, to a swampy, fever-ridden settlement with the Biblical name of Ebenezer. Many found death along with freedom in the sandy soil of the new country before the Lutherans finally obtained a healthier location for their venture. But enough survived to populate the area with their hardy, hard-working progeny, and leave names like Rahn, Gnann, LeBey, Ulmer, and others behind them as a memorial.

Coldbrook had originally been an Ulmer plantation, Milt told us the first time we discussed an excursion there. It has been owned by only two families, the Ulmers and the Kellers, who were related by marriage, for the past two hundred years. Milt had known the last of the Kellers to live there, two aging sisters, who eventually moved to Savannah in the 1950s. They had deeded Coldbrook to the Georgia Baptist Association, who would probably sell it if a suitable buyer for its remaining 1700 acres could be found. What would happen to the old plantation house, now showing its age and inhabited only by caretakers, was anyone's guess.

Milt knew the caretakers, too, a couple named Mr. and Mrs. Jasper Cooler, who had been at Coldbrook since the 1950s. He had visited them, and somehow gotten on the subject of the supernatural enough with Mrs. Cooler to know that she had some interesting stories about the old place. Then we heard that the couple was in the process of moving to their own home, and decided to hurry out and try to talk with them before they left.

The weather, that sunny November afternoon, was just right for a drive in the country: cool enough to have killed most of the insects of the Georgia summer, and with a golden haze over the landscape as we turned off the busy highway. Within a few miles of west Savannah, we had gone from the blighted urban landscape to quiet country roads and old farmhouses, some with modern additions and others in various stages of disrepair. We stopped briefly at one picturesque but sad old frame ruin, which Stephen wanted to photograph, with its collapsed roof around a crumbling chimney.

As he drove, Milt talked of the history of the area, the Salzburgers, the rice plantations, the Revolutionary era of South Carolina Francis Marion's "Swamp Fox" exploits, still recalled by a grocery store of the same name, and the heroic Sergeant William Jasper, who had later died at the Siege of Savannah in 1779. It was

Coldbrook Plantation in Chatham County about 1890, at the time the George A. Keller family lived there.

nearby, at a place called Jasper Spring, that the intrepid patriot and another sergeant are said to have ambushed a detachment of British soldiers, and liberated captured Americans being taken to Savannah.

Later came the divided loyalties of the Civil War, he continued, General William Sherman's march, and reconstruction. Some of the finest brick work in the area, on plantation houses rebuilt in the 1860s, was done by two young Irish immigrants who had first passed through as soldiers with the Union forces, and seen the houses destroyed. When the war ended, and they shivered in the cold winds of New York, their army pay gone, they remembered the sunny weather of Georgia, and came back to help rebuild the houses. . . .

By the time this story ended we three had reached the long country road which leads to Coldbrook, a lane which passes now through uncultivated fields and past an overgrown family cemetery in a small clump of trees. At its end is a white, two-story farmhouse, sturdy and plain, with a red roof, a Savannah grey brick chimney, and sagging shutters. An old weather vane creaked lopsidedly in the wind, and a nondescript mongrel dog came out from behind the shrubbery and barked at us, more from curiosity than hostility.

"Oh, my," Stephen finally said softly. "The next time, Milt, you tell me you have found an old house, I'm going to listen!"

Our friend beamed, opening the car door and making reassuring

39

gestures at the approaching canine. "Well, what do you think?"

"I think it may just be one of the few eighteenth century houses left in Georgia," Stephen replied reverently, unpacking his camera. "The style is called Plantation Plain, and this one appears to be in exceptional condition from the standpoint of the original structure. . . . In other words, where Williamsburg is mostly a reconstruction, this is the real thing!"

While Milton patted the dog, I walked around the enormous camilla tree which dominated the front yard. There was a simple, touching dignity about the weathered home, seen through a tangle of azaleas, holly, wisteria, and other vines and shrubbery. "Of course, the scalloped trim on the porch is later, Victorian," Stephen was saying, "but even that was done by a master craftsman."

I sat on the sagging front porch, already lost in the ambiance of the waiting old house and lush, if overgrown, yard. "I understand this is part of an old Crown land grant," Milt commented. "Mrs. Cooler told me that field out there was part of an Indian burial ground, and that the farmers used to turn up teeth and relics when they plowed. . . . Later on, this was part of a large rice plantation. You can still see some remains of the old dikes and canals out in the fields."

"Well, didn't you find us in a mess!" Mrs. Cooler said reproachfully a few minutes later, when she and her husband arrived in their pickup truck. A small, alert, middle-aged woman with a quick, humorous manner, she seemed to hesitate a moment before inviting us into the house. Her husband, a tall, quiet man who spoke to us courteously but seemed content to let her handle the situation, moved toward the kitchen door, saying something about having to go to work.

"I'd think you'd be sorry to leave a place like this," I commented to Mrs. Cooler as we followed her in the back door. "It's so quiet out here, and such an interesting house."

"I'll tell you, I'm sorry and I'm glad," she replied thoughtfully. "I really like this old place, and I hope that someone gets it who will appreciate it. But my husband and I need something smaller. Life here hasn't been all easy . . . but it has been different."

The house was built on the basic plan of a center hall and stairway off the front porch, a parlor on one side of the hall and a large dining room on the other, and a detached kitchen, featuring what had once been a brick beehive oven, in the back. This was later replaced by a newer attached kitchen, and another small room, off the dining room.

The upstairs was basically as it had been originally, with wide, hand-hewn floor boards, and fireplaces in each room. There was an attic, which Stephen peeked into, and quickly announced was wasp-infected. I did not venture any further up the narrow stairs than the second floor. Halfway up the attic steps, in the bend of the stairway, was an intriguing little window which looked out on the backyard jungle of vines over the old ruined kitchen, and a grove of pecan trees.

"Ummm...." Stephen was saying thoughtfully on the stairs. "Just as I thought, a trick step."

"What's a trick step?" I came back to the present reluctantly from the view out the window.

"It's the way they built stairs a hundred years or so ago. All the steps would be the same height but one, and everyone in the family learned pretty early which it was, and to look out for it. Otherwise, you'd be tripped up. It was an early form of burglar alarm."

"Well, I've tripped there often enough, but I thought it was just happenstance," Mrs. Cooler put in cheerfully as she waited for us in the lower hall.

"Now, that's interesting!" Stephen exclaimed as the tour continued to the downstairs back hall, after we had admired the old Victorian brass chandelier in the entryway. "A cooling board door!"

As we gathered around him, he showed us how the plain, wide-planked door could be easily lifted off its old hinges, and laid over two saw horses, to place a corpse on. "When they prepared bodies for home burial, this was very handy. Notice one side of the door is plain, and the other has two boards nailed across it, which were fitted against the saw horses, to keep the board from slipping as they worked.

"When they were finished, and the body ready to be placed in the casket, the door could easily be replaced...until the next time."

I shivered in the dim, unheated hallway. "Looks old enough to have been used some, too."

"Oh, sure," Stephen said placidly. "In the plantation era, they lived with the fact of sudden death, and were more open and matter-of-fact about it than we are today. This is not to say that they felt any less; they were just more realistic.

"The larger plantations kept a few wide boards on hand, already finished, that could be quickly nailed together to make a coffin to size; the stores sold a coarse type of cloth to line them, called coffin cloth. Services were held in the home, usually in the front parlor, and burial was on the family property like the little graveyard we passed on the way in."

After walking through the rooms, we settled in what had been the large dining room, and was now used by the Coolers as a family room. Mrs. Cooler had visibly relaxed during our brief acquaintance, and now acceded to Milt's request to repeat some of the story she had earlier told him of her twenty-five years in the house.

"Well, every old house has its creaks and groans and drafts and such, and we expected that," she began. "What I'm going to tell you isn't like that at all. Our first experience was not long after we moved in here.

"My husband's nephew was spending the night, sleeping upstairs in the right-hand bedroom going up the stairs. Well, he got up at two a.m. with the most ungodly screech you ever heard! I ran in, and his teeth were shakin' together like he had the flu! Finally he got calmed down enough to tell me that he had wakened up and looked over at the window. He swears there was a man there in white, he could just see his head and shoulders, lookin' in at him . . . and this on the second floor!

"It was a bright, moonlit night. He ran to the window, he said, and looked out just in time to see two men going around the house, both dressed in white with hoods, one with a lantern and one with a torch. Then, another came over to join them . . . three in all.

"He insisted that it wasn't a dream, because he'd been up; those men were out there! He was freezing, though the weather was warm. The windows were all open. He got a blanket and wrapped up in it, and got one of the hunting rifles, and he sat there, with that gun on the window sill, until it started to get daylight, about five o'clock in the morning! Course, we'd already been all around the outside, him with his gun, and not seen anything.

"The rest of that night was quiet, and he was sleepy and grumpy and didn't want to talk about it the next morning. He left right after breakfast, and to this day, he will not set foot in this house after sunset! If he's here, he goes home before it gets dark."

"Have you had any Klan activity around here?" I asked.

"Oh, Lordy, not that I know of! Anyway, if it were real people, how did one get to the second story window without a ladder? And why didn't our dogs bark?

"Anyway," she continued, "my daughter slept upstairs one night in that same bedroom, about that same time. It was still summer; she was sleeping with only a sheet over her, and the window open. Suddenly, about the same time of night, I heard her give a scream you could have heard all the way down the road to the next house! I ran in, and she was shakin' and wrapped up in that sheet so tight, I could hardly pull it off her, to find out what was wrong. She claimed she had wakened up to sense there was a man in the room, though she couldn't see him.

"'Oh, I heard him walking around in here,' she said. 'Then he leaned over, and was breathing in my face.' I turned on the lights, and showed her there was nobody else there, even under the bed. I told her it must have been a bad dream. 'Listen,' she said, 'now he's out on the front porch.' Sure enough, we could hear footsteps down there, like a man walking around, heavy ones. We looked out, but nobody was there. The rest of the night, she slept with me.

"Another time, I woke up about that same time of night to find my two little grandchildren, who were here then, both in bed with me. They said there was a man in that room, walking around and leaning over the foot of the bed, down by their feet. Same room.

"One night, my daughter wouldn't go to the bathroom down here without me. She said there was a man in there, looking at her." Mrs. Cooler indicated a bathroom which had been added later on one end of the dining room-family room, under the hall stairs.

"We also had problems with the children sleeping in that old front parlor, which we were using as a bedroom," she continued. "One night one of the children was sleeping in there, and she woke me up screaming that she heard people coming down the stairs toward her door. She slept with me the rest of that night, on the sofa bed in this room.

"Then there was the summer night when we had all the doors open, it was so warm. My little granddaughter, who was about two-and-a-half at the time, woke me up and said, 'Nan, I hear someone walking around and talking upstairs.' Of course, I looked, and there was nobody there. Another time she said her granddaddy was walking around up there, when there was nobody there but her...that I could see. Once she said she heard a whole bunch of people talking! I asked her what they were saying.

"'Jesus man, Jesus man,' she said. 'We're all a-going to Jesus!'"

"Sounds like a family worship service, or maybe back when they had church meetings at country places like this," said Milt. "I've heard that there were church services held here."

"Anyway," said Mrs. Cooler, "another time I was here by myself. I woke up about that same time and heard beautiful, far-away music...like an outdoor concert, or music for a picnic, you know...pleasant, a long ways off. Old-time fiddle and banjo music. I went outside, thinkin' someone was parked out there with a radio, though it didn't exactly sound like that. But I couldn't hear it outside, and I could, very faintly now, in the house! No radio, TV, record player on to make a sound like that. This was summer again, very hot, about two in the morning. It was nice music, and I would

43

have enjoyed it. If I had known what was the cause of it.

"That's when I started sleepin' with an open Bible by my bed. I thought, if this is anything bad, they don't want to see a Bible, so I'm safe. This was when I was still sleepin' in that front bedroom. So I said my prayers, and went back to sleep.

"Another time," her narration continued, "I was in that same front bedroom, and my little granddaughter, who was about six at the time, was sleeping with me. Well, she was about to crowd me out of the bed! I said to her, she was going to have to move over if she slept with me, and she said she couldn't, that there was another little girl in bed with us. I asked her who the little girl was. 'She says her name's Eliza,' the child said, very sure of herself. 'She says she's nine.' In a few minutes, our little girl rolled over in the place where she wouldn't lie before.

"It's all right, 'Nana,' she said. 'Liza says she has to go now.'

"About that time, my little grandson had what we thought was an imaginary playmate in the house. He was too little to tell us much, but for several months you could see him having a wonderful time with someone or something we couldn't see. Later, we wondered how much of it was imaginary . . . after we found Eliza.

"Well, at least we found out who she had been. I just got curious, and went to poking around out in that old family cemetery, where we hadn't gone before for fear of snakes and poison ivy. It was awful overgrown out there. But after the first frost, I went looking. Sure enough, there was a little stone, 'Eliza Ann Ulmer, age nine, died April, 1818.' But remember, we found the stone after the other happened. No way the child could have seen it; besides, she couldn't have read it."

I shivered involuntarily. "Are you cold in here, Honey?" Mrs. Cooler asked. "Shouldn't wonder if you were; there's parts of this house where it's always cool, even in summer, which is why we started sleepin' in that front parlor; and there's others with warm spots, so's you could just stand there anytime in your bare feet. Sometimes, too, when I'm here by myself in the evenings, the knob turns on that hall door, you can see it. Yet there's nobody there.

"Sometimes, too, my little poodle growls, looking at the door, and nobody's there that I can see. Other times, he goes over in the middle of an empty room and sniffs all around, at about the height of a man's lower pants legs, like he does when someone comes.

"On the other hand, one night I saw a black cat shoot across the room, and he didn't react at all. My daughter was with me, and she didn't see it, either.

"Another time in the summer," she continued, "my daughter

and a fellow were sittin' there on that sofa lookin' at old pictures and things about the house we had found upstairs in a trunk. It was a warm evening, quiet, no breeze. Suddenly, she said she felt a cold wind blowin' on her, like a fan behind her. She got up and walked around, but she said wherever she went, felt chilly for a little while.

"One time in the summer my daughter was sitting on the sofa where you are now, talking to me, and we both noticed a kind of vaporish mass, like cigar smoke, forming in one corner of the room. It kind of divided into two, as we watched it. She nodded at it without saying anything, and looked at me, and I nodded back. 'Yeah,' I said, 'I see it, and it's a spirit of some kind, but I don't know what it is.'

"Another time," she went on, "I looked up from sitting here just in time to catch a glimpse of a little short man in a charcoal-color pinstripe suit, with a black felt hat, walk by. I never saw him again, and have no idea who he was. But I don't think he was an Ulmer; they were all tall, you know. Still are."

During this period, she went on, the family experienced several poltergeist-like raps and blows in the house. "One time, I felt as though I had been hit on the head with a hammer, and my eyes began to burn as though I had pepper seed in them," Mrs. Cooler recalled. "I had to wash them out with ice water, and go sit down for awhile."

"But most of those things happened," she explained, "after we'd been talking about things here in the house. Everytime someone would laugh or joke about what I was tellin', seemed like, somethin' happened to them. One man was sitting in here joking with me, and all at once, he felt like there was a board bumpin' on his feet. . . .He won't come back here any more except in the daylight.

"One time my son-in-law was going up the back steps to the kitchen, and he said he felt like someone was right in front of him, kickin' him in the legs with the toe of a shoe, at each step. He and my daughter were sitting out there in the kitchen and she was jokin' him about it that same day, and she said she felt like all at once an iron bar was hitting her across the back of the legs, and then 'round on the shin bone. She wanted me to move out, and said she wouldn't be back until I did. She stayed away five months, too, but she finally did come back to see me."

We asked Mrs. Cooler if she herself wasn't ready to move by this time.

"Oh, well, yes, I thought about it," she said, "but this was a nice house in those days, and I didn't see where else we would go. I kind of liked it here. I figured whatever was here, wasn't going to hurt me if I let it or them alone. Some of what happened here, the people were just askin' for.

"I mean, like once, a man was here, and he came walkin' in and said, 'I've got me one of those old tombstones from out of the graveyard there, in my car, and I'm going to have me some fun with it come this Halloween.

"I told him he had better not have anything from that graveyard, or he wouldn't wait for tomorrow to bring it back! The people who were buried out there were still keepin' a watch out, I said, and they didn't like people messin' around with them like that.

"Well, he just laughed and wouldn't mind me, and he said, 'Oh, I'm just going to clean it up for you a little bit.' About then, he started to sit down in that chair over there," indicating the chair Milt was sitting in.

"Well, I tell you, he lit up out of that chair like there was a sharp spring stickin' up out of it! Then he went over here to the sofa, and started to sit down. He jumped up yellin' that he was bein' stabbed in the back! With that, he ran out to his car, and threw that old tombstone on the ground, and he was gone! We put it back, but it's all broken now. It was a nice one too, real fancy. Real old.

"Do you know whose it was?" I asked.

"Yeah. It said 'Jane Ulmer, wife of Philip,'" she replied. "I remember it because I felt so bad about the way that cemtery was goin' down. There was some people who had the field there rented out, you see. At that time there was a wire fence around the cemetery, but they just tore it down, and plowed in there everywhere they could reach, for more land, you know. All the stones that are left now are the ones in around the trees, that they couldn't get to. I went out and yelled at them to stop it, but it was too late by then. They all just laughed at me.

"Well, anyway, about that time we had a couple of things happen outside, involving cars. My daughter was here, and left early with her husband, at four in the morning, to take him to work. She said she felt as though there was someone in the back seat, a woman, from the old cemetery to the main road. Only she said she wasn't really afraid, it felt more like somebody that she knew.

"Another time my cousin was here, and he got in the car. At first, the lights wouldn't work, and we finally had to help him get 'em on. They'd been just fine before. Anyway, he said someone was with him in the back seat as he pulled out of here, and stayed with him until he crossed over down there by the railroad tracks where an old house used to be.

"About this time," our hostess continued, "one day my husband was getting ready to go down to the store. I watched him as

46

he went down the back steps and got into the car. Then I glanced out the window just in time to see a tall man, with an old-fashioned black hat, sitting up real stiff beside him in the front seat of the car! Between the tall man and the high hat, you couldn't see the top of the hat, but I saw the man, plain as could be! He was just sitting there in that old Chevy, just looking straight ahead as they went down the road. I thought, 'Now who can that be? I didn't know anyone else was around here.'

"Well, I was watchin' as the car came back, and there's nobody in it now but Jasper! He looked so surprised when I asked him who his passenger had been. He still claims he didn't notice anything. But I know what I saw, and in broad daylight.

"About that same time, my daughter was out in the backyard, and she glanced up and said she saw a tall man, in an old-fashioned black hat, walking around out among the pecan trees. I ran out to see, when she called me, but by then there was no one there.

"She was still wanting me to move," reminisced Mrs. Cooler, "but we'd said we would stay, and I just wasn't going to let someone run me out."

Asked if this had been her first experience with the supernatural, Mrs. Cooler said, "Oh, I suppose that to some extent I've always believed in it, in more than you can see, you know, but there had never been anything like this! What I do believe is, that you have to let them know you're not afraid. When you feel a sudden cool breeze on a hot day, or a sudden chill, you know someone's there. I learned to just say to them, 'Make yourself at home,' when that happens.

"They think they're real, you know. If they're bein' mean, you can always say, 'Oh, go back to the spirit world, you're not alive!' They don't like that, and I wouldn't say it to them unless they were bein' bad, or scary. I would say instead, 'If you're a good spirit, you can stay, but if you're not, then you'll have to go.'

"The tall man dressed in black was the one I sensed the most," she continued. "I had started thinking of him as Philip Ulmer, because the Ulmers are tall, and I knew a man named Philip had built this house. I just figured that when we first came in, he was worried as to what would happen, and was here to see about things. But I learned that he was all right, and could even help me."

Mrs. Cooler went on to explain how she had made peace with the patriarchal Philip. "I was here alone one time, out in the kitchen. I wanted to move the refrigerator out from the wall, and I had gotten tired of waiting for someone to help me. I thought I could just push it and do it myself. Well, I gave it one good push, enough to get it hung up on that old asphalt tile where it's all cracked and chipped in there.

I saw that I couldn't do anything but wait and work on it later when I could get help, and I knew the rest would fuss at me for trying to do it myself. So I just left it, and started puttin' up clean dishes from the sink, into the cupboard.

"All at once, I turned to see the tallest man I've ever laid eyes on, right beside me in the kitchen! He was dressed in that same black old-time hat, and brown dress pants and shoes. My first thought was, 'Oh, God, help me,' because I was afraid some of those convicts had escaped. We're not far from the place they keep them, you know, and three of them had walked about that same time.

"Then I looked again and he was gone. Vanished. So I knew what it was.

"Well, I came in here to this room and sat down in this chair and just sat here, for about fifteen or twenty minutes. Finally it made me mad, and I said out loud, 'I don't care who you are, you're no good scarin' me like that!' Then I thought, that sounds ugly. No use having trouble, it's his house, too. So I said again, out loud, 'Philip, are you there? Now, if you're good, you can go on livin' here, of course you can! I don't know why I let you scare me. If you want to prove that you're good, help me move this refrigerator, and you can stay.'

"Well, with that, I walked right back into that kitchen, got beside the refrigerator, and gave it a little push. It just slid across that old floor, right like I wanted it. I said aloud, 'You are good, Philip.' He's still here, too. In fact, he's here right now.

"Oh, I get along pretty well with all of them," she continued of the presences in the house. "'Course, it's a different story when some others are around. They filmed part of that horror movie *Squirm*, you know, about worms, out here.

"The first night the film people were here, it was just terrible! I walked in this room, and there was a man over there by the door, and people around in this room until you could hardly get through!" I realized with a start she was referring now to presences, not film crew. "I walked through here and said to them, 'Now, don't get upset, they're not going to hurt anything! They won't be here long. Everything will be all right.' But, oh, I was glad to see those film people go! You could just sense the agitated atmosphere."

Real presences also resent pretend ghosts and make-believe scary effects, Mrs. Cooler believes. "One Halloween, the young people from one of the church schools in Savannah got permission to have a party out here. Oh, it was a big thing to them, you know, comin' out in the country at night to a 'real' haunted house!

"They had a casket borrowed from Fox and Weeks over there by the fireplace, and a boy in it with his face all fixed up with some

48

makeup and chalk. They had all kinds of scary stuff around the house, and even lights and stuff out in the old graveyard, where they passed by on the way in here.

"I tell you, now, the real ones didn't like that one bit! They couldn't wait for the foolishness to be over, and all those noisy kids to be out of here, so they could have their own place back!"

We laughed at the thought of authentic spirits resenting amateur imitations, and the somber spell cast by our earlier conversation was somewhat dispelled.

Mrs. Cooler then led us out to what was left of the old plantation cemetery, as the last rays of the fading sunlight struck the old stones. Peering cautiously through a jungle of briars and vines, which we found later included large amounts of still active poison ivy, and brushing moss and dirt from the old markers, we made out most of the ornate carved italic letters and dates.

There was the large headstone of Philip Ulmer, who had died in 1856 at age seventy-three; Jane, his wife, who had died in 1826 at age thirty-four; William P. Ulmer, a son, who died in 1857; and an Elizabeth Ulmer, perhaps Philip's mother, who had died in 1819. There was one for Mary Desveyers, whom we thought might have been a governess or nurse, who died in 1858.

And it was Stephen who found the small headstone of the child. "Eliza Ann Ulmer," it said. "Died, April, 1818. Age nine years."

As we walked back through the field toward the house, Stephen remarked on an old farm basket by the fence. "You like that old basket?" said our guide. "If you do, take it; it's too old to do me any good."

After thanking Mrs. Cooler, we drove home excitedly, talking of Coldbrook and its poignant story. As I checked my notes, Milt asked Stephen what his impressions of the afternoon had been.

"Very interesting. . . .First of all, I think Mrs. Cooler is quite psychic, and probably the children, too. She's right; there's still a lot of activity there. And she's also correct about Philip; he's there. In fact, he was standing behind the sofa where you were sitting, Margaret, when she was talking about him."

"Oh," I said, "that must have been when I was getting a headache. Could you see him?"

"Not see, but sense he was there. I had a feeling, too, that someone walked by my chair as we sat there. Oh, yes, and the black cat is back. I saw it run across the room while she was talking."

"That's when you asked her if she had a black cat," I recalled.

"Right, and of course she doesn't, but I saw one." He added that he was also getting a headache while sitting in the dining-family room. "There was a chill there," he said. "In fact, I felt a definite aversion to some parts of that room.

"There is very definitely a cold spot in the front parlor, right between the front windows where she said she had a bed for awhile. I'd guess that was where they used to place the casket at home funerals. Yet, if I had to live at Coldbrook in order to save it, I would certainly do so. In some parts of it there is also a sense of peace and people having been happy there, of having loved it so much that now they don't want to leave.

"When I walked up the stairs, it was like going back in time," he continued. "I knew what the rooms up there would look like, how it had once looked."

In all our minds that day was born the determination to try to save the historic house, soon to be vacated, if humanly possible. We also planned to find out all that we could about the Ulmers and Kellers who had lived there.

"Just like one of those plantation novels," I said to Stephen as he got out of the car.

"Or a good Gothic," he replied.

"The next time he called me, he prefaced his remarks with, "You're not going to believe this!"

"Try me," I said.

"Remember that old basket I brought in from Coldbrook? Well, I walked in the door with it, and you know how Mother usually likes old things. She took one look at it, in absolute horror, and said, 'Where did you get that!' She won't go near it, and neither will our dog, who is usually so curious about anything different in the house!

"Anyway," he continued, "remember when I told you I was going to a funeral up in Effingham County? Well, I was just standing there, thinking about Coldbrook, when this very tall man came up to me, put out his hand, and said, 'Hello, the name is Ulmer.' It was kind of a shock."

"Not Philip?"

"No, but close. . . George. He's Philip's great-grandson! Says if we come up to his place in Springfield, he'll give us the whole family history."

A subsequent visit to the Springfield Ulmers and other sources, such as the Georgia Historical Society, revealed that the Ulmers were a seafaring family from Ulm, Germany. The first Ulmer to live in Georgia was Philip, Sr., the son of a baron, about 1750. His son, the Philip who built the house at Coldbrook, was born in 1783. He and his wife Jane had several children, including William, Eliza, Charles, and Mary. After Jane's death in 1826, Philip married a woman twenty-seven years his junior, Eliza Mulryne, a year later. They had several more children, among them James, Ben Franklin, Mary Virginia, and Noah.

It is known that the Ulmer's extensive holdings at one time included the famous Mulberry Grove, where one of them is said to be buried. That plantation was bought in order to extend their holdings to the Savannah River. The years between 1840 and 1856 were particularly prosperous ones at Coldbrook, when the cultivation of rice was at an all-time high. They also raised some cotton, and fruits and vegetables. At the time of Philip's death, the family owned fifty-seven slaves.

Family legend says that Philip was a tall, active man who was especially fond of riding his handsome black stallion, and often wore black. His will, written a month before his death in 1856, left his wife Eliza "the summer plantation house to the west of Augusta Road," which is surely Coldbrook.

After his death, his property was divided among his heirs, and much of it sold at public auction. The next couple to live in the house was George Adam Keller and his wife, Martha Wisenbaker Keller of Effingham County. They also raised a family at Coldbrook, which was a prosperous plantation at the time of General Sherman's arrival in 1864.

George Keller, a captain in the home militia, was off with Confederate forces at the time. Martha was at home with her young children when the foraging Federal troops arrived. They took the family livestock, including the horses, and talked about firing the house. Martha asked the Federal officer in charge not to do so, as she was a few months pregnant at the time, and liable to miscarry if forced from her home. While they were talking, her little son George Adam III, in defense of his home and mother, flung himself on the officer and bit him as high as he could reach on his stomach.

"Why, the damned little rebel!" the officer is said to have responded. But he got back on his horse and ordered the men on, sparing the house. However, they had not seen the last of little George, for his pet pony was among the livestock they were driving off to a pen they had commandeered off Monteith Road. Following from a discreet distance, the child is said to have slipped under the fence when no one was looking, and whistled softly. The pony found its master. Suddenly he was on it bareback, crouched low and holding it around the neck, urging it to jump the fence.

Whether he was not seen by the sentries, or because they had no inclination to shoot a child, it is said that the trained pony easily cleared the rails, and trotted home to the boy's anxious mother. In the meantime, the boy's older sister Gertrude had also saved her mount. An expert rider, the girl had sped off at the first sign of the Federal advance party by the back roads, and was at the time on her way to warn the neighbors to conceal their livestock and valuables.

Happily, George Keller survived the war and his wife her pregnancy, being delivered of a daughter named Iola Lee in the summer of 1865 after the war ended. Years later, after her death, her husband married a younger woman and raised a second family at Coldbrook, just as Philip had done.

More interesting highlights on the Keller family were given us by Mrs. Iola Gilbert, Iola's granddaughter and namesake, and her aunt, Mrs. C. E. Oliver, George's daughter by the second marriage, who now lives in Savannah. In a visit arranged by her niece, Mrs. Flossie Oliver ("Dad named me, he said I had such fine, soft hair, like floss....") showed us some of the massive Victorian furniture which had once been at Coldbrook, and her father's desk. She reminisced about happy times there, including her wedding reception, and her father's Confederate army papers. But both women were unyielding on one point.

"We hear that you've been out to Coldbrook," Mrs. Gilbert said to me, "and my aunt wants me to make one thing very clear to you. We understand that you've been talking to the people there about ghosts. Well, here's something to keep in mind. My family lived at Coldbrook for over 100 years, and none of us ever saw a ghost!"

"Not a sign of one," agreed Flossie Oliver.

"Well, some see them and some don't," Stephen commented to me later. "I'd say at the time they lived there, the atmosphere was probably totally different."

"Maybe Philip only comes around when the old place is threatened," I agreed.

We later met with Charles Duncan, the hearty Baptist minister who is now the executive director of the Atlanta-based Georgia Baptist Association. A friendly, sympathetic man, he had also been touched by the atmosphere of Coldbrook, without knowing its full history. At the same time, he pointed out to us, as the head of a non-profit organization whose main function is the management and dispursement of endowment funds for his denomination, he is personally unable to launch a restoration project.

"Believe me, I'd like nothing better than to find the right person to restore Coldbrook," he told us.

Informally dubbing ourselves "the ad hoc committee to save

Coldbrook Plantation House," Stephen, Milt, and I continued our research, which we shared with Mr. Duncan. We also sent copies to the officials of Historic Savannah Foundation and other persons noted for their interest in historic preservation, and Milt took some of them out to see Coldbrook for themselves.

At the present time, negotiations continue for the sale and restoration of what may be one of the most remarkable and unspoiled plantation homes left in the state. Perhaps, Stephen adds, the South. Until it is saved, or destroyed through carelessness, the restless, protective spirit of Philip Ulmer will continue to walk his land, and wait.

"That House"
on East St. Julian Street

The house at 507 East St. Julian Street, Savannah's most famous "haunted house" and the only one known to have had an exorcism, is a solidly-built, four-story frame structure, with shutters at the windows. Behind it is the walled garden, studded with old glass shards on top of the handmade brick, to discourage prowlers.

The home is nearly 200 years old, with a high gambrel roof and a widow's walk, the kind of a house that one would expect to find more in a New England seacoast town than in the South. Its builder, Hampton Lillibridge, was from Rhode Island, and incorporated his boyhood memories into the townhouse which he meant to use when not at his Sea Island plantation.

After his death, his widow married Joseph Grant. He sold the house for $25,000 to James Gould, another New Englander and a plantation owner on St. Simons Island, whose life inspired the first of novelist Eugenia Price's family trilogy, *Lighthouse*. The home is one of the few eighteenth century dwellings to survive the great fire of 1820, when 463 homes were destroyed in thirty-six hours of horror. It later knew numerous owners, was a tenant house, and stood vacant when Savannah decorator and antique dealer Jim Williams bought it in 1963.

It was at the height of Savannah's restoration movement, the heroic efforts to salvage historic but dilapidated homes which won national recognition and made the city's downtown area the largest urban historic landmark area in the nation. Williams, a native of Wilkinson County, Georgia, has been at the forefront of that movement, restoring or refurbishing over thirty old homes.

At the time he purchased the house, it was located some four blocks away on East Bryan Street. Next door was a similar residence; both were made ready for removal to other locations. In moving them, the other house collapsed, and a workman was killed. Some

Savannah's most famous haunted house, the Hampton Lillibridge home on East St. Julian Street, built in 1796. Drawing by Charley Bland, © copyright 1975.

have wondered if the tragedy was an omen. Also, like all old houses, the building had known its share of violence. For instance, it is said that at the time it was a roominghouse, a sailor had hanged himself from the knob of a high brass headboard in one of the upstairs bedrooms.

From the time restoration work began on the house at its new location, strange happenings were reported. Soon the workers were talking among themselves of unusual noises, voices, footsteps, and the feeling of others in the house. Sometimes the unexplained events even drove them into the street. "Half the time they were listening for noises instead of working," Williams later said of this period.

One evening, he and several friends were walking through the vacant house on the ground floor, looking over what had been done during the day. They were surprised to hear what sounded like workmen moving around above them. They climbed each story of the stairs, looking for the source of the noise, but found no one. Finally, standing on the widow's walk of the roof, they realized the sounds were now below them, in the supposedly empty rooms they had just passed.

On another occasion when Williams was out of town, several friends were walking through the house at the garden floor level. Suddenly they heard noises above them, as though people were upstairs. One of the men went up to investigate.

When the others went looking for him, they were shocked to find him lying face down on the floor. He said he felt as though he had just walked into a pool of cold water, and was being overpowered by some force. He had dropped to the floor to try to avoid whatever seemed to be drawing him toward the thirty-foot drop of the unfinished chimney shaft.

Later, across the street, the same men twice heard a woman's scream from the house. A tall, dark-haired man in a black suit and bow tie was seen standing at a third-floor window of what they knew was a vacant house. On another occasion, a grey haired man wearing a grey suit and a white tie, was seen in the home.

After Williams moved in, he was awakened several times to the sound of footsteps around his bed, although no one could be seen. They sounded as though they were walking on sand or broken glass. On another occasion, while talking in the house with a Savannah policeman, Williams heard loud crashing sounds from the room upstairs where a pipe organ was located. When the man rushed up the stairs to investigate, the door to an adjacent store room was seen to open and close by itself, and was then found locked. When it was unlocked with a key, it was empty.

One night, neighbors reported being awakened by the sound of a woman singing. A party appeared to be in progress on the top floor, and they saw lights and dancing figures. Later, when they commented about the festivities, they were told the house had been empty that night. Jim Williams was on a trip to London, and another occupant of the home was visiting in Atlanta.

On December 7, 1963, the house on St. Julian Street had an exorcism rite performed by the Right Reverend Albert Rhett Stewart, a bishop of the Episcopal Diocese of Georgia. He is now deceased. The forty-five-minute Church of England ceremony took place in the partially completed living room, and ended with a blessing of the house. Within ten days, at least some of the phenomena were back. Williams later recalled that he had a difficult time keeping maids. One rainy Friday afternoon, for instance, he came home to find one standing in the carport, afraid to be in the house alone. She complained of the feeling that a masculine presence was in the house, and the sound of chains rattling in the living room.

Williams now lives in another historic Savannah house, the

1861 mansion on Monterey Square which was built by Hugh W. Mercer, Confederate brigadier general and the great-grandfather of composer Johnny Mercer. That house, he says, has been quiet.

Although he generally avoids talking about his experiences in the St. Julian Street home, he did confirm over coffee at Carter's Restaurant on Drayton Street recently that the account of his experiences described by psychic Hans Holzer in *The Phantoms of Dixie*, was correct. Holzer terms Williams "a man of impeccable judgment and taste," and says that researchers concluded "genuine psychic phenomena were indeed taking place in the old house."

Williams then related one incident not previously reported in connection with the house, which he said he had wondered about later after the phenomena began to occur. While working on the foundation at St. Julian Street when the house was being moved, an old crypt was found on the lot, half filled with water. It was made of tabby, a mixture of lime and oyster shells widely used in colonial times. "The workmen later said it was empty," Williams added, "but I will always be sorry I didn't investigate it myself. I was leaving for London as they found it, and I couldn't change my plans. By the time I got back, it was covered up again. Now, I'll never know."

"You mean, why would someone be buried under a house when the city had a cemetery?" I asked. "Well, maybe foul play, suicide— you know they couldn't be buried in consecrated ground then. Are you thinking that something like that might have bad vibrations?"

"Well," Williams said thoughtfully, finishing his coffee, "I thought of Renee Rondolia."

I shivered. Until he said the name, the story of poor ignorant Renee, the boy giant of Foley's Alley, had simply been an early nineteenth century horror story, probably more legend than fact. Something they scared little kids with, especially kids who grew up near the former immigrant section on East Broad Street once known as Old Fort, and now fashionable Trustees' Garden.

"If you're going to write a ghost book, be sure to mention Renee Rondolia," my friend Rusty Fleetwood had said when I first started this book. "When I was growing up, I was more afraid of that character than anything!"

The tale goes that his full name was Renee Rondolia Asch. Large at birth, by the time he was five years old, he was the town curiosity. By adolescence, he weighed over 300 pounds, and stood more than seven feet tall. Worst of all, he had the cruel habit of killing small animals for sport, whenever he could avoid his watchful parents. The neighbors began to be afraid of him, and insisted that he be penned up behind a high wooden fence.

57

When a young girl was found murdered in the area, Renee was blamed, although he was found at home and apparently sound asleep by the mob of angry citizens who confronted his parents. A brick house with iron bars was then constructed, in which to keep Renee confined. Men of the area took turns watching the house, a precaution which was discontinued in the excitement of the 1820 fire. When a second young girl was found murdered in a fashion similar to the first, Renee was killed by the enraged throng, although once again he appeared to be safely locked in and asleep.

Feeling against Renee, even in death, was allegedly so strong that the local cemetery was closed to his body. It is said that he was buried in the marsh east of the city, on a spot later occupied by a ragpicker's tin warehouse. It was also said that on moonless, winter nights when the cold wind blew off the river, a huge hunched form, deprived of final rites, still wandered through his old haunts of East Savannah. . . .

Williams expressed bitterness over one part of his St. Julian Street experience, his invitation to the American Psychical Research Foundation in North Carolina to investigate this house.

"I spent a lot of time on that, and I'll bet they have five-hundred-pages of interviews and information," he said. "I thought it would be available to people who were seriously trying to find out what causes things like this to happen. When we finished, I said, 'Now I'm glad the information is all in one place and available to the public.' The man who had been taking it down just gave me a strange look.

" 'This information is for my research,' he told me. 'It's for a book I plan to write, and I have no intention of showing it to anyone else.' So now I can't send anyone up there to find out about the house. They didn't even tell me much, except that the phenomena appeared to be genuine."

Like Williams, the present owners of the house on St. Julian Street do not desire publicity. "Private Residence" says the discreet plate on the front door, although tour buses regularly go by, and guides with loudspeakers can be heard telling the story of the exorcism. However, psychic Sybil Leek and two other mediums have been in the house at different times. Its present owners did allow Stephen and me to visit the home, now the residence of a young doctor and his family. They added, "We do not give interviews at Halloween any more! We are still interested in serious research on the house, but we have young children, and we do not desire any publicity of the sensational type."

Our hostess, a pleasant, attractive, and apparently very stable young woman, said that her husband had first wanted the house because of its unique lines and downtown location. She was less enthusiastic, because of its recent history. However, she added that she had moved in with the desire to make it a comfortable home, and make peace with any presences which might be there.

"If we do have a presence, I believe that it has accepted us, and likes our children," she told us. "The unusual things which have happened have been generally reported to us by babysitters, guests, and others in the house—as though we were all right, but others are not welcome! One of the strangest things, though, happened when we were moving some things in, but were not living here yet.

"I had a house painter here, a man whom I trusted implicitly to lock up at the end of the day. All the windows were nailed shut. We had put some things in the locked storage area Mr. Williams had installed on the ground floor when he had antiques here. I have a witness, that I locked that door with a combination lock before leaving for the day. The painter says he locked the outside door, and I think he did.

"When I came in early the next morning, the outside door was open, and the storage area, too! Nothing had been taken. Strangest of all, the house door looked as though it had been pried open from the inside! It was almost as though someone was showing us they were still here...but also meant to frighten off anyone who came in to take our things!"

The young woman added that the occupancy of the house had to the most part been quiet, but she had occasionally had the feeling of not being alone. Several times, when she was on the ground floor level, she has heard the unmistakable sound of furniture being moved around overhead...in an empty house.

"I would say it seems like a feminine presence who can't resist showing that it is still her house," she commented. "Our sitters have told us they heard strange things in the house, and one said she felt her trundle bed move one night, but we tried to think it was partly imagination.

"Then, one night when I was alone in the house, I heard the music others had talked about. It was more than two instruments, I don't know how many. It started very softly, from somewhere above me, getting louder...I didn't wait to hear more; I was out of the house!

"Another time," she recalled, "I was leaving the house just at dark, and carefully went around turning off the lights. When I got outside and looked back, lights were on all over the house! I wasn't going back in there alone; I just turned around and left!

"Three different psychics at different times have said they sensed a feminine presence here," she concluded. "They also didn't like the obelisk in the garden, and I don't even know the history of that."

"Sybil Leek described sensing a woman, someone with children, in the house," Jim Williams had told me. "This didn't mean anything to me until Eugenia Price came to town researching *Lighthouse*. She told me she was interested in the home because one of the main characters in that book stayed here awhile, and died in Savannah."

The book adds that Mrs. Jane Harris Gould had come to Savannah for medical care, and was planning to go home when she had to flee the Hampton Lillibridge house in the January weather during the great 1820 Savannah fire, and contracted pneumonia. She died before her anxious husband could arrive from the island. Plans were made to take her body back to St. Simons when Christ Church was dedicated later that year, but were thwarted by a hurricane. She is now buried in an unmarked grave somewhere in the Bunch-Harris family plot at Colonial Cemetery in Savannah.

"Either the exorcism had some effect, or what was there is dormant for the time being," Stephen later commented of the house. He added that he sensed a very low-level energy still present, but it did not seem to be malicious. "Different people have different auras," he added, "and their energy interacts with whatever is in the house. It could be that whatever is there did not accept the initial move or Jim Williams, but is at peace with a young woman in the house."

Willie and Nellie: A Love Story

At the corner of Bull and Oglethorpe Streets in the heart of Savannah's downtown historic district stands an elegant Regency townhouse which many of the townspeople simply call the Birthplace. It was here on October 31, 1860, a night, as she later wrote, "associated with All Halloween, fairies, imps and witches," that Juliette Gordon, founder of the Girl Scouts of the U.S.A., was born to Nellie and William Washington Gordon, II.

Just as the Gordon home stands proudly on its crossroads corner, the family has been prominent in Savannah for nearly two centuries. The first Gordons in America settled in New Jersey prior to the Revolution, where part of the battle of Monmouth was fought on their family farm. After the war Ambrose Gordon found his way to Georgia, and named his first son William Washington after his old commanding officer, a nephew of the first president. Elizabeth, wife of Ambrose, is also known in Savannah history as a spirited woman who defied the government ban on trade with England during the War of 1812. She is said to have shipped her cotton down the Savannah River while sitting on top of the bales in a rocking chair, hoping the soldiers would be too chivalrous to fire at a woman.

Their son William was the first Georgian ever to be graduated from West Point. He was also a founder of the Central of Georgia Railroad, and the first Gordon to live in the house.

The handsome pink stucco home, which was to become Savannah's first National Historic Landmark, was built about 1820 for Judge Moore Wayne, later an associate justice of the Supreme Court, and William's uncle by marriage.

The Gordons bought the Wayne home when the judge left for Washington. Here their son William, II was born, and here he brought his bride, Nellie Kinzie, in 1858. Those who walk through the house museum, now the Juliette Gordon Low Girl Scout National Center, today find the house restored as it was during

Juliette's childhood. It is also rich in family mementos and the feel of a home which knew five generations of Gordons, and a great deal of love.

Beyond the story of Juliette, founder of the scout movement in America and a truly liberated woman of her time, was the tender love story of her parents. They knew the lasting happiness denied Juliette in her marriage to Willy Low, son of a wealthy cotton broker, and playboy friend of English nobility.

It is said that Willie Gordon first decided to marry Nellie, an eighteen-year-old schoolmate of his sister Eliza, in 1853 when she slid down the main staircase of the Yale Library at New Haven where Willie was a student, and crushed his new hat. She maintained the habit of sliding down staircases, along with other high-spirited ways, until her last illness in her house in 1917, when the doctor had told her not to use the stairs.

Her ancestry, as sturdy as his, was an interesting mixture of Puritan New Englanders and frontier pioneers, including some of the founders of the city of Chicago. Her grandmother, Eleanor Lytle, had once been captured by the Indian Chief Cornplanter, who gave her the nickname, "Little Ship Under Full Sail." It became an affectionate term also within the family for both Nellie and Juliette.

In marrying, both Willie and Nellie made some compromises. She was troubled by slavery, but accepted his loyalty to the South. He gave up his Presbyterian membership for her Episcopalian faith. Their disparate backgrounds were soon an issue in what Nellie called The Confederate War. Willie served with the Georgia Hussars, and was wounded at the Battle of Atlanta. Nellie lost one brother, John, in the Union service, and had two brothers captured. Even closer home, her uncle General David Hunter was in charge of the troops who took Fort Pulaski just outside of Savannah in 1862.

During the War, Nellie was to involve both Generals, Robert E. Lee and W. T. Sherman in helping her find her Willie at different times, a record even for her. First, she went to locate her husband in Virginia, where the Confederate leader gallantly gave her an escort of two soldiers. The couple shared a brief reunion before Nellie hurried back to Savannah to hide her family silver and valuables before the arrival of the Federal forces.

After the capture of Savannah, General Sherman came to call, delivering some mail from her family and giving the children their first candy and sugar. His band played "When This Cruel War Is Over," outside the house as he promised to put a guard over the residence. All Confederate officers' wives were being ordered to leave the city. In Nellie's case, General Sherman complied with her

Oglethorpe Street view of the Juliette Gordon Low Girl Scout National Center in Savannah, from a drawing by Peggy Dockery, a great-niece of Juliette's; © copyright by Peggy Dockery.

request to be allowed to go with a flag of truce into South Carolina, to say goodbye to Willie before she and the children left by steamer from Hilton Head for the north.

After their wartime separation, the Gordons returned to Savannah in 1865. Three more children, a total of six in all, were born in the house, and Willie became president of the Savannah Cotton Exchange. Willie later served his country during the Spanish American War, when he was commissioned a brigadier general. Nellie went with him to his command in Miami, and gained national recognition for her work in soldiers' relief. On one occasion, when she learned that a group of sick men had been placed on a train in Florida bound for their homes without nurses or medicine, she went with them herself all the way to Indiana, dosing them with milk punch and brandy.

President William McKinley paid tribute to them both; his successor, William Howard Taft, kept a parade waiting as their house guest in 1909 while he enjoyed lively conversation, waffles and venison in their dining room.

When Nellie visited her daughters Juliette and Mabel in England, Rudyard Kipling put her in a story as "a little old lady with snapping black eyes, who used very bad language," an honor for which she immediately thanked him.

When Willie died in 1912, flags flew at half mast in Savannah. His own Georgia Hussars escorted his body to Laurel Grove Cemetery. Nellie's children feared for her mental state as Juliette wrote her brother Arthur, "She never pretended for a moment that he was not her first and last love, and we as nothing in comparison. I believe Papa thought that the triumph of his life! Maternal love is the inheritance of the ages, but love such as Mamma gave him, was a personal tribute."

Among the many volumes of Nellie's in the Gordon library, there is one on spiritualism. We do not know what Nellie thought of its theories, so widely discussed in the late nineteenth century. At eighty-one, she wrote a cousin: "My strict observance of the fifth Commandment has resulted in my 'living long in the land' according to the promise. . . unless it is because the Lord doesn't want me, and the Devil doesn't want me, either. At any rate, here I remain, very much against my will, for there is nothing I so sincerely desire in this world as to get out of it."

During her last illness, she said to her daughter-in-law Ellie, "When I die, I don't want anybody to wear mourning. I don't want any tears. . . I shall be so happy to be with my Willie again, everyone should celebrate."

Nellie died in the big front bedroom of her home on Washington's birthday, February 22, 1917. At the moment of her death, her five living children were with her. Her daughter-in-law Margaret, who had already said her own goodbye to the frail, fiery little woman, was sitting quietly in an adjoining bedroom, which had been General Gordon's.

As she waited there, according to an account written by her daughter, Mary Stewart Gordon Platt, she was surprised to see a familiar figure. The general, wearing his familiar grey suit, was just coming out of his wife's bedroom. His expression, wrote Mrs. Platt,

Front stairway of the Juliette Gordon Low Girl Scout National Center, where the ghost of General Gordon once appeared to his daughter-in-law, and later startled an elderly butler. From a drawing by Julia Homer Wilson, © copyright by Julia Homer Wilson.

was "one of grave gladness." He walked through his old room and down the front stairs.

In a few minutes, Arthur, Margaret's husband appeared to tell her that his mother was gone. Together they walked down the stairs. Margaret had attempted to tell Arthur what she had seen, but he had gently told her she was only over-wrought, and perhaps had dozed off as she waited. She said no more as they reached the front hallway. There the old family butler was waiting, tears streaming down his worn cheeks.

Before they could speak, he told the same story. He had seen the general, in the grey suit, walk down the stairs just as he always did, and out the front door, "same as allus when de buggy been waiting for him dere," Mrs. Platt quotes him as saying. "Lawd, 'twas good ter see him again....He look so well and happy...happier den I mos' ever seed him....I thought you lake to know de General come fetch her hisself, suh."

Daisy Gordon Lawrence, a niece of Juliette's who later wrote her aunt's biography, *Lady From Savannah*, with Gladys Denny Shultz, also says of Nellie's last moments:

"Her children say that when she died, her face took on the radiance of a bride, going to meet her bridegroom."

Nellie Gordon: A Postscript

Although most people today think of the Juliette Gordon Low Girl Scout National Center as a happy and peaceful place, full of the tourists and Girl Scouts from all over the world who enjoy its Victorian decor and Gordon family antiques, some staff members say that when they are alone in the building, the impressions of the founder's family are still evident. This especially seems to take the form of footsteps on the stairs and through the rooms after the center is closed.

A guide there told me that she had once caught a fleeting and unexpected glimpse of Juliette's mother, Nellie Kinzie Gordon, one afternoon after the woman had just completed her last tour of the day. "I was getting ready to go home," she recalled. "The house was quiet, the lights out. Just as they were locking the door, I remembered a book I had left upstairs. I asked the woman with the keys to please wait for me while I went to get it.

"As she stood in the garden, I stepped inside the back entrance, and hurried up the stairs. I didn't turn on the lights. It was still daylight, but getting a little dim, as it was a late Sunday afternoon in the winter. Well, suddenly I heard a kind of rustle, and a figure was there above me, in the center hall. I recognized Mrs. Gordon from the picture in the library.

"I don't know who was the most startled. She drew back as though to say, 'Oh, I thought you'd all gone!' I turned and hurried down the stairs without my book, or even looking back. When I finally did glance back, at the door, she was gone. It was as though she had simply been waiting to get her house back."

Incidents have also been reported at the Center of long-lost items suddenly turning up in plain sight, and being moved about when the museum is closed. Both Eddie, the maintenance man, and my friend Stephen have heard the faint, far-away sound of a pianoforte playing, recalling the fact that Mrs. Gordon was an accomplished musician. "The instrument which we now have here in the north parlor only has about 20 percent of its keys in working order, but the one which we hear," added Stephen, "is perfectly in tune."

Eddie says that he has frequently caught a glimpse of Mrs. Gordon, "wearing a long blue robe, with flowers all over it," at the dining room table when he comes in early in the morning.

"Sometimes," he says, "I feel as though the whole family were present, just watching me, and then continues 'life as usual' when we all go home. . . especially with the house so much as it was when they were all here."

The Case of the Missing Marbles

The old phrase "Have you lost your marbles?" as a euphemism for mental imbalance has a special meaning for Mr. and Mrs. William H. Pinson Jr., the owners of a handsome brick home at State and Lincoln Streets in Savannah. In their case, it was finding marbles which set off a series of unusual events in their renovated townhouse which they have never been able to explain.

The sturdy four-story double-house is located on one of the original trust lots of the city. Its first owner was Mary Ann Barnard, of the family which gave the name to Barnard Street. The present house on the lot was completed as rental property in Savannah's antebellum boom year of 1856. It had many tenants and owners before Pinson, an attorney, and his wife Maxine moved into the residence in 1974.

The home had been attractively restored when Stephen and I visited Maxine one cold, sunny morning to discuss her experiences. She told us that the renovation, though satisfying, had been more emotionally trying than she could have imagined, when she first saw the house.

As we talked, the energetic young homemaker referred from time to time to a record which she had begun to keep of some of the strange events in the house while they were occurring, to see if some pattern were discernable.

"I must confess that I always felt a bit inadequate when we first moved here, and people would ask me jokingly if we had a ghost," she began. "They say in Savannah that is by no means a necessity, but one certainly adds a degree of character! We had no idea then, how lucky we were!

"As you can see, the house was built of Savannah grey bricks, made by slaves. The carriage house behind had unfortunately been demolished before we came here. The house itself is very solidly built, with its only structural damage a crack in front from an earthquake around the turn of the century.

"Before our incidents began, we were using the first three floors of the house. The top floor had not been occupied in some years. It was simply rented as storage space. There was no electricity up there, and only cold water. With its cracked glass panes, rattling windows, and creaking floor boards, it would have been the perfect setting for a Halloween party!

"I do not consider myself a superstitious person, but I would not have ventured up there alone at night, even with a flashlight! It always had an unpleasant chill, which I thought came from being unheated, and long vacant.

"Our first step in renovation was to remove all the plaster and woodwork, so that only the basic framework was left. When I started to do this, I hoped to uncover some little memento from the past.

"But we found nothing of interest, until my husband removed the last remaining baseboard about four months after we had started the gutting process. When this happened, two blue marbles rolled out! We took this as evidence that it had been the room of a young boy. The top floor in earlier times was often the level on which children had their bedrooms."

Maxine decided to keep the marbles as the single souvenir of her renovation. She placed them proudly in a covered glass dish, on a high, exposed breakfast room shelf downstairs. It was at about that same time that unusual events started to occur, she added, though it took some time for the couple to agree that they must be related to finding the toys.

Twice, after their infant daughter Celia was tucked into her crib for the night and her ceiling light flipped off, it was found to be on again. The child was too young at the time to climb out of the crib, and the light switch was located on the other wall opposite the bed. Twice, on the same floor but in a different room, a deep-heat massage pad was found to be vibrating at high speed under the bed.

On another occasion, Maxine was alone in the house with the baby when her ceiling light on the top floor flickered twice. Then all the lights in the house went out, though they remained on next door.

"If you're wondering about the wiring," Maxine added with a smile, "I will tell you that my husband's father is an electrical contractor. He and Bill did all the wiring themselves."

Shortly after the couple moved their bedroom to the top floor, their bedroom light also came on, two different times, with no one near it. It was a three-way bulb with the lower wattage burnt out, so that it actually had to click twice, in order to light. It was plugged into

70

The 1856 residences of Mr. and Mrs. William H. Pinson, Jr., on State Street, from a drawing by Brenda Zealy.

the same wall from which they had removed the marbles.

When Celia and her mother were out of the house for several days, Bill Pinson stopped by every day at noon to check on the house. He twice found the nursery ceiling light burning on the top floor, although he specifically remembered turning out the light, and closing the door.

Another event was more unsettling, and took place on the

ground floor. While Maxine was upstairs with Celia, she heard a crash in the kitchen area. Directly above the dish with the blue marbles, was a shelf holding a crystal jelly jar with a tight-fitting silver lid. Although nothing else on the shelf was moved, the lid of the dish had fallen to the floor with such force that the little knob on the top was detached. The rest of the dish was still on the shelf.

Another such incident was witnessed by several guests. During a party at her home, Maxine was telling the story of the marbles. She lightly touched the glass dish, secure on its shelf. At that point the shelf above it crashed to the floor for no apparent reason, scattering guests and some of Maxine's best crystal.

During that same period, while her mother and grandmother were in the dining room discussing the dish incident, an autumn wall hanging of Indian corn suddenly crashed to the floor with such force that kernels were scattered into the next room. The string holding it, and the nail on the wall were both found to be intact. On another occasion, an engraved beer stein and a figurine which had been on the mantel in the basement game room, were found shattered on the floor.

"When these events began," Maxine added, "My husband, who is a very analytical attorney, had resisted connecting them with the marbles. Aside from his deep Christian beliefs, Bill is a skeptic. This series of events was beginning to test his logic."

"By this time, I was beginning to get very edgy," our hostess confessed. "Things were getting broken that I really cared about! Also, I was worried about our little girl. I was determined to try to have a talk with whatever might be there, to tell it that we meant no harm. I decided to do this on a night when my husband was going to be gone and I was alone with Celia in the house. My neighbors had invited me to come stay with them, but I was determined not to give in to my fears."

Feeling rather foolish, the young woman began in as calm a voice as possible to address whoever might be listening, explaining that the Pinsons were there to stay. She said that they had made some changes in the rooms upstairs, but she felt that in the end these would make it more comfortable for everyone. She also asked whoever was listening not to play any more pranks, and not to frighten the child.

"Well, just at this point, all the lights went out!" the story continued. "I was ready to cry! Just then the telephone rang. I groped to it in the darkness, and was relieved to hear my neighbor's voice. I looked out the window, and saw that all the lights in the neighborhood were out! I was so relieved. I really don't blame our presence for that!"

72

During this time, something else happened which has never been satisfactorily explained. Maxine had prepared for a club meeting in her home, and had carefully laundered two dozen linen tea napkins. She then placed them in a closet which is part of the first floor bathroom. When she went to get them, she was amazed to find them quite wet. They were on the middle shelf of the closet, with no nearby water pipes. Nothing else was damp in the closet, either above or below them.

"Another major incident happened about this time one evening when we were upstairs in the nursery with Celia," Maxine continued. "Suddenly, we heard a back and forth rocking motion, followed by a loud crash, on the parlor floor!

"We found one of our tall, straight bishop's chairs lying on the floor, next to an overturned plant. Strangest of all, the noise which we had heard had been the chair rocking back and forth several times, before crashing over. As with earlier events, we could find no answers, such as open windows or unusual vibrations.

"The striking thing about these incidents was that they really began after we moved to the renovated top floor, and they happened sooner or later all over the house," Maxine pointed out.

During this time, the Pinsons continued their research on the house. Maxine felt that when she found the family whose children were most likely to have left the marbles, she would know it. They learned that the house had first been rented by Dr. John D. Fish, who had it for at least six years for $600 per year. Another prominent tenant was John McMahon, president of the Southern Bank of the State of Georgia, who moved in about 1871.

"From 1883 to 1909, it was occupied by William H. and Anne Daniel, and their family of three sons and a daughter. At the time, the house belonged to the Catholic diocese of Georgia, and its rent supported two orphanages. Daniel was an insurance agent, later part of the firm of Daniel, Carswell, and Prendergrast. In 1909, the widowed Mrs. Daniel moved to Oglethorpe Avenue," she told us.

"Somehow, it seems likely to me that the marbles belonged to the Daniel boys," Maxine said. "Perhaps one of the children died here. At any rate, about this time, things began to get quiet again."

As we walked about the home, Stephen remarked that it seemed basically peaceful. He even held the two blue marbles, taken down from the shelf in the breakfast room, without incident. However, he did not discount the possibility that a low-level form of energy had been present, or a rather mischievous entity which wanted attention.

"Sometimes they are fascinated by what has been added to a home," he remarked, "such as new light switches, or another bathroom. At other times, they simply use a house as they remember it, which is why you hear stories of presences going through doors that no longer exist, and so forth.

"One should always look for natural explanations first, such as sloping mantels and vibrations from outside traffic, when items fall," he added. However, he agreed with Maxine that the events connected with some of her breakage, was extraordinary.

That involving the water and the tea napkins, was especially puzzling. The theory that the shelf on which they were placed was near where an outside kitchen pump had been at one time, was considered.

"At any rate," said Maxine, "it's encouraging to know that you don't feel anything very strong here at the present time. We feel that for whatever cause, the energy which was present in those cases has lessened now. Perhaps it has accepted us, and the renovation."

"Your mental attitude can make a difference, too," Stephen told her. "When one is nervous and apprehensive, it is like giving an entity which might be present, something to use against you. When you are calm and in control of the situation, it generally improves."

"Well, I learned that looking for a ghost in your house isn't something to joke about," said Maxine with a smile. "You might get more than you bargain for!"

As Stephen and I were later discussing the morning's events outside the townhouse before going our separate ways, he remarked that something else unusual had occurred in connection with the Pinson's. When I had called him and asked him to meet me at the house, I had told him only that some strange events began to occur after some objects were removed from a room upstairs. I had not said what the events were, or the objects.

"Here's the drawing I was idly doodling, at my desk while we were talking on the telephone," Stephen told me, as he opened a large drawing pad. There, as if to illustrate the story, was a sketch of marbles.

"Have you ever drawn marbles before?" I asked as I recovered from my surprise. "They are really quite good!"

"Never! But now I understand why they came to my mind, as we discussed the house."

Another strange thing had happened, that very morning. As Stephen was waiting for me, he told me, he sensed that someone had opened the ground floor door, right behind him on the corner. Thinking I was already there, he turned to say hello, just as it closed again. Then I had appeared from a different direction, and the incident was temporarily forgotten.

Stephen's ESP sketch of the marbles.

"Now I understand," I said as we looked for a moment at the door just off the sidewalk on State Street, "why you asked Maxine if that door was ever opened."

"And you remember her reply, 'Goodness, no, it's so hard to unlock, it hasn't been used in ages!' I didn't tell her why I wanted to know. I felt that incident was directed toward me, and will probably never be repeated again."

Grove Point Plantation: Rumors of Wars and Piracy

South of Savannah, beyond the urban sprawl of shopping centers, real estate developments, and the new campus of Armstrong State College, there are still quiet areas which recall the region's burden of history. Grove Point Road is such an oasis, as it winds through the marsh grass, and among the moss-hung oaks and palmettos of the Low Country. It borders estates such as Wild Heron, whose frame 1756 plantation house is said to be the oldest in Georgia, Grove Hill, and Grove Point Plantation.

Today Grove Point seems peaceful enough, with a handsome white-columned Greek Revival mansion overlooking the marsh of the Little Ogeechee. It is located on a historic land grant made to Joseph Summers in 1757 from King George II of England. But legend says that it was also once a favorite retreat of Edward Teach, also Blackbeard, the pirate for whom one Georgia island is named.

It is known that before his death in 1718, Teach preyed on shipping all the way from the Virgin Islands to Nova Scotia. A legendary member of his savage crew was Israel Hands, who later sailed on the storied Walrus with Robert Louis Stevenson's Long John Silver and Captain Flint. Flint, of course, was the lusty buccaneer who is said to have died in Savannah, singing and calling for more rum.

Blackbeard is supposed to have maintained a slave compound at Grove Point, according to an account written by the daughter of a former owner of the estate, Harriett Elliott van Tess. It is said to have been managed by a lame overseer, "a bold, mean man with a limp," perhaps a former pirate. The overseer was thought to have lived in a hut located about where the main house is now, along with his mistress, "a white lady." There are family accounts of this woman being seen about the grounds, but none after about 1900.

Some believed that buried pirate treasure was still on the property, somewhere between the present location of the house, and

The house at Grove Point Plantation, by Yon Swanson.

the river.

Grove Point was later owned by Stephen E. Habersham of the early merchant family, and was a profitable rice plantation. It was then bought by John R. Cheves of Charleston, who built an unusual brick home on the property about 1830. This was modeled after a German castle, with a tower room, thick walls, a steep pitch roof, and a tiled kitchen.

When the War between the States came, Dr. Cheves is said to have been working on a new type of explosive bomb to assist the Confederacy. As the plantation was overrun by Federal forces in December, 1864, he is supposed to have suffered a stroke, and died the next day. Hurried attempts to bury his experiments are said to have caused the depression in the lawn still visible between two palmetto trees.

Yankee soldiers are also supposed to be buried on the grounds, three of them out on the point near the overseer's house. After occupying the mansion for two months, the invaders left with the family silver and other treasures, firing the house as a last gesture as they decamped. During this period, the property was also used as a signal station between the troops and their ships on the river.

The ruined plantation was acquired by Ralph Elliott in 1882, after nearly two decades of neglect. It was he who built the present two-story brick home there four years later, and who planted the palmettos along the drive to the house. Formal gardens on the property also bloom with camellias, wisteria, magnolias, azaleas, and other flowering plants.

More recent owners of Grove Point have included Judge Henry McAlpin and George A. Mercer of the prominent Savannah family which has included Revolutionary War and Confederate generals, and composer Johnny Mercer. The property was acquired by the Great Dane Corporation in 1956. The tastefully furnished house is now used for corporate entertaining, and is an outstanding example of how a historic property can be both preserved and enjoyed.

During the 1960s, the movie thriller *Cape Fear* was filmed at Grove Point, starring Gregory Peck, Polly Bergen, and Robert Michum. An even more suspenseful film might have been made with the plantation as subject rather than background.

Those who believe that the dramatic events of the past have left their mark on Grove Point include some Great Dane executives, and the estate's caretaker and hostess, Charles and Margaret Edwards.

It is obvious that both the Edwards are fond of the estate and enjoy its natural beauty. Like many people of English birth, Mrs. Edwards believes that the impressions of past owners and their lives can linger on, especially in such a quiet location. Often such presences do not recognize the changes which have occurred since their time, but continue to use the house as they remember it.

Activity in the house at Grove Point now seems to be concentrated around one large upstairs bedroom, which later had a portion walled off for an adjoining bathroom. During work on the house several years ago the paint in this area, especially one bathroom closet, did not want to dry, according to Charles.

"They tried heat lamps and everything else. . . . One day, when I thought the painters were there, I went up to find them gone, brushes all over, nothing put away, lights on, as though they had really left in a hurry! I couldn't figure it out. The next day they were back, looking a little embarrassed. All they said was, 'All at once, we just had to get out of here.'

"When it came to papering the bedroom," he continued, "the paperhanger didn't want to work in there alone! He finally asked me if I would mind staying in the house until he finished."

Charles added that it was in this bedroom that he had clearly heard feminine footsteps in a vacant house, coming from the bath and across the bedroom floor, while he was on the first floor. "One day," he recalled, "the sounds were so clear I was sure Margaret had somehow come in without my knowing it. I finally went part way up the stairs and called to her, but of course there was no one there."

Margaret recalled a summer morning just before dawn, when

she had gone up to the house to get breakfast for early-rising guests. She was driving from her house near the main house with just her parking lights on, so she would not disturb anyone with bright lights as she rounded the house. "Suddenly," she said, "I saw a misty, shadowy form before me on the front lawn...it took off at my approach, around the house. Then, I looked up at the bedroom window upstairs, and saw a light on in the bathroom.

"The window was open, and the shade was up. But, where I should have been seeing a painted wall, instead I saw wallpaper...the old-fashioned kind, with the big, bright flowers, just like a pattern I remember from my mother's house in England. It was like not seeing what is here now, but what had been.

"Another time," she recalled, "I was up there changing the sheets in that room, after we'd had guests. My little grandson, who was about eighteen months old at the time, was leaping and playing about as I tumbled the bedclothes onto the floor. Suddenly he jumped up and stood very serious and straight and still, wide-eyed at something he could see but I couldn't, with such a look of surprise.

"Then I heard, right by my ear, such a soft, feminine sigh, as though someone were saying, 'Oh, look at the child,' sweet, and rather sad. It was not unfriendly, but it startled me so that I snatched that little fellow up, and ran downstairs. I didn't go back up until Charles came in, and by then it was all quiet.

"Another time," she continued, "a couple from the West Coast were staying here. She has told me earlier that she was interested in the psychic and reincarnation, and asked me all about the history of the house. Also, I have several cats, but only one will walk with me into that house. Somehow she sensed that without my saying anything about it, and she asked me if she could take my cat along to keep her company. I said yes, and off they went.

"Well, the next morning, again quite early, I was up there in the kitchen preparing their breakfast, when I heard a funny rattle at the outside back door knob, as though someone wanted to come in. I looked out, wondering what it could be at that hour, but there was no sign of anyone. I went back to the stove, and that rattle came again, this time from the pantry door just off the back porch. I glanced out, in time to see a shadow glide by the window. I turned away, because I didn't want to see any more! I tried to think of something else, and continued my work.

"In a little while, the couple came down who had been staying in that room, the same woman I told you about. She came out and said, 'Tell me, is there anything unusual about the room where we slept last night?'

"'Yes, there's a ghost up there, but you just scared it down here to me,' I tried to say lightly, as she looked rather strange.

"'I thought I had,' she said mysteriously, and that ended the conversation.

"Another time," Margaret continued, "we had a couple who came in very late, remarking how tired they were. They went right upstairs to bed in that room. The next morning, when I slipped in to prepare breakfast, I was surprised to see the husband already up, sitting downstairs in a chair. Just sitting there, with a strange look on his face.

"'Well, you're an early riser,' I tried to say cheerfully.

"'I have reason to be,' he answered, and just sat there. Finally, he asked me the same question, was there anything unusual about his bedroom? I asked him why he wanted to know.

"He told me that he had first fallen into a very deep sleep. He awoke to find the light on in the bathroom, and the door ajar. A woman was standing there. At first he thought it was his wife, in her bath robe. But he looked again, and saw it was someone he had never seen before, in a long dress, and her hair down on her shoulders. According to him, she walked across the room at that point, and out into the hall. . .only she kind of glided through the door without opening it.

"He said that he got up, and hurried to look out after her. Of course, there was no one there. He laid down again, but could not sleep, so that's why he was dressed and downstairs so early."

"I think there may well be a feminine presence at Grove Point," Stephen said when we asked him for his impressions. "But I don't think she's a pirate's lady. I'd say that she is later, more likely Victorian, and someone who still feels at home here. . .perhaps the woman for whom this house was built. I don't think she would harm anyone, and only very sensitive people would be aware of her presence.

"There is a feeling of timelessness here," he continued. "In some areas, around the outbuildings, I do still sense some vibrations of the lame overseer. . . .He may well have been an old pirate, and a cruel man. As one walks about, there is still the feel of what Grove Point must have been like as a working plantation, a busy, prosperous place, with the outbuildings, the cattle, the flower and vegetable gardens. You feel these things are not very far away; you could blink your eyes, and see them all again."

The Faithful Nurse
of the Old Pest House

If buildings can retain in their walls and atmosphere the memories of activities and emotions which they once knew, it is no wonder that the sleep of the residents of an outwardly-comfortable-looking white frame home just off Route 17 south of Savannah, is occasionally troubled. The house, moved and cut down to a story-and-a-half design with a long front porch and contrasting shutters, is well over a century old. It was once called the Pest House, and was a place for the treatment and confinement of people with contagious diseases.

Some say it was a place for the quarantine of sick seamen and immigrants entering the Port of Savannah, and stood east of the city at Lazaretto Creek near Tybee; others say that it was a sanitarium at Thunderbolt. Stephen believes the former theory is probably correct, since it is said that it could be reached only by boat, and that those who died there were quickly buried in unmarked graves near the house.

Stephen and I had heard of strange doings in the old house through my daughter-in-law, Marie, a relative of the present owner. On a pleasant Sunday evening in early March, we three drove out beyond the garish motels and drive-ins of the old coastal route to Florida, to what is now an attractive home in a quiet rural setting. We were welcomed by the young wife, Toby, her two active school-age children by a former marriage, and Joe, the husband, who seemed both quietly interested and yet honestly skeptical of the whole affair.

After a tour of the home, which the family is still in the process of refurbishing, we sat at the long harvest table in the large, comfortable kitchen, as Toby reviewed the unusual events of her nine years there.

"The activity here definitely comes in cycles," she began. "I didn't know much about the history of the house when I came here, as it had been moved several years earlier. I had no idea there might still be something strange about it! At first we were renting, and then we started to buy it. I like the location, and with the work we've done, we are determined to stay if we can.

"Every house has its strange noises at night," she continued sensibly. "I believe now that a lot was always going on here, that I didn't think of as supernatural at the time. I used to hear what sounded like footsteps walking around upstairs, and coming down the steps when no one was there, but I just kept the radio on all night, and tried to ignore it. I never liked the upstairs much. It always felt cold and unpleasant, but I thought that was because it wasn't finished up there yet.

"You know," she explained, "the house was cut down half a story in moving. It still has the original walls, the stairs, and the railing. The house was so old, it had wooden pegs on the walls for clothing! I understand that some old knives, forks, and bottles were found around the place when it was moved, as well as old coins, and these are supposed to be in a museum, but I haven't been able to locate them yet.

"We were also getting strange noises in the foyer, so we put up a door between that and the living room, and we always use the kitchen door now instead of the front one.

"One of the first strange things that happened here," Toby went on, "was when I was here alone with the young children, several years ago. I went in the bathroom, and I couldn't get out the door again! It was like it was being held from the outside! I finally had to climb out the window. At the same time, I had the strangest feeling someone was watching me. But the next time I tried the door, it opened easily. That did scare me, and I spent the night with my family.

"Another time, I was in the living room. Suddenly we heard footsteps coming down the hall and into the foyer, after we had put the door there. I saw the knob turning, as though someone were coming in! But when I opened the door, there was no one there! This was about 1:30 in the morning. They were adult footsteps. Anyway, the children were asleep.

"On another occasion, about a week before Christmas, it sounded like chains rattling around overhead.

"About that time, my son was playing in the foyer. He was three at the time. Suddenly I could tell he was watching something coming down the stairs, that I never saw. All he would say was, 'It had a tail.' Well, that really scared me! I thought of the Devil, of course. After that, when anything happened, I would start to pray.

"Oh, I thought of moving," Toby admitted, "but my first

husband and I had separated, and there was no place this nice that I could afford to go. We like it here—in the daytime!

"The worst time seemed to be about 2:14 in the morning, the sounds, footsteps, and all. It got better, and then much worse after Joe and I were married three years ago. I thought that maybe what was here had accepted me, but not him! One night we heard a terrible crash upstairs, as though a heavy dresser had toppled over! We went tearing upstairs, and there was nothing out of place. We never did figure out what had caused the noise.

"Another time, a friend was staying in the back bedroom. She woke up about that time in the morning, and thought she heard people talking out in the living room. She decided to come out and have a cigarette with us if we were still up, and got into her robe. But when she came out, it was all dark and quiet! We had been asleep for hours.

"Then there was the time my eighteen-year-old nephew was sleeping upstairs," Toby recalled. "He woke up early in the morning, and said he heard noises like people moving around down in the kitchen, getting breakfast. When he came down to see what was happening, same thing. All quiet! About that same time, he felt someone touch his foot in the bed, and place a cold hand on his forehead! That did it! He spent the rest of the night at the foot of our bed, and he hasn't been back.

"One night at 2:14, I woke up and heard someone out in the hall, calling my name," she added. "It sounded like my husband, but he was in bed beside me! I was terrified that someone was trying to lure me out there by impersonating him. Of course, I didn't go."

Marie then told of a strange experience she had known in the house, reminiscent of its history. "I was spending the night here, not very comfortably, on a little mattress on the floor in the living room," she recalled. "I thought about going over to sleep on the sofa, but I could hear someone over there, snoring. I thought it was one of the children, and I tiptoed over in the darkness to see if they were covered.

"When I put my hand out, I could still hear the sound, but I put my hand in thin air! No one was there.

"Well, it scared me so badly, I went back to my mattress and laid down. I couldn't sleep, and I was still lying there, wide awake, when someone came in from the kitchen. She stood in the doorway, and I could see her distinctly. We had left a little light on out in the kitchen, the one on top of the stove, as kind of a night light for the kids during the night.

"She was a rather young woman," Marie went on, "wearing an

old-fashioned white dress, with a high collar, and long, full sleeves, gathered at the wrists. She had long hair, and she was carrying a basin full of water. I had the feeling she was a nurse.

"She looked right at me. 'You know I have to stay here,' she said, 'until they either get well, or they all die.' With that, she turned and crossed the room, toward the door to the foyer...and just disappeared into the door, without opening it."

"That same woman was also seen here by a young man," put in Toby. "Without knowing what Marie had seen, he said the same thing...a young woman, with a long dress and long hair, and in that case, she was walking through the bedroom like she was picking up things and tidying up the place."

After some more discussion and a walk again through the foyer, Toby asked Stephen his opinion of her house. "I think there is certainly psychic activity here," he replied, "and that it has to do with the history of the place. There is layer upon layer of tragedy and suffering here, the pain and despair of people who were kept here knowing they could never be well, and were waiting to die.

"I imagine the upstairs was the wards. The downstairs would have been the common rooms, as they were called, where people ate and were treated. The chains you heard, might have been from those who had to be forcibly restrained at times, the delirious and mentally ill. Also, you're right, Toby. There is a pronounced psychic chill upstairs.

"There is also a definite feminine presence here," he continued, "the young nurse whom you described, Marie. Perhaps she became ill herself, and died while treating others here. She is what we would call earth-bound, kept here by duty, not realizing that she is free to go on."

Toby looked startled. "What can we do?" she whispered, looking at Joe, who put his arm around her shoulders.

"I don't think the presence is malevolent," Stephen tried to comfort her. "I don't get a sense of evil. But she is aware of you, and what is going on.

"At the same time, she sees the house as it used to be. Hence, she walks right through the door to the foyer! The important thing is to stay calm, in control of the situation. Keep a positive attitude. It might help you to hang a cross in a room where you feel a disturbed atmosphere, such as the foyer and the upstairs, and to wear one yourself.

"Also," he went on, "if you can bring yourself to do it, the next time you sense the presence, try to talk to her. Address her in the name of the Lord. Tell her that those she seeks to care for, are gone, that there is no reason for her to stay on here. Tell her she is no longer of this place, that there is a better place waiting for her.

"Tell her to go on, to rest in peace. You may have to repeat this several times. Of course she may not want to hear or believe you, but it won't hurt to try, as long as you do it with a prayer. Also, if you know a priest or minister who would come here, and give a prayer for your house, or read an exorcism which includes a prayer for the dead, I'd do that."

Toby smiled. "My regular minister would think I was crazy, but I think I have a relative who would do it."

"The poor thing, maybe she died during an epidemic like they used to have, and no one could come out to read a service for her," Marie added softly. "Or for some of the others."

We sat there awhile longer, discussing the idea that certain atmospheric conditions lend themselves to the reception of psychic stimuli, and that some people are more receptive than others. "You might notice under what conditions, and at what times, your manifestations generally occur," Stephen suggested. "For instance, the 2:14 a.m. which you mentioned might have been when the nurse died, or some other traumatic event occurred. . . . That is, if you can do this without waiting for something to happen and expecting it."

Asked about the little boy who saw "something with a tail," Stephen commented, "It's always hard to tell what a child sees, because their vocabulary is so limited. For instance, to a young child, a tail might even be a dress with a long train, or a big bustle."

"Oh, I hope that was it!" exclaimed Marie. "What about the voice in the hall?"

"Well, that might have been Joe having an out-of-body experience when he was walking down the hall calling to you, Toby. That's only a guess; of course, it's hard to say about a single occurrence. The important thing is, don't hurt yourself with anxiety. Ghosts can't hurt you. . .the living can."

"Do you think the situation may change when we start renovating upstairs?" Toby asked as we started to leave.

"It could. . .in either direction," Stephen said thoughtfully. "Sometimes a presence resents renovation in 'their' house. Other times, if the work is fairly extensive and really changes the atmosphere, they leave. Sometimes gradually, sometimes all at once.

"Incidentally, I believe both you, Toby, and Marie are psychic, and so is the child who saw the presence in the foyer. I believe it is a gift we are born with, but it fades as we get older, and start using our other senses more."

"Well, here's hoping," Toby said bravely, her hand in Joe's as she told us goodbye. "There's a lot of love in this house, now."

"It really has the potential to be a great country house," I said to Marie as we waved back at Toby, outlined against her lighted kitchen doorway, and drove down the lane towards town. "I'd like to think that a house which has known so much tragedy, can become a real home."

The House on Victory Drive

"There are so many ghosts in Savannah houses, they have a union," one resident said. "It sets up what houses they can haunt, and what hours. Out in the country, though, they are still on their own." Even in such a place, one large white two-story home on Victory Drive is unusual, with its stately front columns and tall, protective azalea bushes. It has not just one presence, but stories of at least five.

The house was built around 1900, one of the first lots laid out in the Baldwin Park neighborhood. At the time, the unpaved street in front was still Estill Avenue, the southern border of the city. It was later renamed Victory Drive after World War I; legend says that a palm tree was planted on its grassy dividing strip of land for every county soldier who died in France. Said to be the world's longest palm-lined road, it is a place of handsome homes, wide lawns, and spectacular floral displays in the spring.

The present owners of the home at Victory and East Broad Streets are Mr. and Mrs. Jim Nettles, who have lived there since the early 1960s. From the summer they moved in, Melba Nettles told us during a visit to the house, unusual things have happened. "The first month, we were alone in the house. The children were in Florida. Jim was upstairs, painting the front bedroom.

"Suddenly, we heard footsteps coming up the stairs and down the hall. Then the knob of the door turned, and the door opened. But there was no one there!"

In the library downstairs, she added, some of the books and bookcases had belonged to a former owner. She thinks that might be why her little son Jimmy said one day, "Mommy, turn on the light here, so the man in the chair can see better."

"Jimmy was precocious from the time he was a baby," she told us. "He was talking at six months, and with complete sentences by the time he was a year old. Once, when I was playing with him in the bathroom, he pointed into space and said, 'See the other mother and the baby!' I carried him to the mirror, thinking that was what he meant. 'That mother and baby?' I asked before our reflection. 'No, no,' he shook his head, pointing at another side of the room."

The most famous presence in the house is one which the Nettles call "The Judge," since the house was once owned by a family with the same last name as a local magistrate. They believe it was The Judge who was seen by Jimmy in the library. They also think they heard his footsteps on the stairs . . . until they got an elevator. From the beginning, the elevator seemed to have a mind of its own, moving from floor to floor apparently at will.

"We would leave it on one floor, and find it on another, for no reason at all," said Mrs. Nettles.

They had the elevator mechanism checked, as well as the wiring in the house, and even the foundations, for anything which might be causing their unusual effects. No explanation could be found.

The elevator was most annoying when it moved alone at night, according to the family. Finally, it seems, Mr. Nettles had to make a house rule, to whoever was listening, that it was not to be run while he was trying to sleep. Since then, things have been considerably more peaceful.

"On two separate occasions, when I went down the stairs, the elevator would go up," said Louis Kincaid, a family friend. "One morning I found the newspaper in the house and open, though I was the first one up." The sound of a piano has also been heard, with no one near the piano.

One night the Nettles returned home from a party to find their maid sitting on a bench in the upstairs hallway. She held a newspaper in front of her, though she was obviously not reading it. When Mrs. Nettles remarked that there were softer chairs downstairs, she explained that she had heard footsteps walking continually up and down in the quiet hall. She felt she should be upstairs closer to the children, where she could watch their rooms.

Footsteps have also been heard in the kitchen early in the morning, and the cheerful rattle of pots and pans, as though someone were preparing breakfast. This is all in an apparently empty kitchen. The sound of a swinging door between the kitchen and the butler's pantry can also be heard. . . .

Sometimes, lights appear in dark rooms, showing under the closed doors. A pool table on the sun porch, after a game, will have the balls lined up in two neat rows, with the 8-ball in the pocket. Rocking chairs move by themselves, especially in the library: this also happened in the house after a large Thanksgiving dinner, as

The Nettles' home on Victory Drive, © copyright by Brenda Zealy.

though others were also present.

From the time the Nettles moved in, there have been incidents where one would think the other was calling, and answer. "I didn't say anything!" would come the reply. This also happened to Kincaid, he reported: "At first, I thought someone was putting me on.

"I am not necessarily 'a believer,' but I do know that three electrical contractors looked at that elevator to see what was causing it to move by itself," he said. "Also, some of the house light switches wouldn't work, and then later for no good reason, they were fine."

Another unusual story has been told of the attic, where the jacket of a West Point midshipman has been found in an old trunk. The story goes, that one night for no apparent reason, it was found stretched out across the trunk. Nearby was an item from another trunk, a wedding gown.

Mrs. Nettles, a calm, kindly person, is a member of the Theosophical Society. She believes young Jimmy had psychic powers as a chld which he has since lost because he preferred not to develop them. "I really feel that some tragedies have been connected with this house," she concluded. "I feel that the bedroom where we hear the footsteps and the door opens, or the light goes on, belonged to a young man who was killed in the war or died at an early age.

"I also believe a young woman and child died here in the early part of the century....I think death is a part of life, and it is very possible to me that afterwards the spirit of the person continues to live on."

After we said goodbye, I asked Stephen what he thought of the house. "Well, I think the Nettles are right in that there are about five presences there," he said. "The man in the chair in the library, who likes the elevator; the young man; the young woman and the baby; and the older woman getting breakfast, who likes the rocking chair.

"I wouldn't care to live with that much 'going on,' but the Nettles seem happy there, and have accepted The Judge like a family friend," he added.

"One thing more. There was definitely a presence in the attic when we were there, and it came down the stairs with us afterwards when we were in the upper hall. Just thought you'd like to know."

"At first we didn't want any publicity about our presences," Melba Nettles told us, "but then we decided, what difference does it make? It's our home, and we plan to go on living here. One thing, we feel safer from burglars now, since several stories have been done on the house."

To Catch a Ghost, Try a Drawing

At first glance the comfortable and affluent neighborhood of Kensington, once fertile farmland and now tree-shaded residential streets, is as unlikely a haunt of old ghosts as could be imagined. Although bordered by busy DeRenne Avenue to the north and the congestion of the southside Savannah traffic around Oglethorpe Mall further on the other side, it is still an area of wide lawns and pleasant homes.

A certain rambling corner white brick house of that neighborhood is only about seventeen years old. Behind it stretches a spacious yard, accented with large oak trees and azaleas. It appears to be a typical American suburban home, with its ranch floor plan of a long, angled hall, a family room, and a carport.

Kim Heffernan, a slender, pretty young woman in her mid-twenties, appears to be as normal and wholesome as the house and its neighborhood. Yet it was there that she says she knew a sad-eyed male presence for several years, one from whom only now she feels she may be free. In her case, too, an off-duty artist from the Savannah Police Department was involved, surely a first even for Savannah ghosts.

During an interview at her in-law's home after she had told her story for the first time on Ed Hartley's radio show, Kim said that she had been born in Texas, but had lived in Savannah for the past ten years.

"This was my first psychic experience" she added, "though I have a grandmother from Savannah who has had several. I always kind of smiled at the whole thing, so I didn't have the nerve to tell her at first when this thing started happening to me." She began her story be recalling that from the time she, her parents, and her two brothers had come to the house when she was a teenager, she had felt a chill in her bedroom. Even on warm days.

The first time she saw what was to become almost her personal

91

ghost, she was dozing off to sleep not long after moving into her room. She awoke suddenly to realize there was a man in her room. Her first instinct was that he was a prowler. Then she realized that he was slowly beginning to fade from her view. . . .

It was always the same man: "tall, broad-shouldered, with a jacket with the padded lines of the 1920s and 1930s. A neat man, with a shirt and tie. I'd say he was middle-aged, maybe in his fifties," she described him. "There was nothing menacing about him. I could never see his eyes clearly. At times, I had the impression that they were bright blue, and piercing. . .at other times, they seemed almost vacant. Not a thin man, or a heavy one, but with a good build, maybe six feet-one.

"There was always a sad look to his face, and he would be gazing at me very intently. It was like he wanted to be near me. As though I were reminding him of someone.

"Another strange thing," she continued. "All the times I saw him in that house, and there were so many I lost count, he had a folded newspaper under his arm. I never could make out the headlines.

"But the time we saw him go down the hall, later on, we could hear the rustle of that paper as he walked.

"I tried to tell myself it was only a bad dream," Kim added. "But then I would see him in my room just as I was getting ready for bed, before I had been asleep. Oh, I tried sleeping out on the sofa in the living room, but Mother said she didn't want me out there every night. I forced myself to go back to the room. Once you get used to it, you know, you are safer with a ghost than with a prowler! But your first instinct is still to get away, to just get out of the room. I even tried asking him what he wanted. There was no answer; he would just disappear."

Kim was the first to see the ghost. Then she went to spend a weekend at Tybee Beach, and her younger brother had a friend over to sleep in her room. Not wanting to scare him, she had not told him of the man with the paper. The next morning, the boy described the presence exactly as she had seen him.

One night after the ghost, whom Kim began to think of as Chester, had appeared to her several times, there was the matter of the music. She was asleep when the room was filled with "sad, slow-moving music. . .not as full as a pipe organ, but more like a spinet. Not exactly a funeral march, but very melancholy."

Her brother, thinking her clock had gone off in the middle of the night, came running into the room with his baseball bat, half-asleep and irritated at being awakened. Instead, he found his sister sitting up in bed, the suspected radio not even in her room. After awhile the sounds ceased, and they all went back to sleep.

By that time," said Kim, "my parents were getting pretty tired of being awakened in the middle of the night by me, and then not sensing anything themselves. I decided, if that music didn't wake them, I was going to let them sleep. So I did.

"When a thing like this begins, you blame yourself. You think maybe it's your imagination, that you're living in a dream world. But as time went on, I could see him in that room without my even having been asleep! Or, I could walk down the hall, glance in the door, and there he would be."

On another occasion, she continued, the presence appeared to her, the young man she later married, and a third young man. Kim was not feeling very well, and was lying on the sofa in the family room. One of the men was playing the guitar. Suddenly they looked up, and saw the man coming down the hall, the newspaper under his arm as usual. Other people were out in the carport and the driveway at the same time, with the hall door open.

"When the men with me saw Chester, they thought he was a prowler, and they jumped up and chased him down the hall," she recalled. "He cast a shadow . . . he blocked the light from the hall into the family room, when he stood there just looking at us. When the fellows ran down the hall, he just disappeared. And the door down the hall, a warped door that you had to force, had closed! None of us had touched it.

"Once about that time, I saw him away from the house. I was very sick, running a temperature. I was at an apartment out in town. I was kind of lying on my left side in a big chair, when I looked up and saw him standing beside me. I was just too sick to care. I closed my eyes, and when I looked up again, he was gone.

"On another occasion, in broad daylight, I was standing talking to my mother, and looking out the big picture window in the back of the house. I glanced out, and there he was, standing in the center of the yard, with his back to us. 'Look, Mother, quick!' I called, and then he vanished."

About six months after the appearance of the ghost, Kim said that she had her dream about the barn for the first time. It was to be repeated about six or seven times, with no variations, while she lived in the house.

"There was always this large barn, with Chester standing in the doorway, looking into the interior. No newspaper," she described the scene. "Inside the barn, with her back to the man, was a slender young girl, about my age. It was summer, and she was wearing a light, printed dress, midcalf style. She had long, loose, brown hair to the shoulders, like mine.

"Then the dream always changed. Somehow I was the girl. You know how you dream that you are falling? Well, in the dream, it would always be a large object, falling from the left, a huge round thing. It would be falling, falling. . .and then I would see the girl, only now she is lying with her hair over her face, and the man is bending over her with the same sad expression. I never saw her face closely, but I always felt that it was like mine."

The morning after the initial dream, Kim was walking about the shady yard, recalling the experience. She nearly fainted when an older neighbor leaned over the fence and said in a pleasant way, "Say, did you know this area used to be a big dairy farm, and there was a barn about there?"

"After that," she continued, "I began finding dairy artifacts. . .a spur, nails, pieces of bottles. I saved them all, on my windowsill, until I moved from that house. Later, I never could find them. I might have lost them, but I don't think I did."

"I always had the feeling, Kim continued, "that the man I was seeing did not mean any harm, but that I reminded him of someone, probably a daughter, that had lived there. I was sure it had to do with the house on that location; I think it had burned. The house we lived in was on the foundation of a much older house. It was built at a strange angle, over the old foundations, like an 'L.'"

After talking with Kim, Stephen and I went out to see the house itself. It was vacant at the time, in the process of renovation. We were told by a neighbor that after Kim's family left, it was used by people suspected of having gambling parties there, and was allegedly raided by the police. On the day we were there, it was quiet, according to Stephen. However, he added that it was not one in which he would choose to live, because of its unusual shape, rather sad atmosphere, and unique purple carpeting.

"This whole area has a sense of not quite being real," he said. "You see something, and yet you feel, if you looked again, it would not be there."

Stephen later met Kim and her husband, and talked with her about her later experience with the sad-eyed man. Kim told Stephen that after she was married, her father-in-law remarked that he knew an artist with the Savannah Police Department who drew people as they were described to him. The sketches were then used in solving crimes. He suggested that the artist try to draw Kim's presence with the newspaper.

Through an additional coincidence, the artist was familiar with the area. He also verified that the house was located on what had been a thriving dairy farm, with a large barn behind the house. After the picture was completed, it was recognized by older persons in the area as that of a former owner, now deceased. He was said to have been very fond of young people; one woman thought he had lost a daughter about Kim's age, around 1940.

Kim also told Stephen that the presence had followed her briefly after her marriage, and that once or twice she had the sensation that he was attempting to form again. "It would start as sort of a vague, smoky column," she recalled, "always when I was alone. I would get out of the room, fast! I didn't want to encourage him, and so I never again saw him develop to full form. I felt it was time that we both went on.

"I don't know the people who live in the house now, but I hope things are peaceful there. I still think he was attracted to me because of my reminding him of another young girl and something that happened in the house. My mother never did see him."

The Message on the Chimney

The modest but striking little white frame house at 310 West Charlton Street has the plain lines and dormer windows of a New England cottage, rather than a southern home in Currie Town Ward, on the west side of the historic district near the Civic Center in Savannah. The first time Suzie Hankins and her husband, Charles, saw the 1839 dwelling, they were struck by its uniqueness, though it had been long neglected. They did not realize that the apparently vacant house, which the last owner had attempted to renovate, but decided to sell instead, already had an occupant.

Charles is a retired Air Force pilot, and Suzie, the mother of several grown children, is also active in Savannah's growing film industry. The two do the hard work of tearing out partitions, stripping, carpentry, and painting themselves, and then rent the Savannah houses which they have restored. As Suzie told Stephen and I when we toured the little house one day, it was their first experience with the supernatural.

To make things worse the presence, whom they have christened Mr. Curly, is a surly character. He has favored them with sudden chills on airless summer days, acrid smells, and even mysterious scratches on the bricks of the red chimney. "We know," Suzie explained the name, "that a Nicholas Curly lived here in 1848. An Elizabeth Curly, perhaps a daughter or sister, lived next door. We know he boarded a slave that year, and sold cotton, so he must have had a plantation out of town, and used this as his town house.

"The first thing I noticed was the smell," Suzie recalled. "It's like...well, passing gas, sewer gas. Very unpleasant! It's acrid; it makes your eyes burn. The first time it happened, Charles and I were working on the third floor. I began to smell it. After awhile, I looked at him and he was looking at me! Then we realized it was much stronger than what we were suspecting, and we started searching for a probable cause, either indoor or out.

Suzie Hankins' photo of the chimney at her Charlton Street House shows the mysterious scratching in the lower left-hand corner, and the unusual blue fog over most of the picture. All other photos taken on the same roll at the same time developed normally.

"We never found another explanation. We noticed after that it was occurring more often on the third level, but sometimes it was on the second, more toward the front of the house. There were times, then, that I could sense a film, or haze on the third floor. Ethereal...I thought I could make out a blue coat, pockets. I never doubted that it was a man. I felt he was unfriendly, though we've had no problems except the smell, and then the scratching on the fireplace." She explained that the latter took place when the house was being gutted inside. Most of the flooring at the second level had been removed, so that it was accessible only by ladder.

"We came to work one morning, and my husband said, 'What's that on the fireplace?' There were five letters scratched on the brick. The first three were in script on one level, SCR, and below them, NW. We were mystified; because with the floor gone, there was no good way to reach that high! The house had been locked overnight. There was no sign of forced entry; nothing else had been disturbed.

"Another thing about the scratches: try as we could, we couldn't find another tool in all Charles's equipment to duplicate it! You know it's hard to scratch brick that deeply. This was deeply scratched in, not just drawn on. It was not done with a nail, or a piece of wood.

"I have a sister in the Midwest whom I consider to be quite psychic," Suzie went on. "When I wrote her about my experiences, she answered, 'I think it means 'Scram now,' and you ought to get out of there! At least be careful when you're on that level alone, and on ladders. Always carry something sharp and metal with you.'

"About that time," Suzie added, "I was working in the house one incredibly hot day. The house was all covered with plastic on the outside, so there was no way any air could get through. I was so hot, on the upper level, I had just said to myself, 'I can't stand this. I'm going to have to go home.' The whole atmosphere was heavy, unpleasant.

"Then suddenly I began to get cool. At first I thought, 'Oh, that's nice, whatever it is,' thinking my husband had rigged a fan or something downstairs for some ventilation. But then I realized it was a deeper, more unpleasant chill. I was really getting cold. I climbed down, and asked Charles if he had done anything to cause a change in temperature. He hadn't. We decided it would be better if I didn't work any more up there that day.

"One thing which we have noticed," she commented, "is that the activity seems to be more pronounced during the period of high tides. I have also had the sensation at times of feeling dizzy as I climbed around the landing. At the same time, something told me not to slow down, but to keep on moving. We have also heard that this is an unmarked cemetery, and slaves were buried in this area.

"But the strangest thing of all happened when we decided, as we always do, to take 'Before and after' pictures of the house. The first was to show it completely gutted, with only the fireplace remaining.

"When the film was developed, the shot that showed the bricks with the scratching on, showed them clearly, but there was a blue fog over the rest of the picture!" She produced a color print close-up of the area, which was exactly as she described it. "This was the only print on which this appeared! These were regular color pictures that we had developed. This was the only shot of the fireplace. Since the initials show through the fog, it is not a mistake in development, or the whole portion of the picture would have been spoiled, wouldn't it? And, the rest of the pictures were normal!

"Whenever we felt his presence, after that, we would always speak politely to him," our hostess added. "It would be, 'Oh, hello, Mr. Curley, I hope you like what we're doing to your house.' I don't know if it helped."

Before Suzie had told her story, Stephen had carefully climbed with her to the third landing, and made his way slowly around the fireplace at all the levels. They both reported encountering the noxious, sultry smell, and were surprised that I had noticed nothing.

"I feel as though we have someone here who is very possessive of his house, and did not like it when he saw parts of it being carried away," Suzie concluded. "We took some of the lumber home with us, to the outside, to refinish. I just hope we can make peace with him, and have him accept us, when he sees that we really like his little house, too." Stephen agreed with her assessment, and thought things might improve when the house was finished, and new energies there, especially if the tenant were a strong, stable person.

But the last time I spoke with Suzie, she told me that they had sustained a costly fire in one of their other properties on East Jones Street. The unexpected expense of that renovation had caused them to temporarily suspend work on the Charlton Street house, leaving Mr. Curly's home quiet once more.

For the time being, at least, he seems to be getting his own way.

"Crashing" A Seance

The sturdy blue frame townhouse at Price and President Streets is one of the oldest buildings in a historic area. It dates from about 1810, and stands on one of the city's original trust lots. It was formerly painted yellow, and is now rented out with separate apartments on different floors.

From the time this project began, we had heard stories of past supernatural experiences there. Several different presences seemed to be involved. When we finally contacted the two young matrons who had taken part in a seance there, they were reluctant to be interviewed. Each had by then moved to a different home; each was married, with a small child. They were anxious to put whatever had happened in the blue house, behind them.

However, the owner of the house, who told us he personally had little experience with such things, gave us the key to investigate the top floor while the apartment was vacant. After this, the two women agreed to talk with us, but at a different location. Stephen and I met the two friends, named Natalie and Victoria, at a most unspectral setting in Ardsley Park.

As they reconstructed the story over coffee, the events in question had occurred several years before, when one of them lived on the top floor of the house, and the other on the ground floor. One of the most persistent oddities which they observed was a "scent that traveled," as one of them put it, "herbal, medicinal. . .like nothing we had experienced before, and which we could trace to nothing in the house on any floor. We finally concluded that the house had been built on an Indian burial ground."

"There was also a sweet, musty smell in the hall occasionally," said one of them. "The only time I ever saw anything was about midnight on Christmas Eve, while going down to the second floor. I caught a glimpse of a woman in an old-fashioned, long, yellow ruffled organdy dress. She was simply there, and then she disappeared. One other person saw her, too. But I did not feel afraid, just a little surprised.

"That same Christmas Eve, we had loud noises in the house, for which we had no explanation," she continued. "It sounded like someone walking around, up and down the stairs, but no one was there! Then there was a terrific crash on the top floor, like all our dishes were broken at once! We went racing up from the ground floor, but nothing was found to be damaged.

"At different times, while we were living there, we would be sure we had burglars, and call the police. They never found anything. Once, when I was alone on the top floor, I felt as though someone had just put their hand on my shoulder. When I turned, no one was there."

Victoria said that she had often felt a presence in her ground floor apartment. "One night I started to pull up the covers, and I felt someone slap my hand! I had a big Labrador at the time, and I once saw him leap on the bed, looking into space and cowering at something that I could not see.

"One night I went to bed, and suddenly for no reason I never could find out, a picture went crashing off the wall! At that point, I pulled up the covers and said aloud to the darkness, "If you are here tonight, let me see you in my dreams." I had heard that would work, and I was very curious. Among other things, items were being put down in my apartment, and then found up to the top floor! At first I thought I was just forgetful, but I soon realized it was more than that.

Well, that very night," she continued, "I dreamed of a little boy! He was a blondish little fellow, in an old-fashioned velvet suit, like you'd see in tintypes of the mid-nineteenth century. I was so surprised. I have never thought of it being a child. And yet, the pranks were often just mischievous. I felt the little boy had lived in that house, maybe died there, too."

Doing research on the old house, the two learned that one of its residents had been an undertaker, W. D. Dickson, who with Donald Ferguson operated a funeral establishment at 138 Broughton Street. The house was later owned by a Mrs. Margaret Ferguson, who owned $19.25 on it in back taxes. It was then bought at a sheriff's sale on New Year's Eve, 1884, for $25 by Donald Ferguson, perhaps her relative.

About this time, the two determined to have a seance with a ouija board, to see if anything more could be learned about the location.

Procuring the board, and putting out all the lights but two candles, they settled down to the task. Appropriately enough, it was a rainy, stormy night. A fierce, cold wind blew off the Savannah River, rattling the panes of glass in the old frames, and lashing the branches of the large oak tree just outside the room.

One of the women asked the first question. "If you are here now, give us a sign."

The pointer did not move. Outside, the wind rose, and a loud crash echoed through the house. A limb of the gnarled old tree nearby had been cracked and broken off in the storm, and went hurtling to the sidewalk. The two ran to the window, but nothing but the broken limb could be seen on the wet pavement below.

Trying to shake off a vague sense of discomfort, one of the women repeated the question. This time, the three-legged planchette began to slowly move. The candles flickered.

"I just did," it spelled out, and stopped again. It was the end of the session. Lights were turned on, and the board was quickly put away. It was not employed again.

Walking through the house earlier, Stephen remarked that he felt a strong feminine aura had been present there for some time, but was less marked at the present. "I don't much care for the stairs," he said as we entered the upper hall. "I feel it would be easy to have an accident there."

He also remarked a certain disoriented feeling in the main room on the top floor, "nothing seems to be at right angles!" Looking out the window at the large oak tree, he continued, "I should stay away from this window, since I get a sense of dizziness here, an inclination to pitch forward. Yet, it draws me." We later learned that was the room, and the tree, whose story we were about to hear.

"I definitely think you both brought some energy to the house, which interacted with whatever was there, and with that of the others in the house," Stephen told Natalie and Victoria. "When I saw it vacant, it of course was quite different. Every old place, and some newer ones, have impressions on its atmosphere. These, with the right people present, make a manifestation more possible. The house is quite quiet now, and the events which you described, may never take place there again."

"The Most Beautiful House in America"

"The most beautiful house in America," some architects and antique lovers have called the elegant and aristocratic Owens-Thomas House on Oglethorpe Square, designed by the young English architect, William Jay. It was completed in 1819 for Richard Richardson, a cotton merchant and banker, and his young wife Frances Bolton, a Savannahian and relative of Jay's by marriage. It was built at a time of civic prosperity and pride, the year the S.S. *Savannah*, the world's first steamship to cross the Atlantic, made her famous voyage.

Unfortunately, Frances Richardson died three years later, and her husband lost the home in a financial depression. It was Mary Maxwell's rooming house at the time its most famous visitor, the Marquis de LaFayette, stopped there for several days in 1825, and made an address to the citizens from the south balcony. It was later home to Congressman George Owens, whose granddaughter, Miss Margaret Thomas, left it to the Telfair Academy of Arts and Sciences as a museum.

My friend Claire believes Miss Thomas is still in residence: "The first time I went there, I felt a distinct chill in her bedroom, although it was spring, and I was very warm when I walked through the door."

The maid at the house museum has also had some unusual experiences. She told of leaving the dining room table neatly set at night. In the morning one chair would be pushed back, as though a diner had just left their place. One morning she found a puddle of water on the dining room floor, though the house had been locked, and all had been normal the night before. The damp area was near neither the window or plumbing. "Let's just say I wouldn't come back here at night," she concluded.

The director of the house museum, Dolly Tison, says that she has never sensed anything unusual. "But I have a little poodle who goes everywhere with me...until we come here. Then it whines at the door, and won't come in; it wants to wait out there for me."

The story used to be told of hearing a tinkling piano in the vacant house later in the night, until the piano was sold. Some have claimed seeing the veiled figure of a woman, wrapped in a grey shawl and wearing a large hat, walking in the garden as though on her way to her carriage. However, this tale may have an earthly explanation.

Among the many pictures at the house is one of Miss Thomas, wearing a rather old-fashioned, long gown and shawl, and walking about the back garden. "She loved to dress up in the old family clothes and have parties with her friends," said one who knew her. Could someone have seen her thus attired, and started a new Savannah spectre on its way?

One humorous anecdote is told of Miss Thomas's fondness for such parties. Since it had been her custom to mark her birthday each year with one, some of her friends decided to carry on the custom with a small celebration on her birthdate the first year after her death in 1951. The editor of the *Savannah Morning News* thought it was a good human interest story, and sent a staff photographer over who did not know the history of the house.

The young man arrived at the old mansion after dark, to find several elderly ladies in old-fashioned long dresses gathered in the dimly-lit front parlor around a small table. Its centerpiece was a cake with flickering candles, which cast grotesque shadows on the walls. "Where is Miss Thomas?' ' he asked as he adjusted his camera.

"Oh, she's dead, poor dear," whispered one of the senior citizens, surprised at the question. Without waiting for his picture, and thinking he was at a seance, the startled man is said to have run all the way back to the newspaper.

REGENCY HOUSE, REGENCY SPIRIT

One eyewitness story of a presence which appeared in the apartment above the museum, once an upstairs sitting room and guest rooms of the home, was told by a young Savannah antique dealer. He and his business partner, who collaborated the story but asked not to be quoted, were visiting the man who rents the apartment of the historic old house. It was, said the first man, about twilight on a peaceful Sunday afternoon. Their host had just served the first drinks of the cocktail hour, and they were sitting talking quietly. Suddenly they were aware that a fourth man was in the room.

"I could clearly see him, what he was wearing and all, yet at the

Owens-Thomas House drawing by Lee Harless; courtesy Owens-Thomas House.

same time, I knew he was not real," said the narrator. "He was a man about thirty or thirty-five, powerfully built, weighing maybe 175 or 180...black hair.

"I had a feeling he was a guest in the home, and had just come in from outside, maybe from riding....He was dressed in the style of about 1830, wearing a cutaway tail coat, black or dark blue, light, tight pants, and a white ruffled shirt. He was at the doorway for two or three minutes, then he kind of moved around the room, and stood behind a sofa. Then he went through the door into what was a guest room at the time the house was new. My partner here and I looked at each other and nodded, to be sure we were both really seeing him.

"Our host never did see him, but he could tell something was going on. None of us spoke or moved, just waiting to see how long we would see him...about ten minutes in all. It was not frightening, just unusual. I'd never had an experience like that before. I was especially surprised that he was in period clothing; somehow, I thought ghosts were kind of white and shapeless!

"Later, we asked our host if he had ever noticed anything else unusual, and all he would say was, 'Well, I wouldn't go downstairs at night!'"

Mary Telfair's Museum

Like the Owens-Thomas house, the handsome Telfair mansion on Barnard Street was designed by architect William Jay around 1818. It was also saved for the public as a museum by the last member of the illustrious family to live there, spinster Mary Telfair, who died in 1875. One of the oldest art museums in the South, its formal opening eleven years later was attended by Jefferson Davis, former president of the Confederacy.

The house has been extensively remodeled as a museum since Mary's time, but still many family furnishings remain. The legend persists among some of the staff that the dynamic Mary is still in evidence, and makes herself known whenever anyone dares to move her huge oil portrait. Most recently, some say, when it was moved from its accustomed place in the dining room, a part of the rotunda ceiling fell through the new lower ceiling below it, and one of the paintings was slightly damaged.

Some told of the sound of harp music in the vacant front parlor when the museum is closed; others spoke of footsteps, and swinging and sliding doors that seem to open of their own accord. When the museum is closed, according to one former staff member, there are occasionally vibrations in the building strong enough to set off the electronic alarm system—for no discernable reason.

Stephen mentioned one incident which occurred to him at the Telfair when he was a student, taking art classes there several years ago. Entering the front hall one quiet afternoon when the museum was closed to the public, he was startled to hear music, and see a party in progress in the large front drawing room. "People in early nineteenth century clothing were moving about," he said, "and there was the sound of laughter and conversation."

After watching the affair for a moment, he walked to the library across the hall to inquire of a staff member about the afternoon costume party. To his surprise, he realized that the large room was

Miss Mary Telfair, from a miniature at the Telfair Academy of Arts and Sciences.

now silent; in fact, there were even dust covers on some of the furniture.

The story goes that Mary and her sister, Margaret, loved the same man, scholar and diplomat William Brown Hodgson, whom they had met in Paris. Margaret, who was younger and prettier, married him on the condition that he move to Savannah. The three lived together in the house on Telfair Square. At his death, Margaret endowed the Georgia Historical Society, one of his favorite organizations, with a new building which was to be named for him.

She died while the three-story porticoed structure at Whitaker and Gaston streets in Savannah was under construction, and her sister Mary oversaw the project. She also died before the building was completed. Her will specified that both Hodgson Hall and the Telfair Museum would have "no eating, drinking, smoking, or amusements of any kind."

At the Telfair, this prohibition is met at receptions after museum events by having catered food in the new lower western

Drawing of the Telfair Academy of Arts and Sciences by Lyda Keller from The Pirates' House Cook Book, © *copyright 1964 by Frances McGrath, courtesy of Herb Traub.*

wing, where the Telfair's carriage house and stables were once located.

On one memorable evening at Hodgson Hall, the issue was resolved by setting out refreshments after a society meeting on the lawn behind the building. However, a sudden storm came up, and there was nothing to be done but to move the tables inside. As the guests began to enjoy the food and drink, the storm intensified, and thunder crashed above the building. The lights flickered.

According to a society account, "A gust of wind blew through the building, a window rattled, a glass fell and broke, and mysterious voices were heard. . . . So now, refreshments and other proscribed amusements are confined to the new annex, whose donors frown on such puritanical prohibitions."

Recently, however, refreshments have been served after the annual spring meeting right in the main room, under Hodgson's own large portrait. Looking at it, one has the feeling he would not have minded so much as Margaret or Mary if a few crumbs got on the rug, so long as people—the right sort, of course—were having a good time in his building.

108

A Spectral Cat at the Davenport House

More than any other house in Savannah, the Georgian Davenport House on East State Street at Columbia Square is symbolic of the successful preservation movement of the city. Built by Isaiah Davenport about 1820, it was a home in which the master builder from Rhode Island raised six sons and a daughter.

After having had many tenants over the years, it was in sad disrepair and scheduled for demolition when rescued by the group of women which later became organized as Historic Savannah Foundation. The first headquarters of the group, it is now a house museum, open to the public in the furnishings of the time in which it was built.

The story about a spectral cat at the house was recalled by Savannah author Gerald Chan Seig, who said she had written a number of ghost stories over the years for various publications, but had never told this one. It had been one she had heard from her father, China-born Robert Chung Chan, who had been a young revolutionary against the corrupt Manchu Dynasty. He had fled China to save his life, and arrived in Savannah at the terrible height of the 1889 Hogan's fire, so called because it began at Hogan's Department Store on Broughton Street.

Seeing the spire of Independence Presbyterian Church on Bull Street in flames, he took it as a sign to join that congregation, which he did.

Chan later lived at the Davenport House, along with several other Chinese families, when it was a boarding house.

"One afternoon Father was coming home from work," Gerald repeated the story. "As he walked up the front steps of the house, a large yellow cat ran in front of him. Startled because he had never noticed a cat there before, he opened the door to go inside. The cat shot through the open door, and disappeared down the hallway. As my father began to look for it, the others in the house heard the story and came out to join the search. It would have been impossible for

109

that cat to get outside again without being seen, yet no sign of it was ever found."

"Do you suppose the Davenports had a yellow cat? With seven children, they probably did!"

Drawing of the Davenport House on State Street as it might have appeared when new; courtesy of Historic Savannah Foundation, Inc.

A Rocking Ghost at the Scarbrough House

In the same heady Regency period of construction as the Owens-Thomas and Telfair houses, architect William Jay designed the stately neo-classic Scarbrough House on West Broad Street in Savannah for a merchant prince who typifies the age, William Scarbrough. It was completed days before the steamship S.S. *Savannah* arrived in her namesake city from New York, before beginning her famous voyage across the Atlantic under steam. A principal promoter of the vessel, Scarbrough entertained President James Monroe and other dignitaries in his new home before the ship departed for England.

By all accounts William's wife, Julia Scarbrough, was beautiful, headstrong, and a social climber. Acquaintances dubbed the North Carolina native "the Countess" for her airs and love of grand parties.

"There was a dinner at which she is reported to have boasted that the ham served cost four times as much as local ham because it was imported," Frank O. Braynard writes in S.S. *Savannah: The Elegant Steamship.* "On another occasion, when the finger bowl reached her, she not only dipped her fingers in, but also washed them vigorously, and then scrubbed her face as well."

"For God's sake, don't ask the Countess to sing, or she will frighten the good people of England," her socialite friend Robert Mackay wrote his wife in London when the Scarbroughs were about to visit her. "She is cursed coarse sometimes, but she has a good heart," he said of her on another occasion.

"Mrs. Scarbrough lately sent out cards of invitation to five hundred persons," another wrote of her. "Three hundred attended. Every room in the large home was newly furnished for the occasion, the beds, etc., sent out; refreshments handed 'round from garret to cellar through the night."

But the S.S. *Savannah* was not a financial success. Sold at auction and ignominiously converted back to sail, she was wrecked near

*Drawing of the restored William Scarbrough House on West Broad Street;
© copyright by Pamela Lee.*

Long Island in 1821. A year earlier, fire had swept through Johnson
Square and then the city from some stables nearby, doing nearly five
million dollars worth of damage. Scarbrough was a heavy loser, and
his elegant house was sold at auction to his brother-in-law. It was
later home to a Scarbrough daughter before being acquired by Mrs.
Margaret Gilespie O'Bryne, a wealthy widow, in 1851.

In his diary her son, Dominick, mentions seeing the ghost of the
first Mrs. Scarbrough in the house, rocking contentedly. It was as
though she had never left, and indeed, perhaps she had not. After the
O'Bryne family, the house where a president danced was used by the
Catholic Diocese of Savannah, and then became a school for black
children. Acquired and restored by Historic Savannah Foundation,
it is now the headquarters of the organization. A registered National
Historic Landmark, it is open to the public.

After its varied history and extensive renovation, its present
owners have not reported any unusual circumstances. However, it
must be assumed that the spirit of the proud Julia would be pleased
to have her beautiful home once more admired, and the center of
glittering social gatherings.

The Doll Museum's Uninvited Guest

The charming and beautifully appointed Museum of Antique Dolls at 505 East President Street in one of Savannah's oldest sections of the downtown Historic District, would seem a likely spot for a resident presence. The townhouse itself dates back to 1856, and houses a collection of antiques and dolls which fill the ground floor with memories of generations of children. But the footsteps which Jo Elizabeth Gerken, an internationally known doll expert, and her husband, Dr. Clay Gerken, have heard, do not come from the exhibits.

However, when the Gerkens are on the ground floor of the building, footsteps can be clearly heard above them. When they go upstairs to investigate, the rooms are vacant.

During their restoration work on the house, they said, dark red stains which appeared to be blood were found on the floor boards. Dr. Gerken, a retired professor of psychology from the University of Nebraska, thought at one time that the proximity of his fireplace chimney to that next door of a vintage 1810 house, might cause echoes in his parlor. So far, he has been unable to substantiate the theory, and no such sounds have been reported next door.

As we visited the museum, Stephen said that he sensed the presence of a middle-aged man, a former owner or tenant who had died there, still walking about in what had been his bedroom.

"I don't think you will ever hear anything more than just footsteps," he remarked. "As presences go, he's really rather dull."

When we asked Dr. Gerken if he as a psychologist believed in a spectre in his house, he answered with a whimsical smile, "Well, I believe that people believe in ghosts."

The Haunted Rectory

"It's rough to live in a haunted rectory if you don't believe in ghosts," Stephen remarked. I knew he was referring to what must be one of the most beautiful and historic church-owned buildings in the country, the stately Gothic Revival Green-Meldrim House on Madison Square.

Once described as "Belle Wattling Baroque," the elegant mansion was completed in 1861 for Charles Green, a wealthy Englishborn cotton merchant. Although Green had once been imprisoned by the Federal forces as a southern sympathizer and perhaps spy, he offered his home to General W. T. Sherman when he rode into Savannah in December, 1864. It was from this home that the red-haired 44-year-old commander wrote his wife, Ellen, "I am at this moment in the elegant chamber of the house of a gentleman named Green. My bedroom has a bath and dressing room attached which look out of proportion to my poor baggage."

It is said that Green may have offered his home to the general in order to save his cotton; records indicate that the canny leader accepted the home and took all the cotton anyway. From this house, too, he penned the famous telegram to President Abraham Lincoln, presenting him with the city of Savannah as a Christmas present.

One person not on hand to welcome the general was the rector of St. John's Episcopal Church next door. The Rev. Farquahar McRae, a stout supporter of The Cause, had hurriedly packed his bags and decamped with the Confederate defenders of the city across the Savannah River into South Carolina.

Happily, what was once the bedroom in which General Sherman wrote Ellen, "It will not be long before I sally forth again on another dangerous and important quixotic venture," and pledged "eternal affection," is now the suite in which excited young brides dress for their weddings at St. John's. The presence said to be in the house dates not from this period, but from the next occupant.

The Green-Meldrim House on Madison Square, by Jean Birnbaum.

After the Greens, the house was next owned by Judge Peter Meldrim, a Confederate veteran, Savannah mayor, state senator, and president of the American Bar Association. Here he and his wife Frances raised four daughters and a son, in a home lively with music and entertaining. Mrs. Meldrim especially enjoyed playing her piano, while the children danced in the large front hall, and she loved planning musical evenings for her friends.

One of her daughters, the late Sophie Shonnard, once recalled that at such times their black butler, Joe, was also fond of the music. Inevitably, as the first notes sounded, a back door would quietly open, and the servant, smiling broadly and tapping a foot quietly in tune, would enjoy the evening as much as the guests.

When the Meldrim family sold the house, it was acquired as a parish house and rectory through the efforts of the Rev. Ernest Risley, then rector of St. John's. The servants' quarters, kitchens, and stables are now connected to the mansion as the rector's house; the street which ran between the house and the church is closed, and a pleasant little garden.

Just as music filled the house during the Meldrim's time, the present bachelor rector says that "music is my passion...the

115

household deity of my life." In addition to owning an extensive collection of classical records, he also plays the harpsichord, piano, and other instruments.

In an interview with a former resident of the rectory, we were told that footsteps could be clearly heard in the night in what had been the servant's quarters, male steps going up and down the stairs and across the old floorboards in the dark. At the present time, the most notable unexplained event is a door that seems to quietly open by itself, when the rector is alone enjoying his music.

"Why, that's just old Joe," Mrs. Shonnard said with a smile when she heard the story. "Joe loved that house so much, took such pride in it...he always told my father he never wanted to leave it. Yes, old Joe always did have an ear for music."

The Presence in the Church

When General Sherman was occupying the Green-Meldrim House, he complained about the noise from the chimes of St. John's next door. The story goes that he had the bells taken down, and was ready to ship them north to be cast into cannon. Then they were saved by presidential decree, through the intervention of the angry ladies of the church and the vestryman who had presented them, Joseph Story Fay.

In discussing the ghosts of Savannah, Stephen and Claire told me that they had one such encounter in the historic 1853 church on Madison Square. When both were singing in the choir there one morning several years ago, Stephen said that he suddenly felt someone give him a very hard push in the back. He turned, but the person behind him gave him only an innocent stare. At the same time, Claire said that she also experienced the feeling of being tapped on the back, and of intense evil in the area.

"At that moment," Stephen said, "I looked across the way, and saw a woman in a long, dark dress, standing in the balcony all by herself. I'd say the period was Victorian. She was a strong, unpleasant-looking, middle-aged woman, with a large hat, upswept hair. Then she was gone, and with her the terrible sense of evil.

"If you accept the Christian idea of a force of good, you also have to accept the premise of evil, and that the two oppose one another, even in the church," Stephen added. "The feeling I got was that she was a very obnoxious woman, who wanted some attention."

He added that one rector of St. John's had told him that he had also experienced a sense of an evil presence nearby when he was alone one night in the quiet church, one which he found so frightening that he prayed until the feeling lifted.

If the lady in black was also one of the indominable church members who rallied to save the chimes of St. John's from Federal destruction, it may well be that she still takes pleasure in checking in

117

occasionally just to make sure that they are still in place and sounding on schedule. Even the general had to admit the power of the women, when he wrote his wife, "There are many fine families in this city, but when I ask for old and familiar names, it marks the sad havoc of war...all gone or in poverty, and yet the girls remain, bright and haughty and proud as ever. There seems no end but utter annihilation will satisfy their hate of the 'sneaking Yankee' and 'ruthless invader'....Although I have come right through the heart of Georgia, they talk as defiant as ever."

One final note on St. John's and its rectory, perhaps entitled "Love Conquors All." In the summer of 1981, it was also the site of the wedding of a local belle, Helen Harris, and William Tecumseh Sherman IV, great-nephew of the general who had remarked on the spirit and pride of Savannah women.

An 1857 drawing of St. John's Episcopal Church, from an old print.

Unrequited Love
at the 17Hundred90

At a shady, pleasant corner of East President and Lincoln streets in Savannah in a fascinating section of the historic area near the old Colonial Cemetery, is located the renovated building complex now known as the 17Hundred90 Inn and Restaurant. The vintage Federal-style buildings are said to be built on the foundations of older ones going back to the 1790s; the name also recalls an early Savannah inn.

The inn, restaurant, and lounge are now tastefully refurnished in antiques and reproductions of the period. The restaurant walls are of old brick, with the original wide beams and flagstone flooring. The garden dining area and kitchen are located in a structure built about 1820 for Steele White, a prominent Savannah merchant, shortly after his marriage to Anna Matthewes Guerard. The building now seems to have two resident feminine presences.

The first and most famous is a girl named Anna. It is said that she fell in love with a seafaring man, and threw herself over the third-floor balcony into the brick courtyard as the sails of his ship dipped out of sight down the Savannah River toward the sea.

One nearby family is said to have seen her sitting one day in "a light, long dress," on the portico of her old home. Others told of unoccupied chairs rocking back and forth, windows opening and closing without apparent cause, and the old stairs creaking as with feminine footsteps.

Chris Jurgensen, the German-born owner of the restaurant and inn, says that he used to sense Anna when he would go in on Sunday afternoons to work alone when he first took over the business. "Anna was definitely here then," he stated. "I would hear footsteps in empty rooms, the toilet flushing with no one there...just the feeling, too, of not being alone.

"I haven't felt her since the inn was opened," he added. "But, I don't come in on Sunday afternoons anymore."

Drawings of the 17Hundred90 inn and restaurant at East President and Lincoln streets; courtesy the 17Hundred90, © copyright by the 17Hundred90.

A former owner, Diane Greenfield Smith, says that she does not believe in ghosts. Yet, she also felt a sensation like a cold wind pass by, several times when she sat alone in the bar area on Sunday afternoons with her books, with all the doors and windows closed. She also said the when she was at work in the kitchen one Sunday afternoon, she heard the jangle of a woman's bracelets behind her. Then someone gave her a hard push, as though to get her out of the way.

Upon visiting the building, Stephen said that the kitchen presence was not Anna. "There are two distinct ones here," he explained as we sat by the fireplace. "One is a young girl, very unhappy, from about the 1820s.... Not a presence that would harm anyone, just one with a great sense of loneliness, sadness, loss.... She may go away in time, but she could also come back when the conditions were right. I'd say she was a servant girl.

"The second presence is a black cook, a big, aggressive woman, from about the 1850s, who wears several bracelets, and does not want another woman in her kitchen. She is really very unpleasant; I'd say the other help was afraid of her.... I would also say she was quite involved with voodoo."

Although the restaurant area of the 17Hundred90 seems more peaceful since the inn opened, innkeeper Jim Cavenaugh says that strange things still happen there, especially late at night and on Sundays. "Sometimes the telephone rings in what was Anna's room," he said, "and there is no one there. We've had the telephone company out to check out the whole thing, and they tell us it is impossible for a phone to ring up there without a call going through our switchboard, yet that is what happens.

"In one instance, a woman in what we call Anna's room says she laid her underwear for the next day out across a chair before she went to sleep. The door was locked, no one went in or out, yet somehow it was gone when she awoke the next morning! Never found a trace of it. We had to blame Anna. Poor thing, if she hasn't had anything new since the 1820s, she probably needed some."

Ghosts A La Carte

The Pirates' House and the 17Hundred90 Restaurant and Inn are not the only Savannah eating places with resident presences. A newer establishment, but in a very old building in a historic area, also has a sad spectre which occasionally frightens the help. It is the Shrimp Factory at 313 East River Street, a popular luncheon and dinner spot with a view of the Savannah riverfront. It is located in the heart of a recently renewed area where shops and art galleries have opened in the old brick cotton warehouses, and modern parks and walkways have been laid out beside the cobblestones, once ballast on English sailing ships, of Georgia's first city.

The Shrimp Factory occupies the first floor of an old early nineteenth century brick warehouse, with the floor above used for storage. Its manager is Janie Harris, whose husband, Frank, operates the Regency Restaurant on Oglethorpe Avenue. According to Mrs. Harris, the ghostly activities are centered in the small room on the second floor now used as a liquor locker for the restaurant. Its main symptom is a low, miserable moaning in the dark, as though someone were in pain. However, when the door is opened and the lights switched on, the room is always empty.

"Having a ghost in the liquor room might be handy for keeping unauthorized persons out," she tried to joke as Stephen and I followed her to the dimly lit and deserted second floor late one autumn afternoon. "However, it is downright inconvenient at busy times, when restaurant employees refuse to come up here alone.

"Even I don't like to come up here, but I wouldn't tell them that," she confided as she searched through the heavy ring of keys to the one for the storage room.

I could understand the feeling. There was a pervasive chill in the old building, with its narrow, dusty windows overlooking the brown waters of the river, a sense of age and absence of life. "Sometimes the keys don't work very well, or maybe I have the wrong one," our guide murmured after an effort to unlock the door. Stephen took the ring, looked at the lock, and easily selected and used the right key. The door opened. I waited at the doorway as he spent a few minutes walking about the small room in silence, and Mrs. Harris selected some bottles to take downstairs.

After a few minutes, Stephen asked her if there was any certain time of the day or year when the moans were more pronounced "Well, it seems to me the help complains more of it in the winter," she replied, "but I thought it was because it gets dark earlier then, and they sometimes have to come up here after dark during our dinner hour. Then, you notice that it is cold up here even now, and of course that is worse in the winter."

"Well, you do have a presence," Stephen told her, "and they are correct that it is sensed more in the winter, because that is when the man died."

Mrs. Harris's eyes widened as Stephen explained the cause of the sounds in the room. "At the time this was a cotton warehouse, the most miserable slaves in Savannah were the ones who had to work down here," he said. "On the plantation, or with house servants, there was the personal relationship that existed. In many cases, the women of the house saw to their food, clothing, and medical care. But the stevedores who had to work loading cotton on the waterfront, had none of that.

"Their overseers were hard, driving men whose only aim was to get the maximum amount of work out of them a day, and feed them just enough to keep them going. Medical care or special food if they were sick, was non-existent. What you had here was a poor slave who came down with pneumonia, and laid here ill and delirious with no one to care for him. He didn't even have enough warm clothes to wear, and only a thin old blanket in an unheated building in midwinter; no wonder he was ill!

"Worst of all, they were not allowed fires up here, because of the fear of igniting the cotton. And they were locked in at night, so they wouldn't try to escape. Anyway, he died, alone and uncared for, in that corner," Stephen poined at a brick wall. "I'd say the time was the early 1860s. . . . The smell of illness is still here, chills and fever.

"His death was so prolonged and painful that its echo was left, especially since the room has structurally changed very little," he added. "But he is not malevolent, or even aware of you. It is more like an imprint of something which happened here, a trauma that is sometimes repeated when the conditions are as they were then."

"Well, I'm glad to know it is not an active ghost," Janie Harris said as she locked the door behind us. "I had noticed that nothing was ever moved, and there was no other signs than the chill, and the moaning sound. I have always felt a little depressed up here, and that's natural enough, given the building's history.''

A House on Monterey Square

Of the many historic Savannah houses of which we spoke that first day at Claire's, one which we later visited was a handsome 1860 mansion at the corner of Bull and Gordon Streets. It was also one where Claire and Stephen had shared a psychic experience.

At the time, the impressive townhouse on Monterey Square was the headquarters of the Savannah Art Association. One gloomy, overcast day when Claire was alone there, she heard a terrible crash on the back stairs. Expecting to find something or someone in bad shape at the bottom of them, she was amazed to turn on the lights and find nothing out of place. Yet it had been too loud to simply be her imagination, and she was sure it had come from within the house.

Not long after that, Stephen had stopped by. Puzzled by some strange vibrations which he had sensed in the house, he asked, "You're not alone here today, are you?" When she nodded that she was, he shook his head and went off to investigate. On the third floor he paused, and walked slowly down the steep inside back steps, the ones reserved for servants.

During this process, he told Claire, he had sensed that a young girl, perhaps fifteen at the time, had once lived on the top floor. She might have been a poor immigrant, or from a Georgia farm family. At any rate, she needed the work, and was anxious to please. Called imperiously by her mistress one day, she had rushed out of her room, missed her footing, and had fallen down the winding, narrow stairs to her death. This tragic event is still repeated from time to time when conditions are right, he believes, such as similar weather, or if a very psychic person is in the house.

As we discussed this, Stephen explained that in some cases the person does not know that they are dead, and continues to repeat their last actions on earth. In others, the events themselves have made an impression that is imprinted on the atmosphere of the house, and the memory of it seems to reoccur from time to time. I

125

wondered which this poor presence might be, and if it were still present.

By the time Stephen and I visited the house it was once again a private residence, and had known two owners since its renovation. We were allowed to tour it from the front hall to the top floor, with its view from the little windows of most of the city. However, Stephen said that the extensive remodeling which had taken place had so changed the atmosphere, that it was now very quiet. What had been Spartan servants' quarters had later been an area for teenagers, with bright hues, psychedelic decorations, and thick wall-to-wall carpeting in vivid colors. The most unusual thing which I noted on this trip was that on one of the huge vertical upright exposed beams of the top floor area, someone had nailed a horizontal board, and painted it, to form a cross.

Whether this or the renovation in general had made a difference, or the impression of tragedy had simply faded with time, it was not possible to say. However, Stephen later told me that our visit had left him feeling very depressed and unhappy. We then learned that the delightful and intelligent young man who had been our guide that day through the home where he occupied the ground floor, was dying of a terminal illness. A year or so later, he was gone.

The other event which I will always recall of that visit occurred while we were being served tea, and discussing our project with the young man of the home and his mother in the front parlor before we went upstairs.

To no one in particular, the uniformed maid suddenly murmured, "I just don't like to be in a house where doors seem to open by themselves, and I feel like someone is looking at me all the time!" a comment that was never explained further.

A Determined Victorian Presence

In the spectral world, as in the real, likes seem to attract. A teenager in Kensington dreams of a young girl who lived there when it was a dairy farm. My friend Mary once felt the presence of another young mother in her child's bedroom, checking on the children. A man not known for his charity winds up in the town miser's home.

Thus it was hardly surprising when Stephen and I visited a sophisticated woman in a downtown Victorian house with striking antiques and a little dog, as well as a ghost of similar tastes. After all, they had both chosen the same house, and one was striving to decorate it as much as possible as it had appeared a hundred years before.

We were invited to tea one afternoon by the owner of a handsome 1880s house on Gordon Street, who wanted to know what Stephen thought of her home and its story. As we sat in the tastefully appointed back parlor overlooking the garden, she told us she had lived with her presence for several years. She thought it was a strong-minded woman who had previously been in the home, and did not want any changes made.

"When I first put iron bars on the ground floor windows, it was just hell," she recalled. "I would hear this terrible rapping at night, like someone running another iron bar across them, but from inside, thump, thump, thump, down in the garden. Then there was a crash at this large window one night like someone had come right through the glass! I came running, but nothing was out of place. I've called the police several times to report prowlers, and then found no sign of anyone.

"Also, things were disappearing, and turning up in odd places. At first I thought it was only me, but I realized it had to be more than that," and she listed several examples. "Oh, and I would sit in this chair at night, and something icy cold would glide by my arm! One night this happened, and then for no reason, the silver picture frame fell off that little table. When I picked it up, the glass was not broken, but the picture in it was wedged between the backing behind the picture, and the back of the frame. That doesn't even make sense!

"Every morning about 3:00 or 3:30, noises occur in one corner of my bedroom. I know it's 'her' room., and she's there. But I've trained myself to go back to sleep. I think she's possessive, but I don't think she means any harm. Perhaps I've encouraged her by decorating like this. But it pleases me to see the house look as it must have when it was new."

What did concern our hostess, she added, was the attitude of the church toward her presence. "I talked to one Episcopalian priest about an exorcism, and he looked at me as though I were crazy," she recalled. "Then I contacted the Psychical Research Foundation at Durham. A young woman came down, and stayed three days.

"She seemed interested, and she told me that she thought I was definitely psychic, and I did have a presence. Then she left.

"I asked her how I was to get rid of it, and she said, 'We don't want you to get rid of it, we want to study it.' That was not my intent in contacting them! They never did let me see the final report.

"I did notice that about this time, and for several months afterwards, I didn't sense my presence so much. I was beginning to think she was gone. But she is back now. I guess she just didn't like being investigated.

"At least, the people from Durham took me seriously! They didn't look as though I were crazy, like the rector did.

"What is unsettling about a situation like this," she went on, "is when you finally realize that you are experiencing something which has no logical, this-world explanation. If you don't have a minister that has some experience in this himself, you have nowhere to turn."

She added that what had also concerned her was a comment she had read that sometimes a presence does not realize it is dead. "That's not my idea of an afterlife," she stated emphatically. "What I want to know, is this a form of hell, to go on haunting your own house? I sit in my living room, and I feel death glide down my arm, and my minister can't tell me what it is supposed to mean."

Stephen repeated the statement he had made earlier about another house on Gordon Street, that sometimes it is a presence which continues to do what it did in life until helped to go on, or made aware of its death. "Other times," he said, "it is simply an echo of something which has occurred in the house."

He then told her that he felt the house did indeed have a presence, "a short, heavy-set woman with long dark hair, dating from about the 1870s or 1880s." He saw her in the sitting room, with a small dog at her feet.

"Well, the church may have its rites of exorcism, but in general it is one that the present-day clergy ignores, because they feel it is contrary to what they believe," said our hostess. "Much more study of all this is required, I think. I do know that for myself, my experience is making me rethink my own beliefs about life and death."

As we left the house and walked down Bull Street, Stephen said that he felt that it was a classic case where the woman's considerable energy was interacting with energy in the house. "If there is enough momentum there to move things around, I really can't blame the rector for not wanting to try an exorcism, though you might say that is his job," he added. "He might only succeed in making the presence angry."

Not long after that, an incident occurred in the house, that is now part of Savannah's vast store of spectral ancedotes. Our hostess was having an evening gathering at her home, with the house at its loveliest, and the women guests in their long dinner skirts, moving gracefully through the rooms. Suddenly, it is said, one woman noticed an interesting-looking guest, a stranger to her, to whom no one else seemed to be paying any attention.

She nudged a companion, and suggested an introduction. The friend turned and said simply, "What woman?"

The first guest, understandably upset, is said to have found her surprised husband, and left as quickly as possible. Our hostess, they say, took it all in good grace. It's the sort of thing which happens when a determined presence decides to attend a nice party. After all, it is still her home.

"Uncle Wilbert," the Loyalist Ghost

Some southern households have presences which have been acquired with the home, passed through the generations with a particular locale. One prominent Savannah family, now living in Ardsley Park and with ancestry dating to colonial Georgia, has "Uncle Wilbert." He seems to come with the family antiques and furniture.

"Uncle Wilbert," the husband and father of the family explained during a recent visit at his home, is a generally benign presence. "I think he came with my wife's side of the family, from Charleston," he commented. "He's been around for several generations. It's like an aura...something you both see, and don't see. I sensed him at her family home on Taylor Street the first time, years ago when I was courting her.

"Some say they've felt him at family weddings and funerals. The last time I noticed it was one night, late, when I went in the kitchen here alone. It was like a presence, just there. It's followed us through many moves, even when we were stationed overseas."

He chuckled. "There's one amusing incident connected with 'Uncle Wilbert,' as we call him. That's not his real name, incidentally.... But we have a pretty good idea who he is, or was; more about that later. Anyway, there is one particular member of the family he doesn't much care for; don't ask me why! And to make matters worse, she can't even carry a tune....But, I'm getting ahead of my story.

"There was a group of us here on night, having a family get-together, and this lady got sleepy and laid down upstairs. Suddenly, she appeared on the stairs blinking her eyes and saying with bored resignation, 'All right, what do you want me to sing?' After our first surprise, we all started to laugh at the poor soul.

"She swears to this day that she was not dreaming, that someone leaned over the bed, shook her awake, and said, 'It's time now for you to sing.' Since no one else was upstairs at the time, we figure it had to be 'Uncle Wilbert,' the old rascal!''

The family story was collaborated by his teenage daughter, who had come in as we were talking. She is the last person to have seen the presence, who now, as our host put it, "appears just often enough to let it be known that he is still with us."

"It was about 3:00 a.m.,'' the girl began, "on a warm night last summer. I had been sitting up reading, in this room,'' she indicated an antique brocade armchair, "when I looked up, and could see this man, across the room from me. I could see him quite clearly, though the light from the table lamp beside me was the only one on in the room. He had auburn hair, or reddish with gold lights in it, and he was wearing a mustard-colored suit. He was just standing there, and then he was gone.''

"During the period of the War for American Independence, there was a split in the family loyalties,'' explained her father. "Though most of the family were ardent patriots, one daughter in Charleston was married to a Loyalist, and she went with him to the Bahamas. After his death, she wrote her father that she wanted to come home. He allowed her to do so, but only on the condition that she and her children could not bring anything from their past lives back with them, even what they were wearing!

"When they arrived in Charleston, his servants met them at the ship with new clothing, and the old had to be symbolically left behind. We think 'Uncle Wilbert' is equally determined, and was from the Loyalist family.

"I have always believed that such things exist,'' he concluded. "As a boy of sixteen, I remember going up to the door of the home of a friend on Gwinnett Street, and seeing a shadowy lady in a long dress, coming down the stairs in the front hallway. I looked again, and she was gone.

MORE LIVES THAN ONE

"I also believe in Extra Sensory Perception, which I have experienced many times, and in reincarnation, though I am a good Episcopalian,'' he added. "It's just a feeling I've always had, of having been here before. Especially in regard to military history....I bought my first sword for twenty-five cents when I was seven. Went back to the War between the States. Oh, that's another thing; I've always called it that. Can't stand the words, you know, 'Civil War.' And I also always say, 'War for American Independence,' not 'Revolutionary War.'

"Sometimes I'm reading history, and I find myself thinking, 'No, it wasn't quite like that!' Or, I know what will be on the next page. . . . I feel that I've known certain people in history, especially in the period of the War between the States, what they were really like.

"In 1963, a group of us decided to ride north to Maryland, following the route Jeb Stewart took to Gettysburg, and it was just incredible. . . the feeling we had at times of having been there before.

"There's a place up there, you know, between The Plains and Haymarket in Virginia, where they say one night in the latter part of June, every year, just at midnight, if you listen, you can still hear Stewart's men go riding by. I can't say that I heard them. . . I knew what it was like to *be* there. I also lived in a haunted plantation house outside of Charlottesville, when I was a student at the University of Virginia, on the GI Bill after World War II.

"There were times during the Second World War," the man continued, "when the sense of déjà vu was almost overwhelming, and the sadness, the despair. I would think, 'I've been here before, but that time, we lost.'

"Also, I did things instinctively in combat which turned out to be right, though I couldn't have told you why I did them. The most dramatic experience was in the Pacific, fighting the Japanese.

"I was in charge of a machine gun nest, and we had to take shelter from enemy bombardment. We were desperately tired, had been without decent food or sleep for what seemed like days. We dug ourselves into the side of the hill in what appeared to be a good spot. But then it hit me, we were all going to be killed!

"My men thought I'd gone crazy, when I started yelling at them to pick up and move out of there. There was some grumbling, but they did it. We dug ourselves into another spot further on. . .just as the first one took a direct hit that would have ended us all. I'll never forget the way they looked at me, with a few cuss words and the question, 'How did you know that was going to happen?'

"'I just did,' was all I could say.

"Another time, after the war, I went to the American Cemetery at Luxembourg. I was looking for a certain grave. There are only 5,800 there! But I walked right to the one I had come to see, by instinct, without looking at the directory. Without knowing of my experience, the very same thing happened to a cousin there, at a different time."

BAD "VIBES" FROM A KILLER

At the end of our conversation, I asked Stephen if he had sensed anything unusual in the comfortable, memorabilia-filled home. "Not what you're thinking," he answered. "But there is something here that has such a sense of evil and death about it, it sets the hairs on the back of my neck right on edge!" He looked toward the adjoining room.

"Oh, that," said our host comfortably, knowing at once what he meant. "Yes. Well it might!" He led us around the corner to the sunroom. There the hide of a giant tiger, the largest jungle cat I had ever seen or imagined, decorated one wall.

"It came from Southeast Asia, and it was a killer," he explained tersely. "The natives asked me to hunt it down after it started preying on their village. It is supposed to have made off with a lot of livestock in its time, and at least two young children."

The Ghosts of Fort Pulaski

The historic forts of Savannah, with their memories of high patriotism, combat, suffering, and sudden death, would seem natural places for presences to linger. Of these military fortifications, the best known is Fort Pulaski on Cockspur Island, guarding the mouth of the Savannah River. The present nineteenth century structure is located on the site of the earlier Fort George, begun in 1761, and Fort Greene, built in 1794 and destroyed by an 1804 hurricane in which some of the garrison was drowned. It is named for Count Casimir Pulaski, the Polish hero who died leading French and American forces at the 1779 Siege of Savannah.

Confederate General Robert E. Lee was stationed at the fort during its years of construction as his first military assignment after graduation from West Point in 1829. He later visited it several times after volunteers from Savannah seized it in 1861, four months before the attack on Fort Sumter. The victory was brief. In April, 1862, the era of coastal masonry forts ended when Federal batteries firing from Tybee Island forced its surrender with the use of new rifled cannon.

The fort was later the site of a barbaric episode in which more than 500 Confederate officers were held as prisoners on a starvation diet in unheated casemates during the bitter winter of 1864-65 in retribution for alleged poor treatment of Federal prisoners by the southern states. At the close of the war, the same dreary iron cages later held Confederate cabinet officers, state governors, a senator and a general, as a nation bent on revenge debated their fate.

After years of neglect, the ruined fort was declared a national monument, and restored during the 1930s as a historic site. It is now open to the public, most dramatically in summer with candlelight tours of the old casemates, and the reenactment of its past in drills and artillery demonstrations on the parade ground by personnel dressed in the uniforms of the 1860s. Its new circular entrance exhibit building is said to be located on the site of the

Drawing from Harper's Pictorial History of the War of 1861 *of Fort Pulaski as it looked before the Federal bombardment.*

former graveyard outside the walls.

One woman who is convinced that the fort is haunted, told me that one summer night during World War II she was coming back from Tybee Beach with a young soldier as the full moon brightened the landscape of the medieval-like fort with its drawbridge and moat. "Suddenly I looked over there," she said, "and we could clearly see a number of men in some type of uniform walking about on top of the walls. We watched them for a few minutes, and then drove on."

One explanation for this sighting might be that during the war the fort was closed to the public, and the island declared a Navy section base, part of the U.S. coastal defense system. After forty years, it is difficult to say to what century those military men belonged, whether they were conscripts of the 1940s or spectres of the Confederacy.

A more detailed account, also concerning an incident on the night of a full moon, was given us by a young man who is now the director of another historic site in the area. "I was stationed at Hunter Field at the time," he recalled. "A friend and I decided to slip over to Cockspur Island one weekend night from Tybee Island with a metal detector, just to see what we could find.

"It was a beautiful night, bright as day, and very quiet. No wind. It was a funny feeling to be out there at night, though, about midnight. We were walking around the outside walls of the fort through the tall marsh grass, when all at once it sounded like someone else was there, on the other side of a clump of bushes. This surprised me, as I had thought we were the only ones there.

"I didn't want to say anything, but I sensed that my friend heard

135

it, too. He was also looking in the direction of the footsteps, and he had also become very quiet, as though he were listening. We both stopped a minute, and the footsteps on the other side stopped, too! Then we started walking again and so did they, long, heavy steps on the grass, like a man's. We realized they were moving in the same direction we were, and so we expected to see someone when we came around this patch of shrubbery.

"We stepped out into the open," he continued, "and so did the footsteps...only we couldn't see anything! As we stood there, we could watch the tall grass mash down, as though someone were walking right in front of us, then past us and on out into the marsh. We both turned, still too startled to speak, and we ran as fast as we could, back towards our boat. We were out of there and down the river in no time, I can tell you! I never went back there at night, you can bet on that!

"But I'll say one thing for that experience," the young bearded man concluded, "though it scared me at the time. Earlier that night, the feeling of walking around the old fort in the moonlight, is why I am here today. At the time, I had no idea of entering the museum field professionally, though I've always been attracted for some reason to old forts and stories of the military, especially the Civil War.

"The feeling I had there, before the footsteps started, was one of completely belonging, of having been there before. I went back to college later, got my degree in history, and here I am. I've never been happier.

"I only have had that feeling of having been in a place before, one other time," he added. "It was at Gettysburg. All at once I knew where I was, where the different regiments had been and where the action took place, without looking at my map. I went directly to each thing I had come to see, with that same feeling of having come back. Maybe I had."

When I asked Stephen to ride out to Fort Pulaski one afternoon with me, he agreed to do so. However, he added, "Frankly, Fort Pulaski has never been one of my favorite places. I find it so depressing. There is such an overpowering sense of sadness from the past, and I get very confusing images of what is there now, compared to how it was.

"For instance," he said later as we stood at the top of one of the wind-swept ramparts, looking down at the parade ground, "you look down there now and you see a quiet yard, and tourists walking around. But what I am also seeing are white tents, arms stacked beside them, wagons, mules, cooking fires, and soldiers.

Federal guns being hauled to the siege of Fort Pulaski, from Harper's Pictorial History of the War of 1861.

"I don't even want to go into the prison casemate," he told me as we walked along the grim corridor outside the great iron gates where men had died needlessly of pneumonia and scurvy. "I don't get the feel of an actual presence as much as just the overwhelming sense of absolute misery, despair, and death.

"I also don't like that stairway," he commented of one leading to the ramparts. "I think there was great suffering, and someone probably died there."

Later, in talking with a member of the Fort Pulaski staff, we learned that a casualty from the 1862 bombardment had undoubtedly been carried down those same stairs from the ramparts above, so badly injured that he died.

"I haven't noticed anything here myself more than you naturally get from a place with so tragic a history," said our guide, "but one of the fellows here absolutely refuses to go into what we still call Colonel Olmstead's quarters, after dark."

No wonder, we thought. It was in those Spartan first floor quarters that the twenty-five-year-old Colonel Charles H. Olmstead of Savannah had faced the agonizing decision of whether to fight to the last man, or surrender the fort, as projectiles from the Federal batteries were passing through the broken walls, sweeping across the parade ground, and striking against the walls of the north magazine where thousands of pounds of gunpowder was stored. They had been under bombardment for thirty hours.

In that same room by candlelight, the officers of the fort later surrendered their swords to the Federal officer in charge of the ceremonies, Major James G. Halpine. Olmstead laid his down with the historic comment, "I yield my sword. I trust I have not disgraced it."

After being kept in the North as a souvenir for 117 years by the Halpine family, the sword was recently given back to the fort for display by a descendant, Mrs. Helen Halpine of Annapolis. Its return must have brought some comfort to the unseen presences of the old fort, especially Colonel Olmstead.

This fanciful Harper's Magazine *drawing depicts a ball held by Federal officers at Fort Pulaski on Thanksgiving in November, 1862. Three steamboats laden with guests, plus supplies for the event, were brought in from Hilton Head, the supply center for the United States Department of the South.*

Remembering Major Gallie

The fall of Fort Pulaski may have ended the era of masonry fortifications, but the long survival of embattled little Fort McAllister on the Ogeechee River some twelve miles south of Savannah proved that simple earthworks could endure the heaviest naval bombardments of the time. Constructed in 1861 to protect the mouth of the river and the coastal plantations, and named for the family on whose land it was located, the fort later withstood the combined assault of Union ironclads, gunboats, and mortar schooners.

It never surrendered, but was overrun by superior forces when General W. T. Sherman deployed nine regiments against its defenders in December, 1864, ending his March to the Sea. Watching from a nearby rice mill, the general called the assault which took the lives of forty Union and Confederate men "The

Fort McAllister is shown as it appeared to Federal troops, from The Story of the Great March, by Brevet Major George Ward Nichols, aide-de-camp to General Sherman, 1865.

"Assault on Fort McAllister," from a Harper's Weekly *drawing; courtesy the Thomas Gamble Collection, Savannah Public Library.*

handsomest thing I have seen in this war!" Seven days later, the Federal forces were in Savannah.

After the war the old fortifications were almost forgotten, until industrialist Henry Ford bought the land as part of his vast holdings at nearby Richmond Hill, and did some restoration. The site was later acquired by the state of Georgia, which now has it open to the public.

It is said that on late summer nights during the full moon at the old Chicamauga battlefield in North Georgia, a dim figure carrying a full picnic basket may be seen making its way over the terrain once so bloodily contested in 1863. Does Fort McAllister, with its gallant defense by both land and sea, have a similar story?

"If we have a presence at Fort McAllister, it ought to be that of Major John B. Gallie," Roger Durham, director of the Richmond Hill site, told us. "He was killed here on February 2, 1863, in a five-hour battle between the guns of the fort and a Union ironclad, the Montauk. I've never seen him, but there are stories . . . a lot has happened here.

"I understand when they were restoring the fort, they wanted the workmen to stay down here at night to prevent vandalism and so forth," he continued. "Well, they never did spend a full night here! Sometime during the first night they were gone, and after that they were out of here every day at sundown. There were stories that they had heard strange sounds and so forth . . . . Let's just say that it gets very dark and very quiet out there on the earthworks at night.

"In honor of Major Gallie, we had Confederate reenactment troops and the Savannah Celtic Pipe Band out here in February," the young man added. "To hear the kilted band marching around the bombproofs playing 'Amazing Grace,' is something I know I'll never forget."

The old fort is also unique for having what must be the only historic marker in the Confederacy to honor an animal casualty. "Tom Cat," the mascot of the defenders, was killed during the shelling which took the major's life. He was later buried with military honors inside the ramparts which now so quietly overlook the wide Ogeechee River at the place called Genesis Point.

Full Moon at Fort Screven

A correlation between full moon, high tides, and spectral sightings was remarked upon by several people during our research for this book. For whatever reason, two more stories concerning coastal forts also involve summer nights and a full moon.

One takes place at Officers' Row, part of old Fort Screven on Tybee Island. Built in the 1880s as part of the coastal defense system, the old concrete fort on the Atlantic Ocean saw service during the Spanish American War and World Wars I and II. During the latter, some German prisoners of war were housed there. Between the world wars, it was home to two officers who were later to gain combat fame, Colonel George Marshall and Captain Dwight D. Eisenhower. It is now a fashionable restored residential area, with a section of the nearby fort used for a museum.

The former resident of Officers' Row who spoke of unusual happenings there, said that on the night he remembers best he had come home from the Savannah Little Theatre about midnight, fixed himself a drink, and gone out on his patio to relax and look at the ocean. Because of the full moon, he had turned off all the house lights in order to enjoy the quiet scene.

"In about five minutes," he recalled, "I saw a light come on downstairs where I had just been. I was positive I had turned that light out! Anyway, I got wearily up, went in, and turned it off again.

"Well, I sat there about five minutes more, and I saw a light come on upstairs! I wondered if someone was in my house. I went inside very warily and called up, 'Now who's playing tricks up there?' but there was no answer. I went up, and there was no one there! I searched around, turned off the light, and went back outside. Notice, I had just fixed my drink and had hardly had time to enjoy it, so I wasn't confused in any way as to what was going on.

"Well, I sat down again, and in about five minutes, I could see a light shining out on the dunes from my driveway. Now, I was

142

positive I had turned that one off! But I went around, and took care of it. I was really tired, and a little disgusted and uneasy. I didn't know what to think. Just then I looked back to the patio where I had been. Would you believe, the light was now on out there, one which I am absolutely positive I had not had on all evening, as it was like daylight out there from the full moon? At that point I just finished my drink, checked the house again, and went to bed.

"That's the only time anything like that ever happened," he concluded, "though of course in a place like that you can hear noises from the wind and storms and so forth. I know also that no one else was in my house that night, because my dog never barked the entire time. But he didn't go with me to turn out the lights, either."

"I SAW YOUR BROTHER WILL!"

One other unusual experience is told in connection with Fort Screven, this dating from the Spanish-American War. At that time, an artillery captain named A. D. Schenck was stationed there. His son was also an army man, a lieutenant serving in the Philippines. As Mrs. Schenck's daughter Elizabeth later told the story, she and her mother were sitting sewing one day in their quarters on old Officers' Row.

Suddenly the mother jumped up and cried, "Oh, I just saw your brother Will! His shoulder disappeared as he fell backwards!" The family was greatly agitated until a news report confirmed the premonition. The young officer had indeed been fatally shot in the shoulder while fighting native insurgents, at about the same time his mother had glimpsed him in her quarters.

The Presences on the
Parade Ground

Further down the coast, across the St. Mary's River at Amelia Island lies old Fort Clinch, whose history somewhat parallels that of Fort Pulaski. Its construction began in 1847, and it was named for General D. L. Clinch, a hero of the War of 1812. The fort was occupied by the Confederacy in 1861, but taken back by Federal forces one year later as the Union blockade effort intensified. It is now open to the public as a historic site, administered by the state of Florida.

It is said by area museum workers that at Fort Clinch on the night of the full moon every July spectral figures can be seen walking across the parade ground. The unusual thing is that they are several persons of different heights, but all appear to be shorter than normal. When one looks closer, it is seen that they only seem to appear from the knees up!

The parade ground is now higher than the original terrain, it is explained. The spectres are thought to be the first settlers who lived

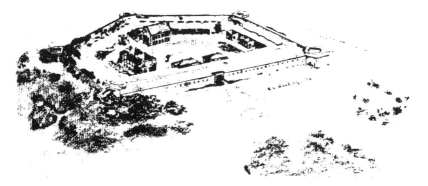

Fort Clinch, Fernandina, is where spectral figures are said to be seen on the parade ground during the full moon in July.

in the area, or soldiers from an earlier time. Why they should appear only in July is not known, unless it was at that time that they met their deaths. Since the island is the only U.S. location to have been under eight flags, and has a violent history including piracy, Indian attack, and colonial and civil wars, that is certainly possible.

We talked about the spectres with George, a member of the fort staff who wears the blue uniform of the First New York Volunteer Engineers, symbolic of the occupation of the fort during the Civil War. George said that he had never seen the presences himself, but had heard the story from those who claimed they had. "All I do know," he added, "is that there is a lady who lives further down the beach and likes to walk up here with her two bull dogs. Neither of them will come in the fort."

Ghost-Hunting at Race Path School

When the editor of the *Savannah Morning News* decided to have one of its best reporters and a photographer stay until midnight in a "haunted house" in the area for a Halloween feature some fifteen years ago, the suggestion sent staff writer Mary Ann Ebberwein, photographer Andrew Hickman, and editor Porter Carswell off to rural Effingham County northwest of Savannah. There they found Race Path School, a one-room abandoned structure said to be visited by the presence of a young schoolmaster who returns every autumn to reenact a tragic event that occurred there in the 1890s.

Mary Ann is now the director of the Savannah chapter of the Heart Association, Carswell is an antique dealer, and Hickman is deceased. As my guest during a recent luncheon interview, Mary Ann recalled the unusual assignment and its eerie setting.

"Just as today, the 1960s was a time of interest in the supernatural and occult," she began. "Naturally, there was a group in Savannah interested in the subject. For one thing, the activity in the house my friend Jim Williams had restored on East St. Julian Street was taking place, and people were following all that. There were seances being held in a house out in Port Wentworth about that same time. One woman was doing tarot card readings, but then a young man killed himself after one of the sessions, and she wouldn't do any more.

"As far as I'm concerned, it's all an open question," she went on. "You might call it suggestion, but there have been times, and that night at Race Path School was one, when I could feel the hair rising on the back of my neck, at nothing I could see. . . . And yet, there was an indication that there was something there."

"First of all," she explained, "Race Path School is in an isolated area, especially at night. No houses near, no street lights, just country road. It really gets dark up there under the pine trees. The wind seems to always blow at that particular spot. . . . Porter says it's the effect of all the trees, an old oak right by the school porch, and a lot of pine saplings in the yard. We went up Route 21 by daylight the first time just to check it all out, and then we went back at dark the next night, and stayed until just past midnight."

Race Path School was built in the 1890s, and used by area students, mostly descendants of the Austrian Lutheran Salzburgers who had settled the county on the Savannah River in the 1730s, until just before World War II. As the name implies, it is located near a wide and deeply curved road once designed for horse racing. There was once also a ball field nearby.

"In the silence of the countryside," Mary Ann had written, "it was easy to imagine the holiday air and excitement of the bygone racing days—families with picnics along the wayside, the shouts of encouragement from the crowds. In the quiet, you can almost hear the hoof beats."

It was during this period, when the building was still new, that a double tragedy is said to have occurred there. It involved a young schoolmaster on his first teaching assignment. As was the custom in those days, he boarded with a family nearby. The household consisted of a well-to-do widower, and his lonely young daughter. She was a beautiful girl with long black hair, according to the story, and violet blue eyes. Soon the two young people were spending their afternoons talking and driving about the countryside.

The father realized what was happening, and tried to speak to each separately about it. But each only spoke of their love for the other, a fact the older man found upsetting, since he already had another wealthy man in the community selected as his daughter's prospective mate. He ordered the young man from his house, and threatened to have him dismissed from the school. The two decided to elope.

On the fall day they had planned to leave, the girl waited until the father was out of the house. Then she hurridly packed her things, and rode to the school as the young teacher was gathering up his books after dismissing classes for the day. But the father returned early to his home, saw his daughter's empty room, and hurried to the school with his loaded gun.

Seeing his intent as he burst in the door, the girl managed to get between him and her lover. In the ensuing excitement the gun was fired, killing her instantly. A second bullet injured the young man. The frantic father picked up her body and went for help, not realizing she was already dead. Her lover lay dying on the school podium, calling her name. With a struggle, he managed to pull himself to the blackboard, and scrawl, "I'll be back."

He went stumbling and crawling out toward the road, bleeding heavily. At the well in the schoolyard, he tried to pull himself erect. It gave way under his weight, and there he died.

"The story goes that true to his threat, he does return in the fall," Mary Ann continued, "On our first trip there, we walked through the deserted school, so quiet now, with its old pot-bellied stove, and then outside. We even located the old well. The brick coping did appear newer on one side. . . but maybe that was just our imagination."

On the return evening trip, the trio took lanterns and flashlights. They also took a camera, coffee, and a piece of chalk for the blackboard, "in case there were any more messages." To set the mood, Porter took along his copy of the Egyptian Book of the Dead, with the idea of reading some passages and incantations to set the mood as they waited.

"It was not just dark, but inky blackness," Mary Ann later wrote. "As we stepped from the car, I heard the wind. At that moment the clouds opened up overhead, and a nearly-full moon cast a kind of sinistral haziness through the trees."

After carrying their equipment inside, and blocking both doors closed so that the wind alone could not open them, they sat down to wait. "Admittedly we were skeptical," Mary Ann recalled, "but we were also curious and open-minded. Being fairly well versed in the parapsychological research under way at many of the leading universities, we felt we were not experimenting without just cause."

For the most part, the wait was uneventful. Once, the trio went outside with a flashlight to find the cause of a persistent scratching sound. It turned out to only be a low-hanging branch, scraping against the tin roof. Later in the evening, the three noticed that a door of the school was now open. The wood strip which they had laid against it to keep it closed, was still behind it. They reasoned that the wind must have done this, very gradually.

Midnight came. Still no ghost, or spirit writing on the blackboard. A funny thing happened, though, according to Mary Ann. The piece of chalk which they had put on the dusty trough under the slate, was now gone. All three denied having taken it; besides, they had been together all evening.

At that point, as midnight came and went, they decided to leave also. "Andy led the way, with the brighter lantern," Mary Ann later told the story. "We had to walk carefully over the porch because of the missing boards. Then Andy abruptly turned and walked to the opposite side of the porch, and stood staring out toward the old well.

"As I joined him near the edge of the porch, he slowly lowered the lantern to the floor. In its glow, there appeared to be wet footprints on the floorboards of the porch, leading toward the well."

After my talk with Mary Ann, Stephen and I were invited to take a ride up to Race Path Road with our good friend and Effingham County native, Milton Rahn. "Some of the people in that story were probably my relatives," he joked. "Most of the folks in Effingham County are, you know."

By daylight, and after so many years, Stephen reported no vibrations in the area but a deep sense of quiet, broken only by the rustling wind in the tall pines. The path to what had been the school, about 100 yards to the left of the paved road, is now impassable without a machete. "I know that's where the well is," Milton said as we stood at the side of the road peering into the vines and underbrush.

"What happened to the schoolhouse?"

"Suspected arson. One day the school burned, and the next day it was a farm house near here, all very mysteriously. That was in the fall, too, I believe."

"The school master returns," I replied as we turned toward the car.

"For such a peaceful area, this place has seen its share of tragedy," our friend continued. "In the 1920s, a horrible murder happened near here. A young girl was working in Savannah, and she came up here to her family one Saturday evening on the train. It used to stop there where we passed the little service station. Well, she started walking toward her home, and was never seen alive again. They said she was raped and murdered by a black man from out of town, who happened to be in the area.

"He never went to trial. He was hunted down with dogs, and lynched, less than a mile from here! They were still talking about it, all in whispers, when I was a child, in the 1930s. I remember straining to hear some of the more gruesome details, and then the adults would change the subject, when they saw I was listening. . . . Yes, a lot of tragedy, for such a quiet little place out here in the country."

Brief Encounters:
A Few More Savannah Ghosts

The Savannah area is remarkable not only for its famous and dramatic stories of spectres, but for its little-known resident presences. These are mostly known only to those now occupying the building, people who accept an occasional chill, doors that seem to open and close of their own accord, and footsteps in the night as part of the locale, like the spring azaleas and the Spanish moss.

Sometimes, if the house is a well-known or historic one, it is inferred to be its most famous late occupant. As in other matters of living, however, the obvious answer is not always the correct one.

For years, stories have been told about the handsome 1870 townhouse at 516 Abercorn Street, just south of Gaston. It was the last home of Alexander Robert Lawton, a handsome and cultivated lawyer, soldier, and diplomat. A graduate of West Point and Harvard Law School, he was a state senator and president of the Augusta and Savannah Railroad before the War between the States. He was then commissioned a brigadier general, charged with the defense of Savannah and the neighboring coast. Badly wounded at Sharpsburg, Virginia, he was afterward quartermaster general of the Confederacy.

After the war Lawton was again a state representative, president of the American Bar Association, and U.S. minister to Austria. For many years, both he and his wife were active in Savannah social affairs, and the name is still a prominent one. What was once the Lawton mansion and carriage house is now the office and studios of a Savannah television station.

Stories have been told for years at the station about "General Lawton's Ghost," the sense of a presence when a staff member is alone in some part of the large building. Some claim to have glimpsed an indistinct figure, or to have sensed cool spots and footsteps about the home.

Then Tom Knight, a staff member doing a series at Halloween on Savannah ghost stories, invited Stephen to tour the facility. After walking about the house, including its little-used upper floor, he remarked, "I think you have a presence here, but it is not General Lawton. What I sense is a feminine one. . . .I would guess it was a female relative who lived with the family, a widow or cousin, or an 'old maid aunt.' The impression I get is of someone who was not very happy in her last years, who felt somewhat neglected and alone, insecure as to her place in the family as the rest went about their own lives.

"This woman is not going to harm anyone. I would say that she is not even aware of present reality. She simply coexists with what is here now. On the other hand, she might cause some electrical equipment to malfunction, or at least startle the staff, in her ramblings about the building. This is the way it is with many presences. They simply stay on in the place that is familiar to them. I get the impression that she wasn't totally happy here, but it was the only home she had."

The Girl in the Bathroom

Those who have shared a bathroom with a family teenager know that it is sometimes a frustrating experience. The situation becomes even more complicated when one also has a young spectral figure flitting down the hallway, and disappearing into the same lavatory. Such was the experience of a Savannah family living in one of the comfortable row houses in the 400 block of East Liberty Street, near Price.

"I was upstairs in our room one evening," said the mother, "when I glanced in the hallway and saw this young girl in a long white dress just flitting by, and into the bathroom. I simply thought it was our daughter in her nightgown, getting ready for bed. But then I realized that I didn't hear anything more, and no one came out. After a few minutes, I rapped on the door. There was no answer. I pushed it open. The room was empty! Our daughter, it turned out, was reading in her room; said she hadn't been out of it for hours. So it wasn't her."

"There is a definite feeling at times of someone around, especially upstairs," said the father. "One night my wife and daughter were in Atlanta, and I was alone here. It was very warm, and I was lying on the bed with no covers over me. But the sense of something in the room, someone looking at me, was so strong that I finally pulled a sheet over myself, feeling rather foolish as I did so. I, too, had the impression of a young girl."

When Stephen walked through the pleasant row house, now attractively furnished with antiques, he said that he did sense a presence, or at least the impression of a young girl. "I'd say she was a servant girl," he commented, "since she is not very much in evidence, but she is here. Yes, I'd say a young girl, 1870s, who quite possibly died here."

152

The Scent of Roses, the Swish of Taffeta

In another 1870s row house on the same East Liberty Street block, tenants in the upstairs part of the house have reported the sound of swishing taffeta and the scent of roses at midnight, in the winter when none are in season. There are also reports of the sounds of laughter, as though whoever was connected with the first two impressions, was still having a pleasant time.

In visiting the house one afternoon, Stephen reported not sensing anything but the patina of years, and the interesting arrangement of family pieces now in the home "Maybe you have to come back at midnight," said the owner, a lifetime resident of Savannah and member of a prominent Irish Catholic family.

"I am told that a murder once occurred in my front hall, and that a policeman lived here," she added, "but I've never checked it out. The thought of the murder did bother me a little at first, but I feel very much at peace and at home here. I don't really believe in ghosts, you know, but if I were to have one, I'd rather have the echo of happy times than of sad ones, wouldn't you?"

The Chill on the Stairs

"I have never been able to sense anything unusual in my house, but others have told me that they can," said the owner of a comfortable and fashionable townhouse in the 400 block of East Macon Street, just off Troop Square. The homes date from 1872, a long, graceful row, each with its outside curving stairs, and a private entryway. Inside, more steps lead from a rather small and dark hallway to the airy living room and dining area, attractively furnished with a quilt wall hanging and antiques.

Walking about the home, Stephen said that the only place he could sense anything was a definite chill on the fourth step of the steep and dimly-lit stairs. "That step also slants a little, and is a little different in height, as they sometimes built them in those days," he pointed out.

"Is there a fan, draft, or some type of air intake that could cause a chill in this one particular spot?" I asked.

"I don't see any," he replied, looking about. The door behind us was closed, and no heating or cooling equipment was in operation on this particular mild, sunny day. "No, I'd say it's more a classic case of the so-called psychic chill, that can't be explained in general scientific ways.

"Anyway, whatever is here is not very tall, I'd say a young child," Stephen said. "My guess is that an accident or tragic event occurred on the steps; perhaps a young child died here. I think it is definitely connected with the stairs, and it is not going anywhere else."

154

The Calculating Ghost on West Perry Street

Some ghosts in Savannah houses seem to be simply there, oblivious of passing time, like the old lady dressed in black who has been seen rocking in a chair and praying with her rosary in a house on East Liberty Street near East Broad. On the other hand, there are those who are still not only aware of their surroundings, but who are fascinated with new electrical and mechanical gadgetry.

A young woman who moved into an apartment in a stately antebellum townhouse on West Perry Street just off Orleans Square, had a presence who especially liked her electric calculator. "I would leave it turned off, on my desk, when I went to sleep, and awake to find it on, and numbers on it," she recalled. "Sometimes I would awaken at night to find the bed shaking. Things would be moved around in the apartment. When I would comment on this to friends, something else would happen, as though someone wanted attention.

"For instance, a wicker basket of dried flowers on my table, would be moved around while I was out. There hasn't been any chills or smells, just a definite feeling of someone 'there.'"

In investigating the house, Stephen said, "I agree that there is a presence here, and it is strongest in what was once the servants' quarters, the upstairs and the back. I don't feel much here except that it is a black man, perhaps a house servant who lived and died here. I don't think he will do any harm, but he is understandably curious about anything new which comes into what he considers to be 'his' house."

The Woman in the Bedroom

In a Victorian row house in the 400 block of East Gordon Street, near Whitfield Square, a young woman awoke one night to find "a lady standing at the foot of my bed! She had on a long robe, and light hair, blonde or grey, down to her waist. I know I wasn't dreaming, because just then my husband came in the door, and he saw her, too. Then she was gone. He also had nightmares concerning a woman and choking, in that room.

"I never saw anything except that one time," she went on, "but it is the kind of a house where you're always looking over your shoulder." When she invited Stephen over to look around, he agreed with her impressions.

"I didn't sense a presence," he commented, "but the house certainly has a busy atmosphere! There was a definite cold spot in the dining room-living room area downstairs. But most of the activity seemed to be in one upstairs bedroom, which I didn't care for at all! There was family furniture in there. My impression was that the bed at one time had been loaned out by a previous owner to a friend, who had died in it. I believe that was the woman which the present owner saw.

"The impression I had was of an invalid woman. It was a very low-level type activity in the room, more like a memory, but I did find it hard to breathe there."

"Be a good animal, true to your animal instincts."
—D. H. Lawrence

Animals, Ghosts, and ESP

Any discussion of the supernatural quickly includes stories of the experiences of animals. One Savannahian told me of his uncomfortable feelings about a house in which he had lived on State Street: "I never saw anything, but my cat, Sinbad, definitely sensed something was there, and he didn't like it at all."

A Tybee Beach resident recalled a beach house there in which his cat "would bristle and stare at nothing I could see. Oh, yes, and I used to find leaves off the plants in the morning. It was not the cat."

A woman told of giving her dog away because "sometimes his hair would stand on end, and he would glare, following nothing that I could see, across a room. I didn't want an animal around that could see things I couldn't!"

"When I lived downtown at Jones and Bull Streets, I used to walk my Shetland sheep dog, Beau, every night," recalled Stephen, "He loved this, but one area where he refused to go, was anywhere around Monterey Square! He would put his tail between his legs, pull back, and refuse to go on. One night very late, I left him cowering there and walked on by myself. I heard the sound of low moaning, just before the square, like someone in terrible pain. It was loudest in the block between Bull and Whittaker Streets, just off the square.

"I really thought someone was there, but could find no one. Then someone remarked that the square is located on land fought over during the Siege of Savannah in 1779, when many wounded and dying would have been there."

"According to your faith, believe that they may receive their reward in the World to come, for they had none on earth."
—George Wymberley Jones DeRenne, at the dedication of the Confederate monument in Forsyth Park extension, 1879.

Shades of the Men in Grey

As a loyal and at times still "unreconstructed" Southern city, it appears that many of Savannah's houses retain memories and even more of the men who wore grey in her streets over a century ago.

At the stately Palmer and Cay Insurance building on Drayton Street, facing Forsyth Park, it is said that one employee has seen an apparition which he has christened "Captain Butler" after the blockade-running sometimes hero of *Gone With The Wind.*

"It happened one morning about 7:30, when he was the only one in the building," a friend recalled the story. "At other times when he was in early, he had the feeling of doors opening and closing behind him, and so forth. But on this occasion he definitely saw a man in grey. He was not trying to be frightening, he was just there. But he seemed to be trying to tell him something, or he wanted the recognition that he was seen.

"The scariest thing about this man was his eyes. They were definitely those of a dead man's, in worse shape than the rest of his face. They had worms and things in them....And yet, my friend says that this main emotion was not fear, but sympathy. He still wonders what the man wanted to tell him."

A similar apparition, of a soldier in a worn Rebel uniform, has been reported many times in a house at Gordon and Lincoln Streets. One version of the story connects him with the nearby Confederate hospital, which was later expanded as Candler General before its move to Reynolds Avenue in 1980.

Another "man in grey," was also said to have been seen many times in a house on the west side of town, just off Broughton Street. The story goes that guests there would sometimes complain of unexpected noises and footsteps, and glimpses of a spectral figure in the hallways or the garden. However, the lady of the house accepted her "star boarder" as an officer and a gentleman, and always nodded graciously to him when she encountered him.

Everything was fine, it seems, until some workmen came to do some carpentry work on the second floor. When they complained of a feeling of being watched by someone behind the door, the woman was quick to explain that it was only her harmless resident ghost. To her surprise and dismay, they left immediately, and never came back.

Another man in grey was reported in an 1850s brick townhouse on East Harris Street. However, it is not known if he is connected to what one matron calls "the late unpleasantness," or a murder which allegedly later took place there. As a Savannah woman told the story to author Gerald Chan Seig for a newspaper feature on Savannah ghosts, she had first lived in the home when it was a rooming house years ago, and she was a bride.

The couple later moved to another city, where the husband died. The wife returned to Savannah, and took the same room until she could decide what to do.

"About two o'clock, one afternoon, in broad daylight, mind you, and very sunny and bright," she recalled, "a friend and I were sitting there talking. She had her back to the door, and I was facing it.

"Suddenly I heard a light knock. Before I could say 'Come in,' the door opened and a man stood there in a grey suit. I couldn't see his features clearly, as there was kind of a luminous haze about them. He moved into the room, looked at me, and simply disappeared. My friend never saw him, but she saw me staring, and said I was suddenly very pale.

"My greatest feeling was one of disappointment. My first thought was that it was my dear husband coming to greet me from the other side, but whoever it was, it was definitely not him."

A "Children of Pride" Ghost Story

The Children of Pride, as thousands of readers know, was a real-life Gone With The Wind, a collection of letters of the Civil War era edited several years ago by Dr. Robert Manson Myers, which told the story of the lives and changing fortunes of the Reverend Charles Colcock Jones family of Liberty County, Georgia. The Reverend Jones was a Presbyterian minister, author, and plantation owner whose special interest was evangelical work among the black slaves. His son, C. C. Jones Jr., a Harvard graduate, was an attorney, mayor of Savannah, Confederate artillery officer, and author, whom historian George Bancroft called "the Macaulay of the South."

An interesting and long unpublished anecdote concerning the young Charles' encounter with a feminine presence in 1857, when he was twenty-six years old, was discovered in the files of the Georgia Historical Society in Savannah in a collection of letters, by Mrs. Lilla M. Hawes, the distinguished former director of the society. In her retirement, she has prepared it for publication by the society, an institution dating to 1839. It is excerpted here by permission of the next director, Anthony R. Dees.

Charles Jones' account of his spectral surprise was included in a letter to Mrs. Henry Jackson, wife of the famous Savannah attorney, diplomat, and Confederate general. It was probably written to her about 1876, as it contains a reference to the dedication of the Georgia Historical Society's Hodgson Hall headquarters on Whitaker Street, at which General Jackson had delivered an address. Jones had evidently told the story earlier, and was putting it in writing at Mrs. Jackson's request under the dramatic heading, "Jones Sees a Ghost!"

As extra documentation, the careful attorney and historian even added a little sketch of the townhouse "on State Street near Bull," where he was living at the time. He shared the rental with his younger brother Joseph, a professor of chemistry at the Savannah Medical College. Both young men were then unmarried.

160

Charles described the house as having belonged to three sisters. One had married and gone to the West Indies, and one had died in the house. The remaining sister, Jane, then raised Savannah eyebrows by marrying a widower much younger than herself, and one with several children. Her relatives were especially concerned that the bridegroom had urged her to make a new will signing over all her property to his children, at the time of the wedding. Their worst fears were confirmed when he turned argumentive and abusive, seemingly caring little for her. Her last years were lonely and unhappy, with only her friends and neighbors for comfort.

After her death in the house, her will was contested by her angry relatives in Charleston whom Jones simply calls "the R. family." Charles found himself not only living in the late Miss Jane's house, but also representing her family in the legal settlement of the property. In the meantime, most of her possessions were stored in the house as sad reminders of her life. "The past claimed all as its own," he wrote, "and there was none to disturb the gloomy memories which cloistered around the gathering dust settling noiselessly there."

On the night he described, he was alone in the house at midnight. Joseph was working late at the hospital on some experiments. Charles sat at the dining room table, with his law books and a cigar. The property case was to be argued the next day, and the young attorney was anxious to make a name for himself as well as satisfying his clients. Suddenly, from out in the hall, he heard light, shuffling footsteps. To his amazement, a woman then entered the dining room from the hallway.

"She was," he wrote, "an utter stranger to myself. She paused upon the threshold, her eyes fixed on the floor, pale of countenance, thin-visaged, and emaciated in figure... attired in a loose morning gown of grave color, confined about the waist with a broad band of the same material, and with a large collar folding back almost to the point of either shoulder. Her hair, lifeless and sandy in its hue, was parted in the middle, drawn back tightly and plainly from the forehead, and disposed behind the ears.

"Her countenance denoted more than sorrow. There was a wanness, a settled dejection, an absence of life and hope and love pitable in the extreme."

As Jones watched in surprise, the thin figure crossed the dining room and disappeared into the dark front parlor. Still not realizing what he was seeing, the young man arose, and courteously called out, asking her if he could be of assistance. There was no answer, and he helplessly repeated the question. The thought crossed his mind, he later said, that he was dealing with a mentally confused person who had somehow wandered into his house from the outside courtyard by mistake.

Taking the light from the table, he followed her into the parlor, only to discover that she had disappeared! First, he went searching under tables and behind furniture, until he had to face the truth. Jones sat down weakly in the dining room, experiencing, "a sensation quite novel, in which wonderment, disappointment, credulity, merit, and skepticism, were strangely blended." What also struck him as unusual, he added, even for supernatural experience, was that he had both heard and seen her.

Then he wondered if he had been dreaming; but no, his fresh cigar was still burning where he had put it down a minute before, and the ink was still wet on his legal papers. Later, he said, he studied the subject of presences enough to be sorry that he had not tried different tests for dispelling the sight.

Then he forced himself back to his studies, and the rest of the night was uneventful. The case was won for the heirs in Charleston. Later, he talked of his experience with one of the neighbors who had been acquainted with the former owner of the house. "To my surprise," he wrote, "she stated that the likeness was that lady . . . Miss Jane, whom she had more than once seen in the long morning gown, with listless air and sad countenance, moving spectre-like about her house, taking note of little, and seemingly holding conversation only with the mournful thoughts which burdened her sorrowing and broken heart."

Jones adds that since the case was favorably settled, "so far as I know or have heard, Miss Jane's perturbed spirit is now at rest."

The Girl Who Came Back

"It wasn't my fault that she died," the young businessman was saying. "I mean, it wasn't like she was my girl friend, though she said she was. You know how kids are. And I don't think I was the one who caused her death. I sure hope I wasn't! But, I really got involved."

We were sitting in a beach apartment at Tybee Island, talking with an articulate, earnest bachelor about some of the ghosts of his life. The main one, he explained, was a girl named Peggy, who had lived in the same apartment building he did in New York City.

"When I was a kid there, eleven or twelve, we played in the hall, the streets, and on top of the building, that was it," he began the story. "Well, there was a very fat girl in our gang named Peggy, and she liked me. I didn't even know what going steady meant, but Peggy told everyone I was her boyfriend.

"One day, we were playing around like kids do, and someone, it may have been me, we were all in it, pushed Peggy pretty hard. She fell against a brick wall, and scratched up her arm. Well, it infected and turned to abscess, and she went to the hospital. They gave her a lot of medication, but she just kept getting worse. Her hair was coming out, and she got very thin. We kids used to go to the hospital and see her. I mean, it was like the least we could do.

"I was scared. She looked so terrible, but she was always glad to see me. Right before she died, she said that she was still my girl friend, and would never leave me. I didn't like that kind of talk, but I went along, because I knew she was dying, and I didn't want to upset her. We kids all went to the funeral. I don't remember much about it but us sitting on the sofa at the funeral home crying and her parents coming up and thanking us for being there.

"Well," the young man continued, serving coffee, "later on, I had a girl named Chris that I really liked, my first real girl friend. I would go to sleep at night thinking of her and wake up to see Peggy's face over my bed in the dark, just the top portion of her body. It kind of glowed enough you could see it in a dark room. It scared me so badly that I quit seeing Chris. When I would hang around with the boys, it wouldn't happen. Then I would get serious with a girl, and there it would be again.

"I eventually started going with another girl, and this was even more serious because I was older.... And there was Peggy at night in my room again! I would always just cover up my head and close my eyes until I would peek out and she'd be gone, but how I hated it! And the dread of seeing her! The funny thing was, I had never been in love with her. I hardly remembered what she looked like, except when she'd come back like that. I had never even had a picture of her to remind me.

"Then I came to Savannah," he continued. "This time, I really liked a woman a lot. One night after all those years, I woke up to see Peggy standing by my bed. Only instead of just the top portion, this time I could see her in full. She was very thin, and wearing a childish short dress, maybe the one she was buried in, I can't say for sure because I don't remember that well. She was still just a kid, and her face never changed when I started talking to her.

"Well, for the first time, I faced up to her! I told her that she would have to realize that she had died, and it was time for me to go on... that she would have to let me go. She was solid; I couldn't see through her. After awhile, she was gone. I guess I was really irritated, and I kind of told her off. I was shouting, and everything. I'd had it! Well, maybe I've exorcised her. I haven't seen her since.

"Incidentally," he added, "you're the first person I've ever told that story to....I didn't even tell the girls I went out with....I do believe in God, and I do call upon Him. As you know from *The Exorcist* and other books, the Catholic Church investigates psychic phenomenon, and is studying how to deal with it. That's enough to tell me it exists. Look how old the rite of exorcism is! I believe in both the spirit of good and of evil in the world. The church should very properly be aware of it and help people deal with it, when they come in contact with situations they can't control.

"My first experience like that was when I was a kid in New York," he went on. "A bunch of us were at the church one weekend morning. We were playing around in there, which we were not supposed to do, hiding from each other and feeling very daring. I slipped into a little room at the side of the altar, one the priests use to dress in or something.

"Well, suddenly, I saw the Virgin Mary! She was about four feet off the ground, over in the one corner, a little smaller than life size.

164

She was all in blue and white, with such a sweet, gentle expression. Kindly, like a mother. She told me I was to be a good boy in church, and not to run and play there.

"I was so frightened, I hid behind the chair until the vision had faded. Then I ran out of the church as fast as I could. But I do know it couldn't have been a nun or a statue, because it appeared and disappeared, and it spoke to me. Needless to say, I never played in the church again!

"I do believe in ESP," he continued. "I know it works. One night on Houston Street in Savannah, I woke up to hear someone calling my name. There was no one there. The next day I called my mother. She said strange I should call, she was just thinking about me. She had had a nightmare the night before, and had wakened up calling my name out loud, or so the family told her. And I had somehow heard it in Savannah!

"I also believe in the feeling of having been in a place before, and sometimes I've felt that here," he added. "The eeriest places are in the downtown, around St. Julian Street, and out about 45th Street in Ardsley Park, between Bull and Abercorn....Have you ever been out there at night, with the old oaks and the Spanish moss, and a dim light coming through the trees?

"I lived down in the 500 block of St. Julian Street, in a house Jim Williams restored," he continued. "I definitely felt a presence there. It was not violent, but it didn't care much for anyone else in the house. We still had the old fireplace, with the metal bars they used to pull out and hang things on. One night I woke up with my dog barking and looking toward the living room. I got up and started in there, and he wouldn't come with me. I was really scared. I could see a soft glow coming from the hearth....there was a fire in the fireplace. Only thing was, I had cleaned out that fireplace the day before, so there was no way it could have started burning again by itself.

"Sometimes the water would turn on by itself in that house in the kitchen, but not in the bath. Then, there was a heavy sliding door between the pantry and the kitchen, and the front room. Sometimes it would open all by itself, though it was a very heavy door!

"One night I had a friend staying with me, and he woke me up hollering that the lights kept going off and on in the bathroom. I used to get an evil feeling in the house when I would go home after work, that something didn't want me there. Sometimes I had to get out for awhile. Then I would have the feeling it was all right to go back. But I never had the feeling that it was a violent spirit, that would harm me.

"Then I lived on Price Street," he went on, "in a two-story brick house. One night I woke up to hear a sound like coins or ball bearings jingling on the patio. I leaned over and looked out, but could see nothing. Then, I saw a black man in my room, standing between the window and the closet. I was terrified; I thought he was a burglar. I tried to cry out, but no words came.

"At that point, I seemed to be above the bed, seeing myself terrified and trying to cry out, looking down at myself. There was the dog, lying by the bed, not moving. . . . I was seeing myself, in my surroundings! Then I was back in my body, sitting up, and then getting out of bed, shaking and perspiring. It was a dream, possibly, I tried to tell myself. . . but I remember so vividly the sensation of being awake and seeing myself! Of course there was never any sign of either coins on the patio, or a man in my room!

"I would like to wear a religious medal," he told me. "But I can't, though I keep a crucifix in my bedroom. In Washington, I was at the Immaculate Conception Cathedral when I saw a medal in the gift shop that I really was fascinated with, Christ and the crown of thorns. I bought it on impulse, and had the priest bless it. I brought it back to Savannah. Well, I was wearing it one night in bed, when I woke up. Another medal, just like it only larger, was floating in the space around my bed. It had a kind of a glow you could see in the dark. I closed my eyes until it went away.

"It happened the same way the second night. I got the medal, and put it in a drawer. On the third night, it happened again, I decided I didn't want that medal in the house any more. I gave it to a friend, and I haven't heard any more about it. I don't understand what it meant, but I haven't seen any more floating medals!

"I think you are more open to psychic experience if you concentrate," he concluded. "I have learned I can put myself to sleep at night that way . . . first the feet, then the ankles, and so on, until the brain is asleep.

"I don't particularly care to discuss things like this with people out of idle curiosity. I think the meaning is deeper than that. But if I met someone who was doing serious research, and they could give me some insight into some of the things that have happened to me, and I could help them, I would be glad to do so."

The Woman in the Chair

Many stories have been told of presences which refused to leave their familiar home surroundings after their deaths. Less common, but definitely experienced by some, including a Savannah woman with some psychic abilities, is the phenomenon of haunted antiques.

Mrs. Doris Pearson, a friend of Stephen's who now lives in Ardsley Park, enjoys buying and fixing up old homes, and furnishing them with period furniture. Her most memorable experience, she told us, was while she was living in Gordonston several years ago. She had just bought a handsome Jacobean Revival armchair, a solid mahogany piece dating from the 1800s. It had been covered originally in deep purple velvet, with a fringe around the bottom.

"The first thing that attracted me to it were the arms," she recalled as she told the story at a house on Bull Street. "The rest of it was dusty, but the arms were shiny at the ends, where you would grasp them to pull yourself out of the chair. It had seen a lot of use; I pictured it as someone's favorite piece of furniture. The seat was completely out of it; there was just a wisp of fabric there."

After buying the chair at a Bay Street shop, Doris took it home and asked her husband to put it in the garage. He misunderstood, and instead carried it into the dining room as Doris was putting dinner on the table. She decided to move it after they ate.

"So we were having dinner," she continued. "Suddenly I looked up, and saw a little, wispy old lady, in a long, chiffon Victorian dress, sitting in the chair. Her gray hair was done up on the top of her head, in a little knot. And my cat was sitting on her lap... although there was no bottom in the chair at the time!

"Well, I screamed, and jumped up from the table. My husband nearly choked, not knowing what was going on. He never saw anything. The cat jumped off the chair in such a rush that the chair tipped over with a crash! I haven't seen the poor lady since. I guess we scared her as badly as she did us.

"Anyway, I couldn't part with the chair, but I had it recovered in a very different material, and painted white, so you wouldn't recognize it. As you see, it is now in the hall.

"One thing, though. I have noticed that my cat still really likes that chair."

Another strange incident at the Pearson home came after the purchase of an old washstand. It was a handsome piece of solid oak. "At first it was in the hall," she said, "and we kept hearing strange noises, children, doors, so forth. . . .We would look, and nothing would be there. I didn't really connect it with the washstand at first.

"Well, we moved it up to the attic, and the noises, bangings and that kind of thing, got worse. One night I woke up, and heard this terrible crash. I thought the cat had knocked over some old picture frames I was working on up there. I went tearing up the stairs, ready to kill the cat! I opened the door, and turned on the light. The cat was there, but sound asleep. . .it just blinked at me. Nothing else was there but the frames and the darned washstand.

"It was a nice piece, but it wasn't worth the trouble. It went off to a dealer the next day."

Her latest experience, she added, happened when she moved to a Savannah house built about 1916. While in the attic one day, she was surprised to see a feminine little china figurine in an otherwise empty space. Dating from the 1920s, the delicate porcelain piece depicts an attractive young woman with bobbed hair, a rope of pearls, red slippers, and a full blue skirt which forms a candy dish. "Although it was a warm day," she recalled, "I shivered for some reason as I picked it up to carry it downstairs. It was cold to the touch. And it was not dusty, though it had to have been there for at least several months."

As Doris placed her new find on the console in the front hall, her cats which had been following her, ran into the next room. Later that night, as she walked down the dark hall toward the powder room under the stairs, she felt a definite "feminine" push at her back, shoving her toward the bathroom door and away from the figurine as she passed it.

"I realized then that I didn't want it in my house, yet I couldn't bear to throw out such a good piece," she recalled. "It both repelled and attracted me. So the next day, I called the woman who had lived there before me, and told her she had left something behind. I asked her if she wanted it.'

"'No!' she said very sharply. 'Put it back up in the attic, or throw it out!' and she hung up on me. Very strange.

"Still feeling restless," she continued, "I carried it into the living

168

room, and tried it out on a table there. Again, the cats were sleeping peacefully until I set it down. They woke up and left the room. I also sensed a feeling of something or someone there. Finally, I put it back out in the hall.

"Later, I had to go out. While I was gone, a friend stopped by to see me. The next day, she called and remarked on my unusual night light.

"'What light?' I asked, puzzled, as the house had been dark when I came home.

"'Why, I looked in through the glass in the front door,' she replied, 'and there was a kind of glow around the figure on your console, in the front hall.'"

Feeling rather nervous, Doris had then gathered up the figurine and taken it over to Stephen's house. He told her that he got no particular vibrations from it, but thought that the fact that it was the same period as the house, was significant. "I understand that the woman for whom the house was built was quite aristocratic, and often felt that she was not given her due in life," he explained. "She died in the house and the husband, a doctor, later remarried.

"My feeling is that the figurine had been a gift to her, and perhaps even resembled her as she saw herself," he went on. "When it was put in the attic, and she was replaced by another woman in the house, naturally she felt some resentment."

In this case, the ending is a happy one. The figurine remained at Stephen's in a place of prominence, where it is often noticed and commented upon by guests. Who could ask for more?

Doris believes that whatever psychic gifts she has, have been inherited from her mother. "My sister in Brunswick is intuitive also, but she doesn't like to discuss it, since some of hers have been unpleasant," she added. "Mine, also."

There was, for example, the time when she vividly seemed to see herself on the wrong side of the road, in an automobile on Victory Drive. "I wasn't afraid," she remembered, "but I was wondering, 'How did I get here?'"

Three days later, she and her husband were hit by a motorist on Victory Drive, whose car hydroplaned in the wet street during a rain storm. It came to rest just as she had pictured it, on the wrong side of the median.

"Another time," she recalled, "I was sitting at home at my dressing table. Suddenly a large glass perfume bottle in front of me simply tipped itself over, while I was looking at it but not touching it, and spilled the perfume. This was just before a young man with whom I was very close, committed suicide."

The Little House
That is Now at Peace

It has been suggested that one reason Savannah and other old southern cities have so many tales of sightings and presences, is a common English heritage. Everyone knows that the British Isles, from the Orkneys to Land's End, have more than their share of stories of the supernatural. One Welsh woman with whom Stephen and I visited in Savannah recalled this theory during our conversation, although she now lives in a cozy little brick home in the mid-town section, near Waters Avenue.

The blue-trimmed, dormer-windowed home is not a very old one, but the interior is attractively furnished with nautical, country and English antiques, recalling the owner's Welsh and English background. After a short tour of the comfortable home on a gusty spring afternoon, we sat with our hostess, Bette, before the living room fire and enjoyed some hot tea. She, too, likes the house now, she told us. But it was not always so.

"When we first arrived here ten years ago, the size and location of the house were just right," she recalled. "But the atmosphere seemed ugly and oppressive. I particularly did not like the stairs! First, my husband lost his footing twice on them, which is not like him at all...and in the same spot, about half-way up. Then, the poodle fell down them, and broke his leg. They are steep, but we've lived in two-story houses before.

"Then Joy, my sister-in-law, came to visit. Joy is quite psychic, and I waited to hear what she would say about the house. Of course, I said nothing of my own feelings to her. She slept on the sofa bed in the famiy room, downstairs. I heard her up once that first night, but I did not go to investigate. The next morning, she came out to the kitchen and said very matter-of-factly, 'Well, I've met your friend.'

"'Oh?' I tried to sound innocent.

"'Yes,' she went on. 'I was lying in bed, but definitely not asleep yet, when I saw a man come into the room. I could clearly see him in

170

the moonlight coming in the window. At first, I thought it was Brother. He looked that real. He was standing by the doorway, wearing a tweed jacket, and smoking a pipe. He just stood there, looking around. Then, he was gone.

"'I got up, and checked all the doors and windows, though I was pretty sure what I had seen. So, you have a presence, but I don't think he will harm you. He just seems curious.'

"After she left," our hostess continued, "I decided to talk with some of the neighbors, and learn his identity. I was sure she was right, for she's had other such experiences. All that I knew was that one owner had died in the house, of a heart attack.

"'Tell me,' I said a few days later to the woman next door, 'did the last man to live here, smoke a pipe?'

"'Oh, no,' she replied. 'He had to give his cigarettes up, even, because of his heart.'

"'Really?' I pressed her. 'I'd gotten the impression somehow that he did.'

"'No,' she said thoughtfully, 'but strange that you should ask! The last owner before you, did smoke a dreadful, smelly old pipe, but he never lived here. He had bought the house, and was planning to move, when he was shot by a woman he'd been seeing, out at Tybee. He was working on an addition to the house, your family room, the summer he was killed.'

"That was my answer," Bette ended the story. "I think he was curious about how his pet project had turned out!"

"Well, I don't feel him here now," Stephen said comfortably, accepting more tea.

"Neither do we. Perhaps he's used to us. As a matter of fact, we haven't sensed anything since that first spring here, when we had two Eucharist cottage services in the house."

"That could do it," Stephen commented. "Perhaps it acted as an exorcism. I recall the service also includes a prayer for the dead."

"Someone suggested to me that they may even have been two presences," Bette concluded. "The unpleasantness on the stairs might have been the man who had the heart attack, and the presence in the family room, of course, the other man. Anyway, may they all rest in peace."

THE TROUBLE WITH ANTIQUES

"I also believe," Bette continued, "that if the vibrations, for good or evil, of a former owner are strong enough, some of them can come with their belongings. This seems particularly true if the owner

171

died violently, or was a suicide. I knew two such cases, and I hope I never know another!

"One day I was browsing through a friend's antique shop, when I saw this lovely old platter. It was just the thing for my collection, and I wanted it very badly. So I bought it, along with a sturdy plate hanger to show it off properly. I was so pleased that my husband fixed it up for me that very day in our dining room.

"Later that afternoon, when the house was quiet, I heard something falling! Fearing the worst, I raced to the dining room. There on the floor, shattered, was my plate! But the hanger was still on the wall, intact! There had been no loud vibrations to cause it to fall, no unexpected jolts; I was the only one in the house. It was as though that plate had been deliberately pushed out from the wall!

"The next time I saw my dealer friend, I complained about the incident, wanting sympathy.

"'Oddest thing I ever heard,' he replied, shaking his head," she continued the story. "'Everything from that wretched estate has been broken, chipped or scratched! Some of the things seem to break of their own accord, or at the least touch, right in my shop. Others give no satisfaction before the same thing happens. I'm ready to rid myself of the lot! But they didn't give the former owner any rest, either.'

"'They say she was a terrible old sour sort,' he went on, 'a retired school teacher with a house full of fine things she'd inherited from her family, but no friends. She even avoided her relatives in her last years, sure they were after her for her possessions or her money. When she was no longer able to stay in the big house alone with her treasures, they say she deliberately took an overdose of her medication, and killed herself.'"

THE UNWANTED CHEST

"Then there was the chest of drawers," continued Bette. "That might interest you, as it also involved my sister-in-law, Joy. A friend had given me this nice, large chest of drawers when we moved out here, you see. At first I was quite pleased, as it was a massive, well-made piece of oak furniture.

"Well, have you ever had something that just didn't seem to fit in anywhere? First, I tried my son's room; he'd have none of it! Said he liked his old one better. Same with our room. Finally, rather than give it back, I put it in one corner of the den. It didn't look right there, either.

"Then Joy came for a visit. She picked it out first thing, and absolutely shuddered. 'Get rid of it,' she told me. 'Sell it, chop it up. I don't like it.'

"After she left, I knew she was right. As tactfully as possible, I told my friend I had changed my mind. Did she want it back?

"'Well, I may as well give it to charity, though I had hoped it would not go among strangers,' she said. 'I can't bear to sell it, because it was my husband's. But I don't want it back in my house, either.'

"That explained it," Bette finished the story. "The husband, poor old chap, had been ill a long time, and then commited suicide."

"COME, SEE OUR HOUSE!"

As the afternoon wore on, Stephen asked Bette if she had ever had a precognitive dream.

"Yes, several," she replied after a moment's thought. "In the most dramatic one, I went to the home of a good friend. But when I got there, nothing was as I remembered it! The house was the same on the outside, but inside, all was changed... furniture, drapes, even the front hallway had been altered. In my dream, my friend came and took my arm and said so cheerfully. 'Oh, Bette, do come see how we've done over our house.'

"This was particularly strange because this couple had antiques, and they had spent years arranging them all exactly as they wanted them. When I woke up, I said to my husband, 'What a confusing dream! But it all seemed so real.'

"Well, a few weeks later, our friends had a terrible fire. They were not hurt, but the old house was damaged, and most of their fine things ruined. However, they decided to stay there, remodel, and get new furnishings.

"Finally, the day came of their little house warming. When my friend opened the door, it was just like walking into my dream. I had seen it all before. And there she was, smiling as she took my arm and said so invitingly, 'Oh, Bette, do come see how we've done over our house.'"

"Into a ward of the whitewashed walls
Where the dead and the dying lay—
Wounded by bayonets, shells and balls—
Somebody's darling was borne one day."
—Marie Ravenal De LaCoste,
"Somebody's Darling"

Déjà Vu at Candler Hospital

Before I knew anything of the long and dramatic history of the oldest part of the Candler General Hospital building at Abercorn and Gaston Streets, I experienced an unusual sense of déjà vu there.

My story begins late on a quiet Sunday afternoon in early winter, as I was reading alone in our home on Oatland Island outside of Savannah. I was surprised to hear my daughter, then sixteen, returning earlier than expected from an afternoon ride with friends to a southside roller skating rink. Generally a mature and efficient young woman, she was trying to speak evenly as she came into my study with her khaki trench coat draped over her shoulders.

"Mother," she began, "I think you'd better call the doctor. It was pretty crowded at the rink, and someone skated into me and knocked me down. . . . I think I've broken my wrist." She was trying to hold it immobile under her coat, against her pocketbook.

"Take her down to the emergency room at Candler," my Wilmington Island physician said briskly and I relayed the message by telephone. Driving as fast as possible through the nearly deserted streets of Savannah, I was soon pulling into the large parking lot of the hospital on Drayton Street for the first time. We left the car, and began walking through the winter dusk toward the oldest part of what had once been The Savannah Poor House and Hospital.

As I reached the building, I instinctively turned and started up the great stairs of the portico. If I had looked up, I would have seen that there was no light on the stairs, and the large doors above them had obviously long been closed. Instead, under them on the ground floor, a lighted sign clearly said, "Emergency Entrance."

"Mother!" my daughter Jennifer said a little impatiently, heading for the correct door. "Look at the sign."

Feeling a little embarrassed at my instinctive turn toward the dark stairs, I followed her through the entrance into the brightly illuminated chrome, glass and white tile of a modern hospital

174

The oldest section of Candler General Hospital was built in 1819.

reception area. After being consigned to the usual waiting rooms, we were then taken to a small private anteroom of a medical suite.

"You know," my daughter said after we had waited there a few minutes, "I was so busy today that I never did eat my lunch between going to the library and the skating rink, as I had meant to do. There's still a peanut butter sandwich in a paper bag in the car. If you could find me something to drink, I would really like to have it."

Grateful that she still had an appetite in spite of her injury, I went back to the now dark parking lot, and to the car. Returning to the hospital, it happened again. This time, of course, I knew where I should be going, inside the ground floor doors to my daughter.

Inexplicably, I once again turned. I found myself hurrying up those great, dark old stairs toward a long-closed entrance way. My former anxiety had vanished. I was suddenly young again, excited, and happy....

In a moment, the feeling passed. Once again I was a suburban matron, with a daughter waiting for me, and carrying a diet bread and peanut butter sandwich. Grateful that no one else had witnessed my second foolish turn of the day, I hurried into the downstairs doorway of the hospital. I fumbled with coins at a vending machine,

175

and got some coffee for myself and a carton of milk for Jennifer.

"Well," she said gratefully when I appeared, "I was beginning to think you had gotten lost!"

The next time I came back to Candler it was daylight, and I took the time to read an old marker that I had noticed in the parking lot. Then I turned and walked slowly up the stairs toward the portico, but in the sunlight, the emotions of that Sunday night were beyond recall. It was just an old building, where perhaps in the stress of the moment I had "flipped into" another time period. But the elation I had so briefly felt had been genuine.

The marker said that the hospital had been the first in Georgia, and was believed to be the second oldest general hospital in continuous operation in the United States. Founded in 1803, it had been on that corner since 1819.

"During the War between the States a portion of the hospital was used for the care of Confederate soldiers," I read with a strange sense of recognition. "In the area to the rear of a stockade was erected in 1864, around the great oak tree that still stands there, for confinement of Union soldiers."

"After Sherman's occupation of Savannah and until 1866, the building served as a Union hospital."

When the Federal forces moved on into South Carolina, they had taken with them all the hospital equipment, and left a black doctor in charge. The building was used as a haven for former slaves until it reopened as a hospital the year after the war ended. Later it had become simply "Savannah Hospital," until the name was changed again in 1931 to honor Methodist Bishop Warren A. Candler.

The hospital had faced its next greatest crisis during the terrible yellow fever epidemic of 1876, the worst in Savannah history. In three months, 247 persons died of the disease, many in hospital corridors while waiting for rooms. Medical and religious personnel who bravely stayed at their posts were stricken, such as Dr. Stephen Harris.

Later the story was told in Savannah by the granddaughter of Dr. Harris, Mrs. James Harrison, and others, that there was an old tunnel which ran under the hospital. It was supposed to go from the oldest part of the building, near the parking lot, across Drayton Street to what was then the woods of Forsyth Park. It was said that during the epidemic, the dead were carried out of the hospital at night through the tunnel and quickly buried, so that the local citizenry would not panic at the sight of so many bodies, as many as fifty-eight in a twenty-four-hour period, being removed. It was also

Savannah Hospital, from an 1877 print.

whispered that the tunnel was haunted by the spirits of those who had died and been hidden there.

When newsman Will Whitten explored the tunnel a hundred years after the epidemic, he found it contained a small stone table and an old sink basin. This led to conjecture that it had also been a place of medical experiments on the indigent dead in the years after 1854 when the hospital served as headquarters for the Savannah Medical College. Others believed it had been used by runaway slaves about the time the Federal forces occupied the building and closed Forsyth Park to the local citizenry.

Papers later found by Mrs. Mary Morrison, a Savannah historian noted for her research into downtown buildings, indicate that the tunnel had once been part of an underground morgue, completed in 1884, with an inclined passageway which opened on Drayton Street. With the assistance of Mrs. Millie Fischer, director of community relations at the hospital, plans were made for Stephen to go into the long unused tunnel.

Slipping bravely into its dark and unventilated depths one sunny afternoon from a small entrance in the parking lot, he disappeared from view with Millie's flashlight. A marble tablet just inside the tunnel read, in Latin, "Have respect for the dead."

He found no ghosts, he told us upon emerging in a few minutes from its fifty-foot brick and mortar length. There was only the damp and deserted darkness of what was once called "a morgue of which there is no superior in the United States."

177

Yet stories persisted in the oldest part of the building later used for medical record storage, and in what was called the old stroke unit, of chills and strange noises and footsteps in the night in empty corridors. It was said that some personnel refused to go up there unaccompanied after darkness fell on the city. "One night I went up there alone," one staff member said, "and I distinctly felt someone quite strong, twisting my arm."

With the hospital's move in 1980 to new facilities on Reynolds Avenue further south, the building will probably be converted into apartments. Only the stories will remain of Confederate and Union soldiers, escaped slaves, and yellow fever victims spirited away in the menacing summer darkness to Forsyth Park.

As for myself, my own experience at Candler that winter afternoon is part of a continuing sense of having been in Savannah before, one more incident in my long love affair with this city. It is known that the famous poem, "Somebody's Darling," later a sentimental Confederate ballad, was written from the author's experiences as a nurse in a Savannah war hospital, "where the dead and the dying lay." My instincts tell me that hospital was the old building later known as Candler.

I also know what it would have been like to have been a woman of that time running up the steps with a little basket of precious wartime delicacies, to see a soldier patient, perhaps one for whom I had traveled some distance. It is only how I happened to somehow walk into the reality and share that emotion, that is the mystery.

An Evening with a Psychic

Emily Trammer, the Wilmington Island psychic, lives in a secluded country home with an intriguing sign on the mail box: "U.S.S. Love."

"Was your husband in the service?" I asked, picturing a retired navy couple, the first time I drove down her winding circular driveway to the small white house surrounded by shrubbery and flowers.

"No, I was just 'told' to name it that," the short, motherly-looking woman in the grey pants suit replied comfortably as she led me inside her pleasant ranch-style house. Her place of work is a glassed-in sunporch at the rear of the home, decorated with several of her original ceramic pieces. I sat with my back to the distracting scenery, a yard ringed with azaleas and a splendid view of the tidal marsh at sunset, as she closed the blinds behind me.

Then she sat down at the formica table opposite me, and picked up a deck of playing cards, closely shadowed by a fat little dog. She invited me to shuffle and cut the deck.

"I was never very good at this," I told her, fumbling at the stack as irreverent thoughts of riverboat gamblers and casinos crossed my mind. "I'm not even a bridge player."

"Oh, that's all right," she assured me kindly. "Some people just like to look at the cards and do it for themselves." Then she spread out the cards I had given her, and began to study them. She was later to tell me that the cards served two purposes. They put the visitor at ease and give them something to do, and they provide her with an object on which to concentrate. The mental images come to her as she looks at the cards.

I had decided to call Mrs. Trammer after a Brunswick teacher, Margaret Lee Dixon, had recommended her to me. Although assured of her absolute integrity, I still felt somewhat self-conscious. Visions of the dreary little signs of "fortune tellers," such as "Palm

179

Readings, $15," and "Madame Clara, knows all, tells all, 9-9 daily," were still in my mind. At the time, Mrs. Trammer and I had not met before, and so far as I knew, she did not yet know the real purpose of my visit. Let it be said, Mrs. Dixon did not know the personal details of my life which Mrs. Trammer then preceded to tell me.

After looking at my cards a few minutes, the kindly, grey-haired woman began to describe my somewhat unsettled family life at the moment. She saw three 'for sale' signs in our development, one in my yard. She warned me not to take the first offer we were about to receive—advice which we later unfortunately disregarded, receiving too late the second offer which she also foretold.

She correctly saw a long-distance move in the offing, north, but added that the location would be only temporary. "Your husband has to do with transportation," she went on, looking at the cards, "but he's not in his regular job just now. I see him at a desk, with a lot of papers. He has the last word on who he will be working with," an accurate picture of my pilot husband at that moment in Montreal, setting up a new office for his company.

After describing our three children, Mrs. Trammer remarked that the eldest was investing in business with another young man. The comment puzzled me, until I learned that he had indeed just advanced some funds to his younger brother so that the latter could work with a soap and vitamin distributorship.

As a spiritualist who believes in reincarnation, Mrs. Trammer includes her insights into past lives in her readings. "You once lived in France," she said to me. "You were a Catholic nun, in a hospital. The daughter you are so close to now, was the Mother Superior, and oh, everything had to be just so! I see old-fashioned cars in the streets outside," she went on, describing a scene reminiscent of World War I.

I thought of my idealistic, perfectionist daughter's interest in different religious philosophies and Biblical history, and her major in French. She had been so anxious to visit Paris, where she had spent three weeks after saving the money from her summer work, the year before. She had come home disillusioned. "It just wasn't what I expected," was all she would tell us.

Commenting on the many girl friends of another son, Mrs. Trammer was saying, "This boy was a monk in the Middle Ages in England. He wasn't a very good monk. . . .I see him getting out of those robes, with a woman. He never took his final vows.

"Later, he was with the Conquistadores in Mexico," she added. "He had a wife and two children in that life, a fine and beautiful woman who loved him, but he wasn't true to her, either. I see him involved with the native women. . . . Then I see him going off on a patrol mission with his men outside of Mexico City, and being killed in an ambush by the natives.

"However, he will meet this girl again, and they will have the opportunity to live out their lives together."

After my reading, I told Mrs. Trammer why I had come. We discussed her working methods and past experiences. She told me that she had always been psychic, but there had been times when she had not worked in it actively. "Then something would draw me back to it," she added. One of these times had been the loss of their only son in the Korean War. "I know he is still with me," she said. "Sometimes I catch a glimpse of him, and tell him to go on, but he says, 'No, I'll wait for you.'

"We used to have some seances here, but we had to give them up because there was one group of very disruptive young people who started coming," she commented of Savannah.

"Our minister when we lived in Richmond was the Reverend Ernest Longest," she said proudly. "He wrote the book *Cosmic Consciousness* and several others. We lived in the Richmond area forty-five years." She added that they had also attended Spiritualist churches in Florida.

"When my husband was shot down over Nazi Germany during World War II, and was a prisoner, I knew he was safe, even when I didn't hear for months at a time," she added. "That was the greatest comfort I have ever had, that and knowing we will be with our son again someday."

Recalling a friend who is also psychic, she said with a smile, "Jennifer likes to work the Ouija board. I think it is so boring; it just takes forever to spell anything out! When it starts, I know what it is going to say. We get half through a word, and, I can't help it, I find myself blurting it out! Oh, she gets angry at me! 'Let the board finish; don't interrupt!' she says. Sometimes she gets up and puts the board away. I don't mean to be rude; I just know what's coming, so why wait?

"The difficult ones are these who come here with a 'show me' attitude," she remarked of her visitors. "If they don't trust me, why do they bother? Their mental attitude makes it very difficult to help them. The worst was two girls and a young man, not long ago. I couldn't get anything from what they were pretending to ask me! Finally I just put the cards down and said, 'You're not telling me the truth about who's married to who, here, and I think you'd better go. I don't have time to play games.'

"Well, sure enough, they confessed then that the fellow was

really married to the one who was pretending to just be a good friend along for the ride, and the girl pretending to be his wife, was his wife's neighbor. They were so surprised! But then they apologized, and begged me to do another reading, so I did."

Later, on several occasions, I visited Mrs. Trammer with other friends. With one, she described an event in her past which she had not even mentioned to me, an unfortunate early marriage, step-children, and an annulment. "This was in another state...north, near the water," she had said, even depicting a little church they had attended in the country.

She also sensed the friend's fondness for her former father-in-law, and described the lay-out of his second floor apartment in the Washington, D.C. area. He was ill, she added, "but don't worry. He will recover this time. But at his age, his days are numbered. Later, he will go very quickly, with a pinpoint stroke."

After going home that evening, the woman called to tell me in a trembling voice that a letter from her former brother-in-law had been in her mailbox when she arrived at her house. "Dad can't write you, as he has to be in the hospital for a few days," he had written, "but he says for you not to worry. We expect a complete recovery."

When another Savannah woman sat down for a reading, Mrs. Trammer announced, "I hear the sound of a piano...it's a child."

"Oh, my God, don't tell me she's back!" exclaimed the woman nervously.

"I am seeing a little girl, a child prodigy," she went on. "She is playing music, and some black people around her are singing and playing too."

On the way home, my friend confided that as a child in Illinois, her mother had indeed been exceptionally gifted. She had been invited to go on the road with a prominent black musical group, but the parents had refused because of her age. "She never forgave them," the woman added bitterly. "Later, she was so disappointed that I hadn't inherited her talent.

"But how did a woman in Georgia, that I had never seen before, know all of this? I had not discussed it here, that's for sure," a comment similar to my other friend's about her first short marriage in New England.

In speaking with a young bachelor, Mrs. Trammer accurately picked out the frustrations at his office. "They expect a lot of education for all they want to pay!" She also saw a difficult personal situation on the staff, "But don't worry, This poor woman doesn't even realize the damage she does. She will be resigning soon, before Christmas." The prediction seemed unlikely at the time, but came true several months later.

When Mrs. Trammer met Stephen, they experienced an immediate rapport. "I believe that you are psychic, and if you knew more about it, you could do more," she told him. "You sometimes have a 'hunch' that something is going to happen, and who is on the telephone. You need to know how to reach 'the other side.'

"But, never sit down to meditate in complete darkness. Always read a verse of scripture, then say a verse or the Lord's Prayer. Always ask, 'If anything comes, let it be good.'

"To mediate," she told him, "imagine yourself in a very peaceful place out in the fields. There are some trees around you. Now, imagine that you can see over the trees. . . .

"Or, imagine that you are in a motel or hotel, in a long hall, with a number of rooms. You are going to go down that hall and look for one room, open the door and get a revelation. What do you see?

"Oh, the revelation won't come at once in full form, or it would scare you to death! But you will see it in your mind's eye. Some are stronger than others. Remember, over there, all things are timeless. Give it time to develop.

"When you get a first and second impression," she went on, "follow the first one. Always give thanks to the spirits for whatever comes and who gives it. A lot of people have passed on, who can help you. . . . You will become psychic to the point of knowing if something is to be, or not to be.

"As you pray, and ask for revelation, this power will get stronger. Some have the potential to be healers. Your gifts are not so much in dreams, as that you hear in your mind, and know."

AN ENCOUNTER WITH JEANNE DIXON

As we talked, I thought of an incident the Savannah artist Peggy Cone had described to me earlier, when psychic Jeanne Dixon spoke in Savannah several years ago. "Afterwards, some of us went up to shake her hand," Peggy said. "But when it was my turn, she just stood there, and held my right hand! Then she said, 'Give me your other one,' and she stood and held that, as though there was no one else in the place but us. Then she looked at my palm.

"'You are not working in the field that will bring you a great deal of recognition, as well as happiness and satisfaction,' she surprised me by saying. 'You have a talent you must be working to develop.'"

"At the time," Peggy went on, "I considered my painting only a relaxing pastime from my other full-time work." Later, she was to devote herself more fully to her studio, and is now one of the area's best known and most popular artists.

THE CROSS ON THE WALL

One other postscript to my meeting with Mrs. Trammer. A few nights later, I was feeling very tired and sleepy as I got ready for bed. I was alone in the house. It was late, sometime between eleven and twelve. As I started to turn out the light on the bedside table, I was looking toward a desk across the room. I saw a plain white wall with a Sierra Club calendar above it, the familiar view I saw every night of my life. Suddenly in its place, and only for an instant, I was looking at an older, rough, plaster surface instead. On it, about the size of the crosses one sees in hospitals and other institutions, hung a large crucifix. I saw it clearly for a few seconds; then it was gone. I was standing staring at my own wall.

Had it been, I wondered, some type of subliminal suggestion or optical illusion, induced by Mrs. Trammer's earlier comment about the French hospital? Whatever it was, it had seemed very real for the time it lasted. Or was it really a memory from the past she had described, one which I do not consciously remember? Throughout my life I have had an un-Protestant interest in cathedrals, chains with crosses, the lights and music of a midnight mass, and even the impulse to form a sign of the cross during moments of tension. However, such things may be subconscious conditioning from friends, or even the genetic memory some writers have described.

I thought of the incident later as I read *Psychics Redux,* the second of a two-part series by author Cliff Bostock in an August 17, 1980 edition of the *Atlanta Journal-Constitution,* Sunday section, *Atlanta Weekly.* In it, he wrote of three accurate interviews with Atlanta psychics, Naunie Batchedler, Jane Hudson, and Frank Rambow. The latter had predicted that a spirit would attempt to reach Bostock, which it later did.

Following that experience, Bostock had been told by a physician affiliated with Duke University that it was "not uncommon for people first researching the field to experience apparent paranormal phenomena as a result of suggestion, if not outright hypnosis."

The author adds, and I could agree from my experience with Mrs. Trammer, that a person consulting a psychic should select one in the same way as a physician, according to reputation and referrals by friends and legitimate organizations.

"It is important to keep in mind that the quality of any psychic reading is influenced by all those factors that affect any other interpersonal experience," Bostock wrote. "It is pointless to

184

approach a psychic with the primary intention of making him or her prove their powers. . . .

"Psychics are not mind readers; they seem to be able to glimpse certain areas of a persons' future, but what they reveal does not emerge with the clear plot of a movie scripted by God. . . . Finally, no professional psychic claims better than 85 percent accuracy, and all believe in the interaction of free will and destiny. Thus, a psychic predicts not so much the inevitable as the highly probable."

A Savannah "House of Usher"

"Would you believe," Stephen said to me one day as we were discussing the houses of Savannah we had visited, "that Mother and I are living in a 'haunted' house? I'm embarrassed to say this, because I always felt it was something I would avoid. All I can tell you in my defense is that I never liked the place, but Mother loves it." I knew their home was a two-story frame house in Ardsley Park, a pleasant area of shade trees and azaleas. It was built in 1914, and they are its fifth owners.

Most of the incidents in the residence which they have dubbed "The House of Usher" concern the front bedroom, now Stephen's, but once that of the former owner. They seem to reach a height of activity in October, the anniversary of his death, and the time when Stephen's sensitivity is increased after the summer humidity.

"One repeated oddity is footsteps, especially in the upstairs front bedroom," said Stephen. "The sound of walking on bare floors can be heard even though the area is now thickly carpeted, and the steps seem to walk directly through a space now occupied by a large double bed! Another recurring sound is heard most often at 10:45 at night, the time when we know this man died. It is a sound like a top being taken off a bottle, and then falling to the floor.

"Since hearing the sound, we have learned that the man walked from the bathroom to the bedroom on the night of his death, and was unscrewing the top of a medicine bottle, just removed from the mantel, when he died."

"I tried having a talk with him once, when the noises got too distracting," Stephen continued. "I told him he was 'what is commonly known as dead,' and it was time for him to go on. It helped for awhile, but now he seems to be back. Sometimes now we hear the footsteps downstairs as well, and after I come in from being out all day, the atmosphere is decidedly heavy.

"We do know," he added, "that the wife of the builder never

liked the house, and moved out after he died. We also hear that he disliked dogs. We have had very bad luck with ours since living there. The very intelligent Sheltie I had when I came, Beau, had always slept in my room. We were practically inseparable. But when I moved here, he hated the house and would only sleep downstairs in the kitchen, right against the back door. He would never go into my room; in fact, he stayed as far from it as possible. Three days after we moved in, he disappeared, and has never been found.

"Our next dog was a Collie who would never go upstairs, though he was used to a two-story house. Our present dog goes everywhere, but will not remain upstairs at night unless he gets locked into a bedroom. You know, they say an animal can detect the presence of the supernatural when a human cannot.

"Right after we got our present dog," he commented, "a whole series of strange incidents happened in the house. We found a clock knocked over in one bedroom, and a light bulb broken where a lamp had fallen from the night stand to the rug; this was with no one in the house, windows closed, and the dog locked in the kitchen.

"Most puzzling of all, someone kept unscrewing the top from my bottle of shaving lotion in the bathroom at odd times. You might say once or twice was an oversight on your part, but not when it happened consistently, with everyone out of the house.

"Other objects were moved around in the house at odd times. Once, Mother had the sensation of someone brushing against her in the hall. She noticed at the same time that the house was very cold.

"On the one occasion that I actually saw anyone," Stephen continued, "I was alone in the house. A dim light was burning out in the hall, which illuminated my room a little. I woke up at 3:00 a.m., feeling that someone had touched me. I sensed someone was there. Then I saw a tall man, wearing a loose-fitting jacket and a dark turtle-necked sweater. He also wore a cap; he did not look like anyone I knew.

"I would have thought it was a prowler, except that he was standing where a bookcase now is! In other words, there is no way, given the present arrangement of the room, that he could be where I saw him. I closed my eyes, and eventually he faded away.

"Then another upsetting event occurred in October of this past year," he added. "I woke up with the distinct impression that two people, a man and a woman, were trying to tell me something urgent. There was this faint, steady murmur, right by my ear, but I couldn't make out the words, like a garbled telephone communication. Then I heard the man say, very distinctly, 'You may as well give up; he can't understand you.'

"This voice sounded as though it had come from just behind me, yet there was no way anyone could have been standing there! The bed was against the wall. I was lying on my side, facing out into the room. Again, it was not a voice that I recognized, at least not from that single sentence.

"I'm still waiting to hear what they wanted to tell me."

The Phantom Thunderbird

Perhaps because we lack the perspective of time, there seems to be fewer supernatural stories involving aircraft than other forms of transportation. However, in *The Ghost of Flight 401*, author John G. Fuller told of a modern commercial airline seemingly plagued with the phantom of a deceased navigator as the result of reusing some pieces of the plane involved in the needless tragedy which took his life. At Biggin Hill, a World War II airfield near London, it is said that on certain quiet nights in midsummer the unmistakable sound of a single Spitfire fighter plane can be heard, as the pilots say, "turning base," toward home.

In the comfortable setting of a southside Savannah restaurant decorated to resemble a British pub, Stephen and I sat by a dying fire late one evening in December and heard the strange story of a phantom aircraft of the Vietnam conflict. Our narrator was Walter Pillsbury, a former Air Force pilot who at the time was the owner and manager of the attractive restaurant with his English-born wife, Pamela. Walter is a native of New England, who decided to settle in Savannah after having been stationed at Hunter Field. A tall, friendly, good-natured man, he told his story with the direct, confident air of the professional pilot.

"It happened several years ago, during the Vietnam War," he said reflectively. "I was with a squadron which was bringing parts of wrecked aircraft back from 'Nam to the aircraft rework facility at Corpus Christi, Texas, to be salvaged for reuse in other planes. Our call letters were Big Mac.

"It was a beautiful, clear moonlit night," he went on. "Bright as day. We were coming into Corpus, and I called the tower for landing instructions, as usual. They came back loud and clear, no problem. Then I heard a second aircraft, with the call letters of Thunderbird, also calling the tower for the same thing. I heard the pilot very distinctly, as though he were right behind me, and from the position

189

he called from, he was.

"I was surprised to notice the tower never answered him! This does occasionally happen, where the pilot can hear another plane but not the tower, though it is rather unusual. As is done in such cases, I relayed the message on to the tower and they came back with the landing instructions for him, right after me. Thunderbird acknowledged this, but still was not heard by the tower.

"Well, we landed and looked behind us for the second plane. There was none, or any reports of one in the vicinity! I couldn't imagine what was going on. I did have a funny feeling though, as they began to unload our cargo, the pieces of wrecked airplanes. I thought of the other pilots who would not be coming back. In some cases, their families would never even know what had happened to them.

"Well, we off-loaded, and started taking the empty plane on into Hunter Field here in Savannah," he continued. "Just outside Hunter, the same thing happened! I called the tower and got my landing instructions, no problem. Then I heard Thunderbird calling the tower! No answer. Once again, it was from our position. Again, I relayed the message, and got the response from the tower.

"By this time, my co-pilot and I were both really puzzled. We didn't see how or why anyone would want to play a practical joke like that. Some things you just don't clown around about. But to make sure, I very quietly walked through the plane at that point, checking out what each of the other crew members were doing. During that time, my co-pilot heard another transmission from Thunderbird, acknowledging landing instructions we'd gotten for him from the tower.

"Once again, we landed and waited. No sign of Thunderbird. The tower personnel told us there were no other reports of aircraft of that description in the area, except what we had relayed. We stopped there for the night. One more strange thing. We clearly heard one last transmission from Thunderbird, on his way on to Jacksonville!

"That was one of my last trips to 'Nam," Pillsbury concluded. "I've made some inquiries, but I've never been able to locate a squadron with those call letters. It sounds like a chopper or attack outfit. You could call it my imagination, except that my co-pilot and I so clearly heard the radio transmission several times, at different parts of the country.

"If you believe in such things, and having lived in England and married a British woman, I have a very open mind on the subject, you might say that 'someone' came back with us with the wrecked aircraft parts we had aboard, and was going on home to Jacksonville. From time to time, I ask pilots who served out there if they ever

190

heard of a Thunderbird outfit. All I can say is that it happened, and remains one of the great mysteries of my life."

Bonaventure:
The Most Elegant Graveyard

"The grand old forest graveyard, so impressive that almost any sensible person would choose to dwell here with the dead rather than with the lazy, disorderly living," naturalist John Muir wrote of Bonaventure Cemetery outside Savannah during a visit there in the late 1860's. Out of funds while waiting for money from his family in the Midwest, he was forced to spend several nights outside in what he called "the weird and beautiful abode of the dead."

As much park as cemetery, with its miles of azalea bushes, entwining oak branches and Spanish moss, the place with the Italian name meaning "good fortune" is the burial place of Georgia governors, statesmen and songwriter Johnny Mercer. It has always enticed the imagination with its natural beauty, unusual history, and legendary ghosts. To keep the peace, the story goes, there is still one spectral Confederate veteran who regularly patrols the grounds at midnight to prevent vandalism to his comrade's graves.

But the most famous story of the cemetery involves the site itself, on a scenic bluff overlooking the Wilmington River. It was one of the great plantations of the Colonial era, part of a 1760 land grant of John Mulryne, the English colonel who built a brick mansion with terraced gardens overlooking the water. It was there that his daughter, Mary, married Josiah Tattnall, son of another prominent early family which had come to Savannah from Charleston. A cherished Savannah tradition, disallowed by some historians, says that the great oaks of the bluff site were planted in a pattern in which the M entwined with a T, symbolic of the union of the two families when Mary and Josiah married at Bonaventure.

Their happiness was ended by the Revolutionary War, which divided so many families. Staunchly loyal, the elder Mulrynes and Tattnalls both left the colony after the British royal governor, James Wright, took refuge at Bonaventure until he could escape to a British ship in the river when patriot forces had placed him under house

Bonaventure Cemetery, from an 1865 print by T. A. Richards in Harper's
Weekly.

arrest. Bonaventure was confiscated by the Americans, but returned
to a son, Josiah Tattnall, Jr., when he arrived from England to fight
under the forces of General Nathaniel Greene.

After the war, Tattnall rose rapidly in state politics, becoming a
militia brigadier general, Congressman, and then governor. He had
married after the war, and for awhile his home became noted for
brilliant entertaining, with guests from other plantations arriving by
carriage or by river for great parties, each group announced by the
distinctive songs of its black boatmen.

The most famous, and, some say, unending dinner party took
place in late November, about 1800. The mansion was decked for
the occasion with dried greenery, as well as fresh flowers. Welcoming
blazes burned cheerfully in the open fireplaces, although the night
was mild and pleasant. At the height of the elegant dinner, a servant
asked to speak to the host in private. He returned to his guests
looking shaken but determined. He had just been told that the
mansion was on fire. Flames were already racing through the roof,

This drawing of Bonaventure Cemetery at Savannah, from an early 1900s picture, shows the former site of the Tattnall family home. Courtesy of Jack Crolly.

and would soon take the house. Nothing could be done.

With unfailing courtesy, Tattnall required his servants to carry the tables and chairs out into the front lawn, followed by the guests. There the party resumed with forced cheer, in the eerie glow of the burning home, until nothing was left of the once-proud residence but glowing embers. Tradition says that in the course of the unusual meal a toast was proposed to the dying house, followed by others. One was for the party itself.

"May the joy of this occasion never end," said one courtly gentleman who had already enjoyed several glasses of the excellent wine, "and may we always be as we are tonight." At the conclusion of the toast, following the lead of their host, all the guests rose and shattered their goblets against a nearby oak tree.

According to the legend, it never has. It is said that on certain quiet nights, especially in the late autumn, one can still hear the tinkle of silver and glassware, the echoes of laughter, and the unmistakable crash of crystal.

The first persons to be buried at Bonaventure were Mrs. Tattnall and her four young children, followed by her husband. His son, also named Josiah, was a U.S. Navy captain and later Confederate commodore. By a quirk of fate, he had the unhappy assignment of destroying the naval shipyards of the city by fire before General Sherman arrived in 1864. Bonaventure was incorporated as a cemetery in 1869, and later acquired by the city.

Like many visitors, John Muir was attracted most of all by the live oaks of the river knoll, though he may not have known their story. "They are the most magnificent planted trees I have ever seen," he wrote. "Long moss drapes all the branches from top to bottom, hanging in silver-gray skeins...when slowly waving in the wind, they produce a solemn funeral effect singularly impressive."

"The Honest Ghost"
of Greenwich

The most famous controversy—and, some say, ghost—of the Greenwich section of Bonaventure Cemetery on the Wilmington River east of Savannah concerns who was, or was not, buried there long before the city acquired the scenic plantation for an extension of Bonaventure Cemetery in the 1930s.

The old estate adjoining Bonaventure to the north already had, like its neighbor, a history of early wealth, war, intrigue, and tragedy. It was first settled by an Englishman named Sam Bowen under a land grant from King George II, and named for the town near London on the Thames River. As with their friends the Mulrynes, the family peace was shattered by the War for Independence.

Allied troops established a supply depot at nearby Thunderbolt before the combined French and American attack on British-held Savannah in October 1779. Jane Bowen at Greenwich assured the French leader, Count Charles d'Estaing, of her cooperation and willingness to furnish "everything in my power for the Troops under your command" including "beds & blankets, fodder for the Cavalry and Boats and Negroes for obtaining provisions for the Hospital," as well as "horses for the Dragoons," and housing for naval officers.

All she asked in return was that her home not be used as a hospital, as was the Mulryne's, where, despite the presence of the mistress, the French troops had pillaged it in a shocking manner. Perhaps this was not too surprising, when one considers the known Loyalist sympathies of the absent Colonel Mulryne. At any rate, despite her pleas, Greenwich's plantation house did become a crowded hospital, as casualties overwhelmed Thunderbolt after the American defeat at the city's fortifications on October 9. The battle was the second bloodiest of the war, exceeded only by Bunker Hill in the number of casualties suffered by a single side. The most famous patient at Greenwich was the discouraged French leader d'Estaing himself, who pointed at his heart and said to his attending surgeon,

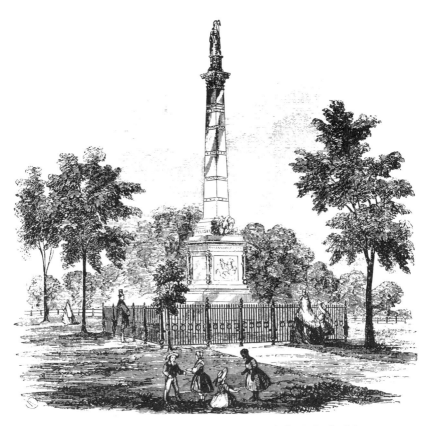

This is an 1857 drawing of Monterey Square and the Pulaski Monument.

"I have a deep wound, which it is not in your power to cure."

The wound in the admiral-general's leg, said one of his officers, was "rendered dangerous by the state of his blood, and, I think, that of his soul."

But the handsome Count survived his wounds and departed with his navy, only to die with other aristocratic friends in the French Revolution. The Greenwich controversy for over 200 years has surrounded another nobleman casualty of that warm October morning, the dashing Brigadier General Casimir Pulaski. The Polish rebel had first fought for freedom in his own country before it was overwhelmed by the combined forces of Russia, Prussia, and Austria. "...Know that as I could not submit to stoop before the sovereigns of Europe," he wrote. "So, I came to hazard all for the freedom of America."

Some say he was fatally wounded by grapeshot from a British

197

ship in the Savannah River while leading a brave but suicidal cavalry charge against the defenses of the city. Count d'Estaing, less sympathetic, said that the Polish officer fell "by his own fault in placing himself where he should not have been at the moment," and that he had "prematurely advanced in order to avail himself more promptly of the passage we were to open for him."

"He was a young and noble gentleman, a very daring horseman, and feared nothing in this world," recalled one of his dragoons. Some believe that the impulsive thirty-two-year-old officer had a death wish. Others said he was a fatalist, who had always believed he would not survive the war.

Colonel "Light-Horse Harry" Lee, the father of Robert E. Lee, recalled that the count, while being "amiable in heart," was "very reserved, and when alone, betrayed strong evidence of deep melancholy."

As many legends surround Pulaski's death as his short, adventurous life. After his wound was dressed by Dr. James Lynah, he expressed a desire to be convalescent with the French rather than the American forces. When his doctor protested, wanting to keep him under his care, Pulaski answered that he feared if he were an army stretcher case, he might be captured by the British and turned over to his most hated enemy, the Russians.

Here his path is lost in the confusion of retreat and the mists of history. Some Savannahans still say that he was indeed carried aboard the U.S. Navy brig *Wasp*, bound for Charleston, but was too ill to travel, and dying of gangrene. Brought secretly ashore because of his fear of the British, he died at the house hospital at Greenwich and was buried in the Bowen orchard. Others say that he died at sea, and was buried off Tybee Island. Still other legends put his final resting place at St. Helena Island off Beaufort, under a large oak tree.

What is known is that the *Wasp* entered Charleston harbor a few days later with her flag at half-mast, and general mourning ensued. Funeral services, without the body but with the horse on which the officer had received his fatal wound, were held in the city with military honors. General George Washington designated the watch-word "Pulaski" for the day's guard, with the countersign to be, "Poland."

"His death," wrote d'Estaing, was "an incalculable loss for the American cause."

"Pulaski has died as he lived-a hero-but an enemy of Kings," said the king of Poland.

After the death of Sam Bowen, Greenwich was purchased by Dr. John Bancroft, a former British army surgeon who married

Brigadier General Casimir Pulaski . . . if he died and was buried at sea, who was buried under his monument in Monterey Square in Savannah?

Bowen's daughter. The property was later divided among the family heirs. A hint of unusual happenings at the old plantation is in a poem of uncertain date, "on old Greenwich," written by Ann Elizabeth Bowen:

> "Say, have you lived within
> Savannah's bounds

And not heard of 'Old Greenwich'
    Home and grounds?
Such skeptics are we now
    of the place
In which an honest ghost dare
    Show his face.
This is the haunted house, this
    ruined spot
Was on the tablet of my childhood
    memory traced."

Was the "honest ghost" to whom the writer referred, Pulaski? The problem is dating the poem. If it was written, as some researchers believe, by 1765, then Greenwich had a ghost even before it became a hospital. But if it were later, then it may refer to the restless young nobleman, denied even the satisfaction of a monument.

In an effort to resolve the dispute, the orchard grave thought to be Pulaski's was opened in 1854 by Colonel William Bowen and two Savannah physicians, Dr. William Bullock and Dr. James Reed. To the surprise of some, a skeleton was indeed unearthed which bore what was called a striking resemblance to a lithograph of the late officer. This and other relics found at the site were placed in a metal container, and buried under the Pulaski Monument in Monterey Square in Savannah. The cornerstone of this monument, on the site of part of the ill-fated battle, had been laid thirty years earlier by another European nobleman and old comrade in arms of Pulaski's, the Marquis de Lafayette.

But the controversy, like Pulaski's fabled courage, lives on. If the young nobleman was, as some insist, buried at sea, then who was in the orchard grave at Greenwich, and later buried with full honors in Monterey Square? Who haunted the grounds of Greenwich? As mysterious in death as life, the impulsive young count is still, as one writer called him during a discussion of the matter in the city newspapers over fifty years ago, "Savannah's unknown soldier."

The Haunted Library

The story has long been told in Savannah of a haunted house which was located near Bonaventure Cemetery. Although the tale first saw print in *Stories of Old Savannah*, by Margaret Godley of the Savannah Public Library and Lillian C. Bragg in 1949 without the name of the estate involved, some believe that it was Greenwich.

"The house stood about a quarter of a mile from one of the avenues of oaks at Bonaventure," the story began. "It was large and strongly built, much defaced by time in its last days. The wild swallows made their nests in its chimneys; its court was overgrown with weeds, and vines clambered over the windows. It was finally removed, and a neat, small mansion erected not far from its site."

The narrator states that her father "had always been one to laugh at the idea of ghosts in haunted houses. Such things in Savannah in the nineteenth century—impossible!" Then one chilly February afternoon, as the early winter darkness came on, he found himself weary after a day of hunting near Bonaventure, in the time when it was still largely woods and marsh. The young man suggested to his companions that they seek hospitality for the night at the old house, whose owner was known to one of them, rather than ride back to Savannah in the dark.

The others objected, telling him that they had always heard the residence was haunted. He hooted in reply, and turned his tired horse toward its walled garden.

It was an area, added the writer, which had been "one of the old Colonial estates, rich in history, legend, romance, and beauty." Many years before the residence had been an elegant one, tastefully and expensively furnished and surrounded by fruit trees and flowers. Shortly after the War between the States, there had been a quarrel among the heirs. Those whom most of Savannah felt had the best claim to the property were unable to produce the necessary documents, and lost their home.

Heartbroken, they left the area. So, in time, did the next resident. Stories of unusual happenings in the old house under the oaks began to be told and embellished. As the young men were thinking of these things, the present owner appeared and graciously invited them all in for supper. Under the influence of some fine wine, they later admitted to him their misgivings about ringing his bell. He laughed easily, saying that he thought the idea of such things "exploded at the present day," and that he regretted he had no ghosts to show them. He did, however, suggest that the young man who had proposed the visit spend the night in the house library apartment, formerly the bedroom and study of the host's late father, where there were a number of rare volumes on the subject.

The others laughingly agreed, arranging to meet the next day and further discuss the matter over dinner in Savannah. Then they asked for their horses and rode on, leaving their friend alone with his host.

At first, the tale continues, the young man was comfortable in the combined library and bedroom. He examined its volumes, many now long out of print, and its excellent prints and paintings. These included several life-sized portraits of various members of the family, now long gone. There was a strong, virile-looking man in the regimental dress of the recent war; a beautiful young woman in a bridal veil; an older woman in brocade; a middle-aged man holding a roll of parchment in his hand, and several more. Finally, worn by the days' exertions, he fell asleep.

He awoke a few hours later to the sound of the great striking clock. A full moon shone in the windows, illuminating the room. As he glanced about his strange surroundings, he was startled to see a man—the man of the portrait, in uniform—now seated near him in a large leather arm chair. The frame of the painting above him was empty.

Then he realized in terror that the other elaborate frames were vacant as well, for the persons who had occupied them were now moving about the room. There was the matron, whose brocade skirts rustled as she walked; the young woman more beautiful than ever under her bridal veil; a feminine relative who complained, "Are we to have no music or dancing anymore?" and the man with the rolled parchment. It was between he and the officer that a conflict was ensuing, the watcher realized. Finally the veteran urged him, "Be just! Yield up what is not your own! Let not the innocent suffer!"

The man with the papers only shook his head. The handsome features of the other were now contorted with rage. Then, continues the story, the scene began to change. "The outlines of the figures first became tremulous and indistinct, and then they seemed to melt into one another. At length, all was dark, as the moon had gone behind the tall trees."

Exhausted by emotion, the young man managed to sleep again. He awoke to a servant entering the chambers, and a room full of sunlight. An uneasy glance told him that the ancestral pictures were solidly in their frames, although he felt as though they all were looking directly at him. At breakfast, and the later meeting with his friends, he found himself unable to speak of the night's events. He was, however, more interested than ever in what he could learn of the history of the house and family.

The old residence, the story continues, was eventually removed, "and a neat, small mansion was erected not far from its site." If this was indeed the last house to be built at Greenwich, it was, like the one at Bonaventure, destroyed by fire in 1923. Its occupants, the Torrey family, narrowly escaped with their lives.

Years later, after the older house was demolished, workmen excavating near where its foundations had been found a molding and nearly illegible piece of rolled parchment. Perhaps hidden in the confusion of the war years, it was one of the lost papers which might have helped the dispossessed heirs. But since the original estate had by then been divided and was decreased in value, nothing was done with the document.

It did, however, serve to convince the guest who had slept in the library during what songwriters Sir William Gilbert and Arthur Sullivan called "the ghosts' high noon," that such documents did exist. To the end of his days, the man who had once scoffed at ghosts, was unable to look at a lifesize portrait without a feeling of horror.

Sunlight and Shadow
at Colonial Cemetery

"The first time I ever walked through Colonial Cemetery," said Claire, "it was a beautiful day, and I was strolling along enjoying the quaint old monuments and inscriptions, the sense of history. Suddenly I turned icy cold, and started to shiver. I was overwhelmed with sad feelings, just in one particular area. But I walked on and came out of it, back into the sunlight, so to speak.

"I looked around, realizing that something unusual was there. Then I saw the marker that had been erected to the memory of nearly 700 victims of the terrible yellow fever epidemic of 1820, who were buried in a mass gravesite. No wonder there is a sense of tragedy."

Colonial Park Cemetery on Oglethorpe Avenue is the second oldest in the city of Savannah, and was the main burial ground after 1750 for over 100 years. Here lie Georgia's Revolutionary War statesmen, including five governors, soldiers, and many prominent early citizens, such as James Johnson, the state's first printer, of the *Georgia Gazette.* Just beyond its southern border, where children now play basketball, is reputed to be the spot where Button Gwinnett, a signer of the Declaration of Independence, was mortally wounded in a dual with his political rival Lachlan McIntosh.

Because of his short life, the forty-two year old Gwinnett is most famous in death for the scarcity of his autograph. One of Savannah's most celebrated scandals a hundred years later involved a local historian who is alleged to have sold a legal document from the state files with the signature to a collector for about $50,000. A law hastily passed to avoid a reoccurrence of the incident, but the signature itself was never recovered.

In disgrace after the duel, Colonel McIntosh was sent out of the state to serve on the staff of General George Washington, who called him "an officer of great worth and merit" after the shared misery of the ensuing winter at Valley Forge. He later participated in the Siege of Savannah in 1779, and was captured by the British at Charleston a year later. He is buried in Colonial Cemetery near his great-nephew, Colonel James McIntosh, who said during the Mexican War when wounded, "Just give me some water and show me my regiment." The gravesite of Gwinnett is unknown, but is reportedly in the Savannah area.

The state enacted a law against dueling in 1809, which was signed by the Scottish-born governor, Colonel David Mitchell. Ironically, Mitchell had been a duelist in his youth, and killed William Hunter, a Savannah businessman, in the old Jewish Cemetery west of the city in 1802.

That the law did not halt the practice of "affairs of honor" is witnessed by one of the famous markers in the cemetery. It belongs to a young Army paymaster named James Wilde, who died in a duel with another officer on the South Carolina side of the Savannah River in 1815 at age twenty-three. "He fell," says his epitaph, "by the hand of a man who a short time before, would have been friendless but for him."

Upon seeing those lines over one hundred years later, author William Dean Howells wrote in *Harper's Magazine* in 1919, "They wrung my heart with abhorrence for the custom which wronged him and his victim alike, and made me feel its atrocity and stupidity as never before."

Wilde's life was also memorialized by his brother, the Baltimore poet Richard Henry Wilde, in a long unfinished poem. It contains the famous lines.

> "My life is like the summer rose,
> That opens to the morning sky;
> And ere the shades of evening close,
> Is scattered on the ground- to die."

"No finer American poem has met my eye," said Lord Byron when he heard the tragic story.

Another famous, and long defaced, tombstone in the cemetery belongs to duelist Odrey Miller, a Kentucky horse trader who now lies on the west side of the cemetery, near the Abercorn and Hull Streets intersection. "A just, honest, and benevolent man," says his huge, flat granite stone, "who died from a wound inflicted by _____ on the 13th July, 1831, aged 33 years and three months."

Who killed Odrey Miller? The newspapers of the time, as was common with such affairs, do not even mention his death. Whoever's name was on the marker resented the fact that his crime had been fixed in stone, enough to slip into the burial ground at night and chip away at the inscription. He was obviously more afraid of the censure of posterity than any lingering presences, including Miller's.

"The chipping of the name," said one writer, "has done more to centre attention on the inscription and awaken comment and conjecture than if it still told the passer-by who it was that slew Odrey Miller."

During the nineteenth century, popular area dueling places included Screvens Ferry, near what is now the Eugene Talmadge Bridge between Georgia and South Carolina, and Tybee Island, near the old lighthouse. City records show that Aaron Mendes, late of Charleston, died in 1818 at the corner of Barnard Street and Bay Lane after a duel. As late as 1855, in an encounter at Fort Pulaski, John Chaplin of South Carolina killed his brother-in-law, a Dr. Kirk of Savannah.

The last duel fought in Savannah was in 1877, between two young lawyers who wisely avoided bloodshed, and later resumed at least a polite professional relationship.

For many years Hutchinson Island in the Savannah River between Georgia and South Carolina has been said to be haunted. Whether this was from its former fame as a dueling place, or because it is said to have been the site of colonial Georgia's first murder, is not known. In that case, a planter living there was killed by his two indentured servants, who were later hanged.

While I was working on this book, a friend with some psychic abilities came to visit from Virginia Beach, Virginia. She especially wanted to see more of the sites I had researched, she said. After touring Colonial Cemetery, and the Trustees' Garden and Pirates' House area, she surprised me by walking around what is left of the high brick walls of old Fort Wayne, where it is bordered by Bay Street and the Savannah River.

"I just know something happened here that involved death and young men," she insisted, and was disappointed when I told her I did not know of any historic happenings at that particular spot, except for possible fighting during the 1779 Siege of Savannah. Later I learned that east of the fort, like Hutchinson and Tybee Islands, had been a popular location in the early nineteenth century for what was called "the aristocrat's crime."

Many duels are said to have originated at the old City Hotel building on West Bay Street, an 1821 structure designed by architect William Jay and now an office supply house. Under the influence of a few drinks at its fashionable bar, bored young men of the times are reported to have dramatically given and taken offense, and gone off for weapons and seconds as their friends tried to resolve the difficulty.

One Kensington woman told me of a spectral story of the building as she had heard it from her grandmother. It concerns a young seamstress who worked there at a tailor shop in the 1890s. She had fallen in love with a mysterious young man whom she sometimes encountered in the dim and little-used upper hallways of the structure. One evening, she decided to follow him home.

Alarmed by her obsession with the man, two friends quietly trailed her from a distance. After several blocks, they found her at twilight, standing alone in tears outside the iron fence of Colonial Cemetery.

Echoes from Laurel Grove Cemetery

Just as Bonaventure Cemetery borders Savannah to the east, on its western limits Laurel Grove has been waiting for its citizens since 1854. Under its wide oaks and Spanish moss rest such famous natives as Juliette Gordon Low, founder of the Girl Scouts of the USA, and General Francis S. Bartow, who fell at First Manassas in Virginia saying, "They have killed me, boys, but don't give up the fight." Here James Pierpont, son of a Unitarian abolitionist and the composer of "Jingle Bells" and Confederate martial music, lies beside his wife, Eliza, the daughter of Savannah Mayor Thomas Purse, and his young brother-in-law, Thomas Jr., who also died in the 1861 battle the defeated Yankees called First Bull Run.

There, in what has traditionally been the black section, is the grave of "Old Tom," described as "Faithful servant for over fifty years of Captain John F. Wheaton, died, February 11, 1904, age ninety-six." The marker was decorated every southern Memorial Day by the "Men of The Confederate," who had erected it, because Tom had followed his master to war. There is also the grave of Andrew Bryan, who founded the first black Baptist Church in America in the western Yamacraw section of Savannah in 1788.

Two ghost stories are connected with Laurel Grove, both involving children. Savannah author Gerald Chan Seig recalls hearing that a horse-drawn trolley car once followed a route along Montgomery Street, and then out by the tall iron fence of the cemetery.

"They say that one day a little Jewish boy from Liberty Square was run over and killed by the trolley," she said. "He was buried in the cemetery.

"Well, the next day as the horses trotted leisurely toward the burial ground, I'm told that a wailing voice on Gwinnett Street, right at the foot of the cemetery, could be clearly heard crying out, 'You killed me! You killed me!'

208

"The horses reared up, and refused to go on. The driver frantically beat them, but they only whinnied and stood on their hind legs, pawing the air. Passengers and passersby were terrified. The whole trolley, driver, car, and horses, were transferred to another line.

"To my knowledge, no one on the street has heard the child since."

The next story concerning the cemetery was told Mrs. Seig by Mrs. Marinda Bullard, a Savannah laundry woman and expert ironer. Mrs. Bullard says that she has been able to "see things," since an early age, because she was born with a caul, or membrane, over her face. Most of the spirits which she sees are unpleasant, "people who died bad, by killing, or hard drinking, or something. They come around me frowning, with such sad looks, they're starting to get me nervous after all these years. They know who can see them, you know. Oh, yes, they know."

The children, the three little girls, were the happiest ones she had ever seen, she went on. "One day I was walking out Henry Street, and these pretty little girls in starched white dresses came up and joined me. They didn't say a word, but they were just so sweet. One took me by the hand, and they all skipped along like regular little girls. When we reached the end of the block, they turned off toward Laurel Grove. I stood and watched them until they reached the big iron gates. They turned to wave goodbye, and then they went inside, and were gone."

Memories of a Ship Builder

One intriguing aspect of Savannah history is the number of houses which have been moved from one downtown location to another. Among these is the charming restored frame cottage at 426 East St. Julian Street, which formerly stood on Price Street south of Oglethorpe Avenue. A story told of the house concerns its first occupant, shipbuilder Henry F. Willink.

It seems that as a young shipwright, Henry wanted his own vessel. It is said that one day while he was working on the ship in the Savannah River, his wife was aboard, helping him by handing him tools. But as she did so, she tripped over some lumber, and fell into the water. Weighed down by her heavy clothing, and unable to swim, she was swept away with the outgoing tide, though Henry jumped into the river and tried to save her.

After that, they say that on nights when he could not sleep, he would often slam his front door at strange hours, and go off to work on his ship. He began to think of it as a memorial to his wife, and decided to name it in her honor. But one day when it was almost completed, he was amazed to look up from his work and see the woman on the deck watching him. She was standing just where she had fallen. He was so startled that he took a step backward in fright, and fell into the water. He was fortunately rescued; by that time, the apparition had vanished.

Years later, Willink went on to own a Confederate shipyard just east of the Savannah bluff, building such ships as the *Georgia*, the *Macon*, and the *Milledgeville*. As for his house, it was said that especially before it was moved, one could hear the door slam at strange hours in the night, and heavy footsteps leaving it in the direction of the river. It was just Henry, they would say then, walking down to the waterfront and to the ship where his young wife had died.

This drawing by Ralph J. Mitchell shows the Henry F. Willink cottage at 426 East St. Julian Street in Savannah.

The Psychic Life of John Wesley

Visitors to Savannah are frequently surprised to see a Reynolds Square statue of the Reverend John Wesley, so well known for his evangelism which foreshadowed Methodism, in the Church of England attire which he wore during his brief Georgia ministry at Christ Church. Those who view all interest in the supernatural as diabolic, would be even more startled to know that the devout clergyman was both repelled and fascinated by the subject during his long and productive life.

Wesley, one of the nineteen children of the English Reverend Samuel and Susanna Wesley of Lincolnshire, had from childhood considered himself divinely spared and marked for greatness. A fire, some say set by disgruntled parishioners, had swept his birthplace at Epworth rectory in 1709 when he was five years old. At first, those who gathered to watch the blaze were sure they could not save the child asleep on the second floor. The stairs were already in flames, and his father knelt in prayer for his soul.

But little John, waking to find his bed on fire and none to help him, sensibly climbed over a chest to the casement window, where he was seen by the crowd below. As he later told the story.

"One in the yard saw me, and proposed running to fetch a ladder. Another answered, 'There will be no time, but I have thought of another expedient. Here I will fix myself against the wall: lift a light man, and set him on my shoulders.' They did so, and took me out the window. Just then the whole roof fell in: but it fell inward, or we would all have been crushed at once.

"When they brought me into the house where my father was, he cried out, 'Come neighbors! Let us give thanks to God! He has given me all my eight children! Let the house go; I am rich enough!'"

His pious mother also noted in her diary, ". . . With the soul of this child that Thou hast so mercifully provided for, I do intend to be more particularly careful than ever I have been; that I may do my endeavor to instill into his mind the principles of true religion and virtue.''

THE POLTERGEIST IN THE RECTORY

The stable, sensible Samuel and his efficient wife Susanna, a woman ahead of her time in such matters as putting her household and large family on a daily schedule, would seem unlikely subjects to host a poltergeist. But that is exactly what happened to the family in the brick, two-story rectory at Epworth, which had been built in 1695, and rebuilt after the fire. Letters and journals of various family members, carefully saved by John's brother Samuel, record that the problem began in early December, 1716, and ended by the next March. John was thirteen at the time, and a student at Charterhouse School.

Some students on the subject of the unwelcome "noisy ghost" of the German term, point out that they are generally found in a house with a great deal of repressed and or adolescent energy, which was certainly the case at the rectory. The manifestations included groanings and loud knocking from different parts of the house, the sound of breaking bottles at the foot of the stairs, chains rattling, a carpenter's plane, and even a jack being wound.

One night the rector and his wife went down the stairs together to investigate. When they reached the downstairs hall, according to Susanna, she heard what sounded like "a large pot of money poured out at my waist, to run jingling down my nightgown to my feet."

"Have you dug in the place where the money seemed poured at your feet?" wrote back her son Samuel, for the family was always very poor.

That same night, according to author Rebecca Lamar Harmon, in *Susanna, Mother of the Wesleys*, the couple went on to investigate in the kitchen. As they did so, "their mastiff came whining to them and wedged himself between them, cowering with fear. They searched every room in the house, and saw nothing unusual, but the 'rattle and thunder' continued for more than an hour."

At first, the practical mother attributed the problem to rats, and blew a large horn about the house to frighten them off. Later as the manifestations involved all members of the family and the servants, both separately and in groups in the house, there was no explanation except the supernatural. Susanna thought that it might be an omen of death or disaster, but such was fortunately not the case. Her daughter Emilia tried to see the bright side.

"I am so far from being superstitious that I was too much

inclined to infidelity; so that I heartily rejoice at having such an opportunity of convincing myself of the existence of some beings beside those we see."

It was Emilia who named the spirit "Old Jeffrey," as he harassed the family. Terrified at first, the children in time accepted him. "They found they could tease and anger him by making personal remarks about him," writes author Harman, "and this turned into a sport. To little Kezzy, Old Jeffrey became a favorite playmate. She chased his tappings from room to room, gleefully stamping on the floor with her tiny feet, and hearing the answering knock in return.

"Nancy reported that the ghost walked behind her as she swept the room, seeming to repeat the sweeping after her. On one occasion, the bed on which she was sitting was lifted several times. This performance was in the presence of several others in the family." Sometimes the Wesley girls would hear a gentle tapping on the heads of their beds between nine and ten at night. "Jeffrey is coming," they would say. "It is time to go to sleep."

The mother was annoyed at the interruption in her well-regulated home. "If they could instruct us how to avoid any danger, or put us in the way of being wiser or better, there would be a sense in it," she said of such apparitions, "but to appear to no end that we know of unless to frighten people almost out of their wits, seems altogether unreasonable.

"I cannot imagine how you should be so curious about our unwelcomed guest," she wrote young Samuel at his school. "For my part, I am quite tired with hearing or speaking of it; but if you come among us, you will find enough to satisfy all your scruples, and perhaps may hear or see it yourself."

But Samuel never saw Old Jeffrey. Neither did the elder Wesley's clergyman friend, a Reverend Hoole, who persuaded the distraught rector that it was useless to threaten a spirit with a pistol. After that, Hoole even spent a night in the rectory at the Reverend Wesley's request, in order to try and "conjure" the ghost.

Susanna saw the presence once, under a bed, in the form of a headless badger, according to her biographer. "Robin Brown, the manservant, caught a glimpse of the same figure near the kitchen fireplace, and at another time a creature like a small rabbit came out from behind the dining room fireplace beside Robin, turned swiftly around five times, and disappeared. To Sukey and Hetty, the apparition resembled a man in a long, trailing nightgown.

"Jeffrey had his favorites, too. The door latches would be opened by a mysterious hand to let the girls pass through. Susanna, always practical, expressed the wish that she not be disturbed from five to six during her private devotions, and oddly enough, the wish was granted," writes Harmon.

There was no lack of theories about this curiously well-documented presence. "Wit, I fancy, might find many interpretations, but wisdom none," concluded Samuel Jr. "It would make a glorious penny book," said his father. John Wesley was interested in the fact that the spirit had Stuart leanings, and made its worst rackets when the Reverend prayed for King George and the prince at family prayers. Angrily, the father would repeat the prayers, but with the same result.

Was it coincidence that fourteen years before, the couple had quarreled bitterly over the same subject, when Susannah had refused to say "amen" to that same prayer for King William? Her husband, when she refused to recant, had left her for London, where he hoped to receive a chaplaincy in the army or navy. Though they were now reconciled, his son thought Jeffrey might still be a reminder of this marital rift. A modern parapsychologist might suspect that the wife still unconsciously harbored some resentment, which found expression in the noise at prayers.

"Thou deaf and dumb devil," Samuel Wesley cried in exasperation, "why dost thou frighten the children that cannot answer thee? Come to me in my study, that am a man."

The ghost answered by mocking the pastor with the particular knock which the father used on his own gate and door each evening when he returned to the family, only much louder, "as if it would shiver the boards in pieces." After that it particularly annoyed the Reverend in his study, which had been quiet until then.

If an exorcism was attempted, it was not immediately successful. But the visits became less frequent in time, and then ceased. However, thirty-four years later, in 1750, Emilia wrote John that she sometimes sensed a presence nearby, "but so little is known of the invisible world that I, at least, am not able to judge whether it be a friendly or an evil spirit."

Strangely enough, over one hundred years later, a recurrence of the Epworth Rectory presence was reported. It proved so troublesome that the occupants of the home moved to London for quiet.

As for John Wesley, he never forgot the experience. Andrew Lang, a biographer, wrote, "Old Jeffrey made a thoroughfare for the supernatural through John Wesley's brain."

During their student years at Oxford, John and Charles Wesley and the other devout youths who formed the Holy Club there, engaged in such activities as investigating reports of levitations, and attempting to exorcise haunted houses, along with holding prayer meetings and trying to reform prostitutes. Wesley believed in the reality of ghosts and angels as in the Devil, for he found them all in his well-thumbed Bible.

The two brothers came to the colony of Georgia in 1736, after the death of their father. John, recruited by the Society for the Propagation of the Gospel in London, hoped to be a missionary to the Indians as well as rector at Christ Church in Savannah. His brother was to be a personal secretary to the colony's founder, James Oglethorpe, as well as the pastor at Frederica on St. Simons Island, and secretary for Indian affairs.

John was anxious to know the native Georgian's beliefs on a supreme being and life after death. According to his journal, edited long afterward by Nehemiah Curnock of London, he soon interviewed five "Chicasaw" Indians, including two chiefs, in Savannah through an interpreter, probably the Reverend Mr. Andrews. They told Wesley that they believed in One in the sky, who "made all men at first...out of the ground."

They also believed this One had the ability to save them in battle, if he chose: "Many bullets have gone on this side, and on that side, but He would never let them hurt me....Many have gone into these young men here, but they are still alive."

The chief Paustoobee also believed that the "beloved ones" who had died in battle continued with them in spirit. "When our enemies came against us, then the beloved clouds came for us. And often much rain, and sometimes hail, on them, and that on a very hot day...I saw, when many French and Choctaws and other nations came against one of our towns, and the ground made a noise under them, and the beloved ones in the air behind them, and they went away, and left their meat and drink and their guns....All these here saw it, too."

The warrior continued that he had heard such sounds at other times, "before and after almost every battle...like the noise of drums, and guns, and shouting." Four days after their last battle with the French he had heard it, and also the night before, when "I dreamed I heard many drums up there, and trumpets, and much stamping of feet and shouting...I thought we would all die. But then I thought the beloved ones had come to help us. And the next day I heard about a hundred guns go off before the fight began, and I said, 'the beloved ones will help us, and we shall conquor our enemies,' and we did so."

"We think of them always, wherever we are," he added of the warriors of his tribe who had died. "We talk of them, at home and

This statue of John Wesley depicts his brief Church of England ministry in Savannah. Constructed by Marshall Daugherty and dedicated in 1969, it is located in Reynolds' Square near the site of Wesley's 1736 church and parsonage. Wilhoit photo courtesy of Savannah Visitors Center.

217

abroad; in peace and war, before and after the fight, and wherever we meet together."

When Wesley asked him where he believed the souls of red men go after death, the chief answered, "We believe that the souls of red men walk up and down, near where they died, or where their bodies lie; for we have often heard noises near the place where any prisoners had been burned."

"As for the souls of white men," he added, "we cannot tell. We have not seen."

"Our belief is, that the souls of bad men only walk up and down, but the souls of good men go up," commented Wesley.

"I believe so, too," replied the Indian. "But I told you the talk of the nation."

Despite their sometimes misguided youthful zeal, or perhaps because of it, the Wesley mission in Georgia was not a success. Neither brother was emotionally or physically suited for the rough life of the frontier. Charles irritated the settlers at Frederica by preaching to them of the sinfulness of hunting on Sunday, and Oglethorpe soon sent him back to England with the frank advice that he would be a better minister if he found a congenial woman and married.

Perhaps because he had seen the demands a large family made on his father's time and small salary, John had resolved to live a celibate life for the church. But in Georgia as in England, the thirty-two-year-old man found himself continually tempted and frustrated. He was soon desperately in love with an eighteen-year-old girl named Sophy Hopkey, the niece and ward of the town storekeeper and jailer, Thomas Causton. Both the girl and her family was ready for the match, but the clergyman was torn between love and duty. His friends the Moravians, a group of devout Protestants from Bohemia who had come to the colony on the same ship as the Wesleys, counseled against marriage. They thought the pretty, high-spirited Sophy was not suited to be a minister's wife.

Later, when she eloped to South Carolina with another man, the heartbroken Wesley denied her communion on a technicality. Her uncle sued him for defamation of character, and Wesley left the colony in temporary disgrace and with only one comfort. "He that made the heart," he noted, "can heal the heart."

Brief though his ministry was in Georgia, some twenty-one months, he began the first Sunday School, and wrote the first hymnal used in Georgia. He later credited his difficult time in Savannah with broadening both his personal and theological horizons, particularly in his conversations with the pacifist Moravians and the Indians. "They humbled me and proved me," he later wrote, "and showed me what was in my heart."

Just as Wesley continued to believe in Divine intervention in his own life, he maintained an interest in such supernatural manifestations as diabolic possession, and "evil spirits, that infect mankind with sin and doubt." He never forgot the puzzle of Old Jeffrey, and published an account of the affair in his Methodist *Arminian Magazine* in 1769, when he was sixty-six years old. Time proved him right in his premonition against marriage. He did finally marry, to an English widow. It was not a happy union, and the couple were separated when Mrs. Wesley died.

Another unusual event happened to Wesley in later years, after he had begun the "open air ministry" and constant travel of "the world's first circuit rider." As one of his friends of the clergy, the Reverend Samuel Smith, later told the story, Wesley was preparing to leave on a preaching trip one day in late February, 1772, when a letter arrived for him.

He opened it, and saw with surprise that it was from the eminent Swedish scientist and theologian Emanuel Swedenborg, then in London.

As Reverend Smith later often told the story, the note said that Swedenborg had been informed "in the world of the spirits," that Wesley had a strong desire to converse with him. He added that he would be pleased to see the clergyman if he would care to call at his address in Coldbath Fields.

Wesley admitted to Smith that he had indeed wanted for a long time to meet the Swedish philosopher, but had never told this to anyone. He quickly dispatched a note saying that he was in the act of leaving for a six-month preaching tour, but that he would be pleased to call upon Swedenborg on his return.

The mystery deepened when the eighty-four year-old Swede wrote back that it would be much too late by then. He expected to "enter into the world of the spirits on the twenty-ninth day of next month, never to return." The prophecy came true, and the two never met—at least in this life.

Who is Lady Huntingdon, and Why is She Walking at Bethesda?

Tales are frequently told concerning persons whose spirits are said to return after death to the place they loved and frequented in life. Stranger still is the legend recounted at Bethesda Home for Boys, the nation's oldest orphanage in continuous existence, located nine miles from Savannah along the Vernon River.

Countless "Bethesda Boys," and there have been over 8,000 of them in the past 240 years, have heard of Lady Selina, the British Countess of Huntingdon and benefactor of the home. She is honored at the school by a landscaped amphitheater, and by a pathway shadowed by large oaks, which follows the water's edge around the pleasant campus. It is here, according to tradition, that the thin wraith of the Countess may be seen on certain clear, crisp nights when a full moon hangs over the marsh, and Bethesda is quiet after the day's work and play.

But who is Lady Huntingdon, and with a perfectly good castle at home, why is she walking so far from her ancestral land? The answer lies in the unique history of the school, and the hardships of the Colonial era in which is was founded.

In early years of the Georgia colony, many children were left homeless because of the deaths of their parents. The need for a charitable institution, molded after the "widows and orphans house" of the thrifty Lutheran Salzburgers at Ebenezer, was quickly realized by founder James Oglethorpe and his two clergymen, John and Charles Wesley. They recruited an old friend from Oxford, the Reverend George Whitefield, to organize the charity which John had already begun by taking some orphan boys into his home.

The institution quickly received the approval of the Georgia Trustees in London, along with a land grant of 500 acres. Whitefield collected a staff of eleven persons, and planned a self-sufficient operation "in an open place upon the salts, where wicked influences of the city are no longer with us."

This portrait of the Countess of Huntingdon was presented to Bethesda in 1773 and is now at the Georgia Historical Society. Courtesy Bethesda Alumni Association.

The cornerstone of the main building at Bethesda, or "House of Mercy," was laid in 1740. Even the kindly Yamacraw Indians helped, by sending venison and other foods when Spanish pirates seized an English ship laden with provisions for the home.

The orphanage soon had its own livestock and gardens. James Habersham, Whitefield's "fellow traveler and invariable friend," from England was installed as the schoolmaster and administrator. This left the Reverend Whitefield time to become the school's chief fund-raiser, and he traveled widely on its behalf.

His preaching moved the economical Benjamin Franklin so that after one session, when the printer had planned to contribute sparingly, he found himself impulsively emptying his pockets, "gold and all." However, Franklin believed that the children would have done better in Philadelphia, since Georgia was known to be the home of vagrants and debtors.

His travelers also brought him in close contact with his English benefactor, Lady Huntingdon, and he became her personal chaplain.

A daughter of Washington Shirley, Earl of Ferrars, Selina Hastings was a distant cousin of George Washington, and wrote him concerning her Georgia charity. She was married to the ninth Earl of Huntingdon, a mild, good-natured man who did not share her enthusiasm for the revival movement then sweeping England. However, recognizing his wife's interest in the cause, he accepted the fact that their home was the site of religious services, and open to crusading ministers such as the Wesleys, especially Charles, and Whitefield when he was in England.

Her titled friends were less indulgent. The haughty Duchess of Buckingham is said to have turned from her proselytizing with, "It is monstrous to be told you have a heart as sinful as the common wretches who crawl the earth!"

Selina found comfort in her new faith from personal sorrow. Two young sons perished of smallpox. Her beloved daughter, Selina, died as a young woman. At age thirty-nine, Lord Huntingdon had a nightmare in which he saw a gruesome figure representing death open his bed curtains one night. Then it crawled in, and laid down between him and his lady. His wife tried in vain to cheer him from the uncharacteristic depression into which he lapsed upon awakening, but he died soon after of apoplexy.

Her eldest son, the new earl, hated Methodism. Selina reduced her personal expenditures in order to finance her charities, including a number of chapels she had founded in England. She also contributed to Princeton University, Indian education, and helped establish Trevecka College in Wales for ministerial training.

This is Bethesda's main gate. From a drawing by Chris Fredeman; courtesy Bethesda Alumni Association.

Both Selina and Whitefield dreamed of a college at Bethesda, chartered after the plan of Princeton. Workmen were sent over from England to erect additions to the original building, and the royal governor of Georgia laid the cornerstone. But a charter for the school was never granted. Whitefield opposed giving control to the Church of England, declaring, "It should be founded on a broad base, or not at all."

Exhausted by years of travel, he died unexpectedly in 1770 at age fifty-six, while on his way to Boston. His will left Bethesda to Lady Huntingdon, with the request that she still pursue plans for the college. She accepted the challenge, and the Georgia Legislature passed a bill enabling her to hold property in Georgia.

More bad news was ahead. Lightning struck the main building in 1773, and left only fire-blackened ruins. The president, William Percy of St. Paul's, Charleston, had badly mismanaged the school's money. At this point Selina sold her jewelry to help rebuild the school, and even sent over her own housekeeper to set things right. Bethesda was rebuilt, but on a smaller scale. Selina still dreamed of her college, and saw Bethesda as the base of a great missionary movement among the planters and the Indians.

She also sent the school a life-size, full-length portrait of herself, done about 1772 by John Russell in the style of Sir Joshua Reynolds. Elegant in its gold leaf frame, it depicts her with one sandal-clad foot on a coronet, showing her lack of interest in wealth.

The portrait, which now hangs at the Georgia Historical Society, is credited with saving Bethesda during the Revolutionary War, when the children were evacuated and British troops ravaged the area. They are said to have spared the school building because they thought the picture indicated allegiance to England. Bethesda was also visited prior to the Siege of Savannah by French troops, who carried off livestock, poultry, and twenty gallons of Jamaica rum.

After the war, Selina sent the Reverend David Phillips from England to try once more to organize the college. But the "Mother of Methodism," exhausted by her good works and the strain of the war years, died in 1791 at age eighty-four. The control of the school passed to trustees, who located it for a time in Savannah, and agreed to have a separate institution for females.

Bethesda was later relocated at its old site, just in time for the fire and hurricane of 1805 which demolished the building and flooded the rice fields with salt water. After again operating in Savannah for a time, the orphanage was reestablished on its Vernon River land in the 1850s, before the orphans were removed inland during the War between the States. The story goes that it was saved from Federal pillage by the name of its governing body, the Union Society.

Originally formed in 1750 as St. George's Club, the group was later renamed to indicate a union of all sects. Three of its original members had been Benjamin Sheftall, a Jew; Richard Milledge, a member of the Church of England; and Peter Tondee, a Catholic and "Bethesda Boy" as well as one of the Sons of Liberty before his death during the Revolutionary War.

The building became a Confederate hospital. When foraging Union troops were sacking coastal plantations, it is said that they found a black caretaker at the gates of Bethesda. When asked who owned the property, he quickly replied, "The Union Society, Captain!"

"Imagine finding loyal sentiment in the heart of the Rebellion!" their surprised leader exclaimed, and ordered the men to march on.

Bethesda was later occupied by freed blacks, in accordance with General W. T. Sherman's directives giving them the sea islands. But after some legal maneuvering, the Society gained control and brought the boys home.

This drawing of the Lady Huntingdon Ampitheatre in Bethesda is by Chris Fredemen; courtesy of Bethesda Alumni Association.

Today, Bethesda Home For Boys is on the National Register of Historic Places. It is still operated by the Union Society, with wide community support, and receives youths who are victims of temporary dislocation as well as orphans. New buildings on its attractive campus attest to the generosity and success of some of its alumni, and its status as a fashionable and respected Savannah charity.

Its handsome, arched gateway is a well-known landmark, with an oak-lined drive to the school buildings and cottages. Whitefield is remembered in the handsome little non-sectarian chapel which bears his name, built on the ruins of a 1755 structure. A stained glass chancel window is dedicated to Habersham. Part of its design shows the burning bush which Moses saw, "consumed by fire, but not destroyed," a symbol of Bethesda's many trials.

It is a place where visitors remark on a certain peaceful timelessness. Recalling its British past, the old English traditions of the Yule log, caroling, and the ceremonial boar's head at Christmas, are still maintained. The name of its chief benefactor is remembered in Savannah with the prestigious Huntingdon Club, said to be the oldest for women in the city, and by Huntingdon Street in the downtown area.

Walking about the campus, one thinks that if Lady Huntingdon could, or did, come back, she would be pleased and surprised with what she sees, although her original dream of a college was not realized. I was unable to find a "Bethesda Boy" who could actually say he had ever seen the self-sacrificing noblewoman. And yet, as the director and former "Boy" William Ford says, "Oh, she's here. At least, that's what they say."

The present and 15th Countess of Huntingdon, author Margaret Lane, has visited Bethesda twice recently, and is fascinated by stories of her husband's famous ancestor. She also has an attractive young daughter, Lady Selina Hastings, who bears a strong resemblance to the other Selina, who died tragically and too young.

When told the tradition of Lady Huntingdon's walk, the Countess exclaimed, "I've never heard that before, but she was a very strong minded woman, and she did love Bethesda. She longed to come here, to see it all for herself."

"If only I'd known that story sooner," she mused with a twinkle in her blue eyes, "I could have dressed in a long gown, and strolled the path in the moonlight. That would have given the tale new credibility for another two hundred years."

The Possessive Presence at the Pink House

James Habersham Jr.'s pink-complexioned, long-jowled portrait still hangs in the foyer of the 1771 building on Abercorn Street which he had remodeled to his specifications before moving in about 1779. "The gentleman of the family," his father once proudly called him, adding in a letter, "he is a youth of strict honor and of uncommon sweetness of temper, perhaps too much so." On another occasion, the parent wrote a friend in London. "James is out of all kinds of business at present, as he is married."

There is no doubt that James the younger was proud of his mansion, which has survived as Savannah's most elegant eighteenth century building. In fact, Herschel McCallar, Jr., co-owner of the Olde Pink House Restaurant and Planters Tavern now in the building, believes that he has never really left it.

James Habersham, Sr. was a leading merchant, planter, and public servant during the Colonial era, when the Reverend George Whitefield appointed him first supervisor of Bethesda Orphanage. Of his ten children, only three sons survived. James, Joseph, and John all opposed him politically during the stormy months preceding the outbreak of the War for Independence. Though he privately disapproved of some of the oppressive acts of Parliament, the elder Habersham was faithful to the Crown.

But James, who like his father had made a fortune in rice and shipping, helped finance the war effort. During his residence at what is now the Pink House, it was the location of secret and desperate meetings of the local Sons of Liberty. These helped lay plans for the raid on the King's powder machine in 1775, and the arrest of the royal governor, Sir James Wright, by Joseph and his men in 1776. Both he and John served in the Continental Army in the war which their father said, "arrays father against son, and son against father." Reconciled in death, all are now buried together in Colonial Cemetery.

227

The Olde Pink House on Reynolds' Square was sketched by Mark Lindsay. Courtesy of Lady Print Shop, © copyright 1974 by Lady Print Shop.

Later the building became the Planter's Bank, the first in the state. In that same year, 1812, the British brig *Expervier*, loaded with $110,000 in gold to finance the English war effort, was attacked by the American vessel *Peacock* and forced to surrender. The gold was paraded through the streets of Savannah in triumph, and deposited in the vault at the bank which is now the wine cellar of the restaurant.

During the Federal occupation of Savannah in 1864, the building was a Yankee general's headquarters. That same year, two of James's great-nephews, the brothers Joseph Clay and William Neyle Habersham, were killed on the same day during the Battle of Atlanta. Their deaths are thought to have been the inspiration for the fictional brave Tarleton twins of Margaret Mitchell's epic *Gone With The Wind*, brothers who met the same fate.

The old building was later an attorney's office, a bookstore, and a tearoom. One Savannahian, sure it was about to be torn down, built an architectural copy of it on Gaston Street. But it somehow survived, and was extensively restored by McCallar and his partner, Jeffrey Keith, in time for its 200th anniversary celebration, by opening as a restaurant and colonial tavern in furnishings of the period.

Over the years, the native brick under the plastered walls has bled through the stucco, changing its color to a soft pink. In the same way, McCallar believes that the traumatic emotions which the building has known in over 200 years, has become as much a part of its atmosphere as the old heart pine flooring and Georgian staircase.

"James is definitely still here as a presence at times," he said, "according to different people who have been in the building when it was very quiet....Especially on Sunday afternoons. This building has been involved with three wars, and a lot of money...those old bank vaults are now our wine cellars. All those things, war, money, and good wine, touch our deepest emotions....I think it's only natural that James checks in occasionally to see what has happened to his old home. I'd like to think that he approves."

Close Encounters of the Spectral Kind on Jones Street

"Friendly ghosts haunt this restored townhouse," reads a Savannah newspaper advertisement from a local realty company for a West Jones Street home. The ad acknowledges the fact that Jones Street, along with St. Julian Street in the downtown historic area further north, seems to have more than its share of supernatural stories. The street is a pleasant, tree-lined area of brick townhouses, many built in the prosperous 1850s "Before the War," and others with the 1870s recovery of the cotton market.

One persistent presence, thought to be feminine, was encountered by an attractive young divorcee from Florida who moved into an 1873 brick house, designed for two families, on West Jones near Tattnall Street. It seemed to be centered around the upper stairs of the front hallway. "From the beginning, I didn't like those stairs," she began her story.

"They were too dark; too narrow. You would go up about four of them, and then one would slant toward you," perhaps describing that early burglar alarm, the irregular trick-step. "The bottom of the stairs and lower hall were all right, but from the landing on, it just felt unfriendly. This had never happened to me in a house before."

"Sometimes when I went up those stairs at night," she went on, "I swear, I would feel something reaching out for me, as though trying to stop me from going up! This only seemed to be for women; my teenage daughter and I noticed it, my son didn't. But she didn't like the house, and didn't even like to ask her friends over."

"Sometimes when I would sit in the TV room on the first floor at night, I had the feeling someone was watching me from the stairs. Then I started waking up at night, around two in the morning, and I would be terrified. I would hear what sounded like a woman's light footsteps, going up the stairs, always at the same time. My daughter heard them, too. If I would sit downstairs late watching TV, sometimes I would hear them on the stairs from there.

230

"Later, I learned that one former resident of the house was so upset by the noises and so forth that he moved out, with his girl friend, right in the middle of the night.

"Once when my mother came to visit me, she woke up to what sounded to her like a heavy chandelier falling inside the house. She got up and searched everywhere, but found nothing out of place.

"Then I heard that in the other half of the double house, up on the third floor, they also had the feeling that something was there," she went on. "In that case, it seemed to be mostly the son and his grandmother who sensed things. Anyway, we left.

"Later, I understand they renovated the place so there is one apartment upstairs and one down and the stairs is kind of blocked off," she continued. "I haven't been back, so I don't know if that has changed the atmosphere or not."

THE NAME ON THE WINDOW

Another young woman who lived in a brick two-story 1852 townhouse at West Jones near Whittaker Street, said that by her count, six couples had rented it in the past eighteen months. She and her husband had moved in as newlyweds in July, and spent six depressing months there. "I went in all enthusiastic about making a new home," she recalled, "but it didn't work out that way. Looking back, I can see that there were certain things I never unpacked to make it pleasant. . . like my mirrors.

"I never saw or heard anything, but it was just a weird feeling, like I didn't want to be in the house by myself. I would leave it about as soon as my husband did in the morning, and people would comment how early I got to work. I just didn't want to be there alone.

"There was a window in the bathroom with a name scratched on it," she recalled. "I always felt particularly uncomfortable in there, and I've never had that type of feeling before." Her older sister corroborated the story.

"I was in the bathroom one day," she added, "as the rest of the family was getting ready to leave. I could hear them all going out the door. I had the silliest impulse to yell after them, 'Hey! Wait! Don't leave me here alone!' But I didn't. As I was hurrying to follow them, I looked at the bathroom window curtain, and saw it just flip out from the bottom, as though someone were behind it. The window itself was closed. There were no pets in the house, no draft, no breeze, nothing to cause this. I was out of there, dressing as I went, I can tell you!"

"All my plants died there, though I've been successful with

231

them other places, and consider myself to have a bit of a 'green thumb'," the woman went on. "It just had an oppressive feeling. If you get in a place like that, the only thing to do is to leave, lease or no lease. I really felt my personality changing there. I wanted to eat out more, instead of going into the kitchen to cook. . . . I'm sure something quite depressing happened there, or a very 'down' person lived there."

There have also been reports of unusual activity in East Jones Street houses a few blocks away. A Confederate soldier is said to be seen from time to time in an 1850 house with dormer windows near Bull Street. One block further on, in an 1852 double brick house, the young son of the family has reported seeing "a little old lady" on the top floor in his room. When contacted, his mother confirmed this, and said she believed the child, but added that her husband did not desire any publicity for the family.

Another young bachelor, Rusty Conner, spoke of the feeling of never being comfortable in a house on East Jones between Bull and Drayton streets: "I found myself talking in whispers all the time. And the house was always cold."

"There are many unusual houses in Savannah," a writer said to me, "but the strangest of all for my money, and the coldest house in town, is located on East Jones Street near Abercorn.

"Oh, it is a nice-looking stucco townhouse, and one of the coldest I've ever lived in! There seemed to be no way to get it warm, or even homelike. One upstairs bedroom, one with a southern exposure, too, was especially chilly.

"The house had been built in the 1850s, and then remodeled in the Victorian style in the 1870s, with a bay window and so forth. This particular upstairs bedroom had the old glass in the windows, from the 1850s.

"We lived there about six months, and then we moved. Later we heard that a young girl had been kept locked up for years in the one upstairs room which we found so depressing. The old windows would be the same ones through which she had looked so often. Maybe she's still there."

Enough Ghosts on Which to Build a Reputation

In the vacation business, ghosts are now "in." The Travel Service of the U.S. Department of Commerce has published a "Traveler's Guide to the Supernatural: Haunted Houses and Legendary Ghosts," with stories of historic homes from that of General P. G. T. Beauregard in New Orleans, to Belle Grove Plantation in Virginia.

"Travel Tips in Georgia: The Classic South," a brochure published by the Georgia Department of Industry and Travel, speaks of "rambling antebellum mansions. Boulevards lined with blossoming trees. The Southern sun flickering on well-kept gardens. . . . " Its cover shows an elegant nineteenth century stairway, with a pretty young girl gliding sedately down to meet a handsome soldier in a jaunty field cap. Both are transparent. . . .

"Beware of a house that will haunt you!" says a Georgia Power Company ad from a Savannah newspaper. It turns out they are talking about energy loss.

Outside of Savannah, as in the downtown historic area, there seems to be enough spectral activity to uphold the regional reputation. Ghosts here tend to be somewhat less famous and dramatic, but more personal.

On once-rural Whitfield Avenue, the sounds of footsteps running as though to catch a train, can still be heard late at night near the spot where a commuter train once crossed the marsh. Later, the area is said to have known bootleg whiskey activity during the era of Prohibition. Whether an accident occurred at the crossing, or if it is simply an echo of the steps of a past commuter who caught the train at that particular spot, has never been determined.

At Hoover Road, on the southside of town, the presence of a young man, "as kind of a grey fog drifting through," has been glimpsed occasionally by the family. Though the residence is new, it is of old brick, and is said to be near a plantation graveyard.

233

"Oh, strange things also happen in newer buildings," Stephen remarked of an Italian restaurant on Skidaway Road, where he says a bottle of rosé was once poured on him by a rather spiteful spirit. "I know people won't believe me unless they were there, but I do have witnesses. One minute I was simply looking at the wine, and the next, it was all over my good slacks! I can't explain it, except that a presence was there who didn't like me."

On Wilmington Island, a resident who says she has had no other psychic experiences, reports a terrible feeling of sadness and loss on Wingate Road, in the comfortable and comparatively new residential subdivision of Wilmington Park. This occurs, she says, whether she is walking, biking, or in a car as she passes it. "All at once, the words are in my mind, 'something old, something old,' and it is very sad."

One Savannah military historian suggests that for years a legend has persisted that a Yankee patrol party from Fort Pulaski was ambushed and buried on the island by Confederate forces after the fort fell in 1862. "Maybe she's found the spot," he commented.

"One night I was driving home quite late alone on a rather desolate stretch of old Louisville Road," said a westside Garden City resident. "All at once there appeared to be a group of people just ahead, walking toward me in the road! There were several, adults and children. It all happened so fast. I screamed, and slammed on the brakes. I was sure I was going to hit them.

"They were, I swear, right in front of me, in the headlights, and then they were gone! I squealed my tires, and slammed to a stop in thin air. . . . No, I hadn't been drinking! There was nothing, neither cars nor people, to be seen in any direction. I was both relieved and frightened, and I still can't explain it."

One Savannah businesswoman said that her husband, an attorney, had always laughed at ghost stories, until they went down to Liberty County to spend a quiet weekend in a small secluded cottage that had been in the family for generations. "There had been stories of the place being haunted," she recalled. "Two sisters were supposed to have burned to death there, then that part of the house had been rebuilt. My husband didn't believe any of it, he said.

"Well, we got there, and I decided to go for a walk. He was going in the house to take a nap. When I got back, I was surprised to see him outside in the road, walking up and down waiting for me! 'I never heard such a racket as in that bedroom,' he said. 'There are two women in there, and they really hate each other! Lying there in the quiet, I could distinctly hear the voices. I just had to leave.'"

Stories have also been told of unusual sounds and sensations at another Liberty County plantation, located on one of the old colonial land grants. There the present rambling and comfortable country home is built on the foundation of a much older structure, which burned. "I believe there may be energy there," the owner said of the house, "but I also believe that the power of suggestion operates in some of the stories about old houses and so forth."

In walking about the home, and a nearby 1850s overseer's house where a resident had left his diary of being there during Sherman's march to the sea, Stephen said that he found the place basically quiet. "There is a layer of energy here, from the many people who have been here in the past," he commented.

"This is not unusual for a house of this period. It will probably continue to be peaceful, unless the energy at some time interacts with the sensitivity and psychic energy of a person who chanced to be here."

> "Savannah is more than a city; it's a state of mind."
> —Arthur Gordon

Shadows on the Brick

There are places in the port city's walls and buildings, on the sun-dried, slave-made brick of past centuries, where one can still see the imprint of even older houses which stood beside them, and are now long gone. Like everything else in the place where, as William Faulkner said, "the past isn't even the past yet," these are not forgotten. Just as Historic Savannah Foundation mourns some of the elegant structures which were demolished before the present successful preservation movement, older citizens recall stories connected with some of the lost buildings.

For instance, those who remember the 1835 Pulaski House, the famed hotel which stood for a century at Johnson Square, say that the presence of a winsome little girl was reported there occasionally. To those who remarked on glimpsing a child in an old-fashioned ruffled dress and high-top shoes in the hotel's long corridors, it was explained that her name was Gracie Watson. Gracie had been the only child of a former hotel manager, W. J. Watson, and had died there of pneumonia just before Easter in 1889, at age five.

An unusually bright and appealing child, she had been a favorite with hotel guests and townspeople. After her death her parents moved on to the new DeSoto Hotel, and eventually left the city. But a life-size sculpture by John Walz on Gracie's little grave at Bonaventure Cemetery still captures the city's heart, as did the eager, round-faced child.

Grimmer tales are also connected with the Pulaski Hotel. According to Savannah author Gerald Chan Seig, moans and cries of unforgettable misery used to be heard occasionally at night, coming from the empty cellar area. It was thought that they dated from the time when desolate Africans were confined there, chained to heavy iron rings imbedded in the walls until they could be taken to the nearby slave markets.

It is also said that clanking chains used to sound eerily at a house

236

on Lincoln Street, just behind the Owens-Thomas House museum. It seems that they could be heard most clearly on the stairs in the middle of the night. In one instance, a family who had just moved in, is said to have left because of the weird noise. Whether they were also from the city's past as a place where slaves were smuggled through the coastal islands and sold long after the slave trade was officially ended has never been determined.

A similar gruesome disturbance which is said to have sent a family packing, was also told of an elegant 1830s townhouse, later a private club and now an apartment building, on Bull and Perry streets at Chippewa Square. It seems that when it was still a one-family rental, the occupants had just moved in when they heard a terrible scream in the empty upstairs. This was followed by a sobbing cry, "Oh, so much blood! So much blood!" After searching the home, nothing could be found to account for the voices. The family is said to have spent the night in a hotel, and moved their furnishings out the next day.

It is also said that a feminine presence used to be in residence at Miss Ellen McAlpin's boarding house, at the northwest corner of Oglethorpe and Barnard streets. Sometimes she is supposed to have been seen lying languidly down in the upstairs bedroom which had been hers; at least once, she and some friends were heard singing in the parlor in an innocent musical evening...except that no one appeared to be there.

Author Lillian Bragg of Savannah told of another feminine wraith, a fragile old lady, who used to be in residence with the grocer Slater family and their seven children at a home near Broughton and Jefferson streets. They said she spent most of her time in a Boston rocker in front of the dormer windows in the attic, or walking about the upstairs. But occasionally, the writer added, she would join the family in the kitchen, where they accepted her as one of them.

Historian Bragg also told of a Savannah family of a generation ago who had a mischievious boy spirit in the house. He delighted in harmless pranks, such as pulling the covers off the beds, hiding one of a pair of shoes, and other childish tricks. He was especially fond of the mother of the family, who good-naturedly accepted his play along with the antics of her own family. Then she became ill, and was rewarded for her patience.

"Every now and then," as Mrs. Bragg told the story, "ripe Florida oranges would appear on the bedside table overnight." Fresh fruit was more of a luxury then, and in many homes, oranges appeared only in the toes of Christmas stockings. Every member of the family disclaimed knowledge of the gift. Finally it was accepted as a childish love offering from their invisible friend.

Several Savannahians clearly recall glimpses and stories of presences which startled them as children. "I remember a house at Bolton and Barnard streets," said one. "It was a double house. I was there once, going up the stairs, and I passed a lady with long, full skirts, who drew them aside to let me pass. When I realized what had happened, and turned to look back, she was gone."

Another told of going to meet a friend at a house at the corner of Liberty and Barnard streets. "I saw a woman in the hallway. I could see her quite clearly through the glass, and wondered why she didn't respond to my knock. She had on a long, dark dress, and her hair was off the back of her neck in a bun on her head. Then my friend came to the door and replied, in answer to my question, 'What woman? There's no one here but me?'"

Sargeant Al Henry of the Savannah Police Department told author Gerald Chan Seig of a two-story frame house with glass in the front door at the corner of Park Avenue and Burroughs Street. There, it was said, if one looked through the glass, a dim face could be seen staring back.

"I only saw it one time," he recalled. "It was not a reflection. I don't know if it were male or female; I was gone!"

Another described a now-vacant house at East Gwinnet and Lincoln streets, where the ghostly image of a face was said to appear in a hall mirror every afternoon as the level rays of the sun touched the glass. "I never stayed there long enough to find out if it were a man or woman," he said, "but there was definitely something there. I wonder who it was?"

My friend Claire recalled an experience at Laura's House, a small and charming early nineteenth century frame house which was once located at State and Houston streets, but is now on East State Street near Columbia Square. "It used to be a tea room," she told me, "and quick, feminine steps could sometimes be heard overhead in the empty upstairs. I was there once, and both the waitress and I heard it, as she served me.

"The girl looked at me and murmured, 'She's really busy today, isn't she?'" The building is now a private residence, the tea room long closed, and no more recent stories have been reported.

One Savannah matron told me that she looked out one day from a rear window in the St. John's Episcopal Church Sunday School, and saw a man sitting in the window of an old house across from her on Whittaker Street.

"He was rather swarthy and foreign-looking," she recalled, "obviously a workman. He had a dirty, white jersey shirt. The next time I looked, he was gone, like that! Then I realized that the window sill where I had seen him sitting, was hanging in the house so loosely that there was no way he could have been sitting there! The whole scene was deserted."

Savannah spirits in what Alfred Lord Tennyson called "beyond the veil" seem to be as varied in personality as its current residents. One man told of a house on Gaston Street where covers were pulled off the bed at night by a jealous former owner, and other feelings of a presence in residence took place while the family was attempting to settle the estate.

In a large house at Gwinnett and Barnard Streets, it is said that charming operatic music may occasionally be heard in the quiet hours of the early morning. Some, but not the owner, say that they have also sensed the presence of the cultivated, music-loving man who built the house and died there of malaria.

In the same home, what one dinner guest, Lulu Waters, described as "a large sun spot, a globe of light," was seen by the guests as it flickered about the walls and then drifted down the hall while a dinner party was in progress.

"The strange thing," said Lulu, "is that that house with such beautiful mysterious music in it, was later a school for deaf children."

At a large building on Drayton Street near Bay, now occupied by attorneys' offices, a Savannah janitor says he has encountered the presence of a former businessman occupant in a quiet office on the top floor.

"There are definitely ghosts in Savannah houses," said one Savannah writer who with his wife has lived in several in the downtown historic area in the past few years. "When we lived in a frame double house in Trustees' Garden, I would awaken about two every morning to the sound of footsteps coming up the stairs.

"One night at that same time, we heard this shattering noise in the house, as though all of our glassware was broken! We both got up and looked around, but we could find absolutely nothing out of place. We couldn't understand it. Finally we decided it had to be on the neighbors' side, though it had certainly sounded much nearer.

"The next morning, when I saw my neighbor, and was just ready to ask him about it, he had the same question for me! They had also heard it, and were sure it came from our house. We never did figure it out.

"Also, when we lived on Taylor Court," he went on, "we could definitely sense a presence there from time to time. All I can tell you is, it was female, and seemed to be mostly in one doorway.

"There is also a frame house, very old, on Houston Street that is quite strange. It is supposed to be built over a well. The story goes that an old sea captain lived there, and hid his life savings in the well in his last days. I understand he still comes back from time to time, to make sure they haven't been disturbed."

A house near 38th and Waters streets is said to be haunted as a result of a fight there between two men, in which one was killed. The murderer then allegedly dismembered the body of his former friend, and hid it in various parts of the city, but was apprehended by the police. The spirit of the wronged man is said to still be in residence, with such manifestations as doors which will first not open, and then fly open of their accord, and other unsettling activity.

In a handsome antebellum Bull Street townhouse which is now the location of a bookstore, there have been stories of volumes found off the shelves and in disarray in the morning by the owners of the house and store. "The first time I ever came in here and turned on the lights, they all started to flicker," commented the proprietor. "I said to myself, 'I'm not going to have any of that foolishness,' because I had heard stories about some of the old houses here. So I looked at the lights, and said 'Stop that!' and they did."

Her attitude was similar to a Bluffton, South Carolina, resident who told me of strange noises in her home, but added that she did not want to be interviewed: "I'm getting along all right with whatever is there now. I don't want to get them 'riled up!'"

But it was a member of one of Savannah's oldest families who had the ultimate put-down when asked if her ancestral plantation home just outside town at Isle of Hope had a ghost. "Certainly we do," she sniffed, "and we have *no* intention of talking about it!"

"Oh, I believe in ghosts," said James Morgan of Ardsley Park. "I believe that some of them are from persons possessed by the Devil. I'm an Episcopalian. When I feel evil forces, I ask my friends to join with me in forming a circle, holding hands. Then we silently pray for the White Light of Christ to protect us, calling on the saints, John of the Cross; Teresa of Avila; Francis of Assisi; David of Wales, and Jesus Christ. David of Wales is my personal saint, which is why I wear this Celtic cross. After we do this, we feel safe. It works every time."

Through the Eyes of Children

"Children and fools speak true," the English dramatist John Lyly wrote in the sixteenth century. In talking with people about psychic experiences, a number always involved the perceptions of children. As to why these are not repeated as the child grows older, a hint may be found in a column published in the *Savannah News-Press* on August 30, 1964.

When ten citizens were asked if they believed in ghosts, the majority said that they did not. "I was taught not to, when I was young," said Irving Rubnitz.

"No, I believed in ghosts as a little girl," replied Faye Page, "but my parents soon changed that!"

"Unless the parent has some idea of why the child is talking of 'imaginary playmates' and things which they can see but the adult cannot, they may be ridiculed, or punished for lying," Stephen commented. "In time, told that such things do not exist, they lose whatever abilities they possess."

An example of the sensitive child was Kevin, a bright little boy who moved into a 1900 brick duplex in the area of York and President streets a few years ago with his mother, Eleanor. From the beginning, she recalled, it seemed that Kevin could see something in the house which she could not.

"It was not a frightening presence," she went on. "It seemed to be mostly on the landing of the stairs, and upstairs. He would say, 'Can't you see the witch?' which I took to mean a woman dressed in black. He would be so frustrated that he could point, but I still couldn't see anything!

"He would also refer to going upstairs to play with her. I never saw anything, but I did realize it was a strange house. Every time I would go out, I would come home to find all the toilet paper off the roller! This of course was with the house locked, and Kevin with me. Once I even found my hair brush on top, as though to call attention to the mess.

"After awhile I just gave up, and left the paper all piled in the wastebasket. Then my refrigerator door started coming open at night! I tried putting a chair against it, but when I'd wake in the morning, it would still be open. The house did have kind of a slant to it, but why only at night? Finally, we moved. I understand the people who came in after us, also had strange experiences there."

"That sounds like a possessive presence hanging on to its house," replied Stephen. "It doesn't sound destructive enough to be a poltergeist. I do believe that emotions leave their imprints on the atmosphere, and the spaces we occupy."

"Kevin used to be able to predict things," his mother went on, "but he lost this ability, or didn't speak of it, as he became older. He had an 'imaginary' dog named Herman, and he would say Herman told him this or that was going to happen. It did!"

Three months after moving from the York Street address, Kevin developed leukemia. Through his long illness he was a patient, cheerful little boy, his mother added. "He was greatly interested in oceanography, and especially whales, and efforts to study and save them."

"Sounds like an 'old soul,'" said Stephen. "Maybe even a former whaler."

"After he was gone," his mother stated, "we had a good friend who grieved so, and didn't seem to be able to accept it even as well as the family. One night he was sitting in his chair at his home, and he said suddenly it was as though everything material had fallen away, and he was all alone, kind of in space. He couldn't see anything, but he could hear Kevin's voice so clearly, 'Uncle, don't grieve for me. I'm all right.'

"Our friend's wife saw him sitting there staring, as in a trance, with cold sweat on his brow. She thought he was having a heart attack. Finally he was able to speak to her, and try to tell her what he had experienced. Since then, he has been much more at peace.

"Kevin's step-father says he often feels a loving, guiding presence, though he can't see anything," she told us. "His sister, who is five now, sleeps in the same bed he once had. She tells me that Kevin sometimes comes into her room at night, sits on her bed, and talks with her. Then there was the time we were out for a drive, and had to stop for a funeral procession.

"'You know,' she later said to me, 'when that big car that took Kevin to Heaven [the hearse, of course] passed us, there he was in the back. He leaned out and waved at me. He was in there helping someone else go to Heaven.'"

A VISITING ANGEL

"That reminds me of some friends of mine in North Carolina who had two children, four and ten," said Stephen. "The oldest, a bright, otherwise pretty little girl, had a disfiguring malignancy on her face, a terrible thing for a child to have to endure. She was very brave. One night she said to her mother, in a matter-of-fact way, 'I'm going to die next week,' and she named the day.

"She went on to explain that an angel had come into her room the night before, and told her that she was one who worked with children about to die. The girl went on to tell her mother things about her condition that she couldn't possibly have known from the parents. And she did die just one week later as she had said...on Christmas Eve."

A VISION OF THE VIRGIN MARY

One Savannah man told me that he had decided to study for the priesthood, though he had later given it up for family reasons, as a result of seeing the image of the Virgin Mary when he was about five.

"It was in our home in Scranton, Pennsylvania," he recalled. "One day I looked up, and there it was, very clearly, on a window in our house. I'd say it lasted about five minutes....Oh, I definitely saw her. She was very beautiful. She didn't speak; she was just there."

"Did you tell your parents?"

"I told my mother. She believed me, like a good Catholic, and very gently replied that she hoped it would be an inspiration in my life. It has."

"AN EASTER BASKET WITH WINGS"

Not all of the psychic experiences recalled from childhood are happy ones. A Victory Drive resident who lives in a handsome corner brick home there told me that his daughter had found one front corner upstairs bedroom unpleasant, from the time they moved there when she was four years old. "Julie never wanted to sleep in that room," he said. "She was terrified in there, which was not like her at all. One evening she came screaming out, telling us that 'an Easter basket with wings,' had flown out of the fireplace at her, around the room, and behind the heater.

"We went up and searched, but we never could find anything

unusual there. Later, though, other things happened to people who came to visit, but only in that room. A mature young teenage cousin, a boy, wet the bed when he stayed there. He was so embarrassed! Another, a 12-year-old girl, got sick in the night and vomited in the bed. A young adult cousin in her early twenties spent the night there with her little boy, and became deathly ill in the middle of the night. She woke up and said she felt as though she were choking to death. Our dog died.

"These were all healthy when they came, remember, so far as we know. But the rest of the house seems very comfortable, and we've been happy here."

Walking about the pleasantly furnished bedroom, Stephen said that he felt "one damp, cold spot," and the impression of a woman who had felt neglected and unhappy, and spent a great deal of time in that one area, perhaps in a favorite chair.

Our host then confirmed that he had heard that the former owners of the house had marital troubles and separate bedrooms; that room had been the wife's. It was said that she spent a great deal of time alone there, while her husband was with his mistress across the river in South Carolina.

"OH, HIS FACE! HIS FACE!"

The same child, who was undoubtedly psychic, had another interesting experience in the neighborhood which they had never been able to explain, her father continued. "She was six at the time, and had been having a wonderful time at a children's birthday party in the back yard. Unwilling to end the day, she and her sister and a few cousins were romping around the yard at twilight playing an old game called 'Ain't no boys out tonight,' around the shrubbery between our yard and a neighbor's."

Hearing the fun, he went on, a young man who was home on leave jokingly stuck his head over the fence from next door as though he wanted to join the game. "My daughter took one look at him, screamed, whirled, and started for the house, as hard as she could go! All she could gasp out was, 'His face...his face was so terrible!' and then she would cry.

"Well, the young man worried about it, and came over to see what was wrong. The strange part was that they knew him, and he had often joined in their games in just that way when he was home from the service. Well, we put her to bed, and the others went home. She cried herself to sleep.

"The next week, that fine young man was killed in an aviation training accident. I have always felt that our daughter had some forboding of this, and his fatal head injuries, when she looked at his face for the last time.''

"Sometimes They Want to Help You"

In contrast with persons who have only had one or two psychic encounters in their lives, there are others who quietly accept their sensitivity as part of a way of life. One of these is Lu Waters, a civil service worker who lives in the Kensington area in Savannah.

"Some children are very gifted psychically," she commented as we talked at her home. "This has always been something of which I was aware. My grandmother read tea leaves; my mother had a crysal ball. When I lived at what had been my family home in Bloomingdale, in west Chatham County, I knew there were spirits there. One day when my little grandson told me that he'd just felt someone put 'a cold hand' in his, I knew he had it, too.

"This is not something which frightens me," she went on. "It is something which I try to understand. I know that each of us has a spirit, and that it is more than the body; it is eternal. I was in the hospital with a relative who was very close to me when he passed away. His spirit, like a bluish-white vapor, hovered there over his body for a minute, and then rose toward the ceiling, and disappeared.

"I also believe that the spirits of our loved ones sometimes come back when they are needed," she went on. "For instance, one night about two a.m. in the house in Bloomingdale, my husband was quite ill. I hurried downstairs to get his medicine. As I went toward the stairs, it was suddenly like there was a dense blue fog around my feet. But I was so sleepy and anxious, I didn't pay any attention. Consequently, I misjudged my distance from the stairs, and fell down twenty-two of them.

"Someone was trying to slow me down, but I didn't heed the warning."

She added that she had also experienced warning dreams, such as one of a terrible storm and flood, "a dark night, and rushing water," a few nights before the recent flood and dam break at Toccoa, in north Georgia, where several people were killed. "I told

246

my dream the next day to the friends in my car pool," she went on, "and how depressed I was, but I didn't know the location. Later, when I heard the news, I again felt that someone was trying to tell me something, but I had not been able to understand it in time."

As a member of the Theosophical Society, Lu believes in reincarnation. "I feel that I have lived many times before; I'm what you'd call an 'old soul.' I believe one recent life was in the near East. I feel very drawn to spicy foods, olives, dates, and so forth from that area. I believe we are put here to learn, to work out what we missed another time. But the next time, I don't care if I come back or not! I'm getting tired."

"LIKE AN INSTANT REPLAY"

Another member of the Savannah area Theosophical Society, Rusty Conner, a young bachelor, also believes in reincarnation. He not only feels that he has known the "lost" continent of Atlantis, and ancient Egypt, but "a life having to do with snow, wolves, and a sled; I keep getting these very realistic flashbacks about a cold place.

"It's like an instant replay," he went on. "It all seems so familiar. I get these mental pictures of an area, and I know how it was. It's been like this all my life.

"Sometimes I find myself asking 'Why me?' when I get an impression I'd rather not have. But there it is. For instance, I once had a sudden, intense pain in my left hand. Then I learned that a cousin had been badly hurt in an accident, in the same place on his hand. Another time I had chest pains, and my mother was having heart trouble in Statesboro.

"She still denies the psychic realm, even though she once saw my grandfather after his death."

Rusty added that his psychic feelings had made him uncomfortable in some of the places where he had lived. "There was a place in Metter," he recalled, "where the lampshades would tilt at an angle for no reason, and I would hear footsteps at night in a supposedly empty hall. I later found out that a young boy had killed himself there.

"I also lived in a new house at Hilton Head, where I could hear footsteps and doors opening and closing at odd times during the night. I found out it was built on the site of an old plantation house that had been occupied by Yankees during the Civil War. I'm sure the sounds were from that period.

"One night on a dare, some of us went out one Halloween to a cemetery on Hilton Head. We were going to take pictures of each other there at midnight, to prove we'd been there. But we came to a place where neither our cameras or flashlights would work, and we got out of there!"

Stephen and I were talking with Rusty in a contemporary development ranch house style home on the southside of Savannah. He had not been in it long, and it seemed like an unlikely haunt, no pun intended, for a presence. Suddenly he motioned to Stephen. "I wish you'd come sit here in my chair for awhile and tell me what you think."

Stephen got up from the sofa where he had been, and took the large armchair across the room which had just been vacated. The conversation resumed. After a few minutes, Rusty turned back to Stephen. "Well?" he asked.

"My arm hurts. It feels kind of numb and prickly, partly paralyzed . . . the right one. I feel like it would be hard for me to get up now . . . kind of depressed, and . . . old."

"That's exactly the way I feel when I sit there," Rusty told him. "What do you make of it?"

"I get the impression of a woman," Stephen replied. "No form that I can see, just feminine. I'd say older, someone who sat in this spot a lot, looking across the room at the TV. I'd say she had a stroke here . . . and is probably dead by now."

"That was my impression," Rusty agreed almost cheerfully, with obvious relief at having his instincts confirmed. "When I first moved here, I got several pieces of mail at this address that seemed to be for an older person, Medicare stuff and so forth. So whoever lived here, left without a change of address."

As the evening went on, Rusty and Stephen agreed on another point. "I want nothing to do with Ouija boards," our host stated. "I had a bad experience with one in Statesboro, when some friends insisted I try it. I didn't want to. It seemed I was soon in contact with a very nasty German, a Nazi colonel who talked about abusing and killing a Jewish boy during World War II. Had I been either one of these people? I can't tell you how I came to get the particular message, but it was very frightening. I believe there are some unpleasant spirit entities about, as well as some good ones.

"I don't want to encourage the connection. But I've been aware all my life, that these things exist."

A Few More Selected
Savannah Ghosts

"I will never forget the first time I saw Savannah," Claire said as Stephen and I sat comfortably in her living room before the fire, and she served us some of her homemade ginger cookies and hot tea. "I came down on the passenger ship from New England which ran in the 1930s, before the war. We entered the harbor just at dawn, and I saw it all on the bluff above me, a sleepy, picturesque, little Southern city. I think I knew then that I would finally live here.

"It really hasn't changed that much, in some ways," she went on. "It has a certain timeless quality."

"That may be why it has so many ghost stories," I commented, and invited her to tell some of the ones she had formerly used in a magazine article. The first concerned a nineteenth century brick warehouse once used in the cotton business, and later a bar and restaurant in the west side of downtown Savannah.

"Legend has it," Claire began, "that a Mr. Pringle, who died in the mid-1800s, was the black sheep of a prominent family and worked as a clerk there. He was also fond, as the Irish say, 'of the drink.'

"When it later opened as a bar, they tell me that they used to place all the stools on the counter at night for the sweeping up, and so forth. But in the morning, a single stool could be found turned over on the floor, and an empty glass tipped over at the bar! They suspected that old Pringle was still at it. How happy he must have been to find alcohol so close his old office!

"Then there's another bar story, this one on West Congress Street. It seems that the luminous figure of a slight young girl has been seen, going along there, swinging her purse.

"They say she is dressed in the style of the eighteenth century, and is locally known by those who have seen her in the area late at night as Susie Sheets, a member of the oldest profession.

"It is said that Susie usually turns in at one of the bars on the street, in a very old brick building. It was once the site of a house that seamen headed for when they came off their ships, and needed relaxation after their journeys to far places. It is also thought that poor Susie met her death there, strangled by a jealous lover."

We then discussed the plight of a Savannah woman shopkeeper whom we all knew, who had unfortunately moved into what had been an alleged house of ill repute on Williamson Street, near the waterfront. She awoke one night to the presence of a tall, thin, dark-haired man in her room, about to get into bed with her. 'Old habits are hard to break," someone quipped of the story.

However, it was the living seamen who remembered the address, and not the deceased ones, who were the problem. The woman became so annoyed at the knocking at her door at all hours, mostly from very real people, that she later took an apartment in Trustees' Garden.

Incidentally, I added, the same woman had told me that she had a presence in the van which she used to pick up antiques for her shop. She believed it was a helpful male one, and had come with her from Michigan, where she had lived in a new house near a very old one, in an isolated wooden area. She had brought many of the furnishings from that house to Savannah.

We had later made an appointment to discuss the matter further. However, I had found when I arrived at her shop on a Sunday afternoon at closing time, that she had changed her mind. "I feel that it is definitely there, maybe even more than one," she told me. "It is a helpful presence now, and real company to me when I'm out alone. I'm about to take a long drive in that van, to Texas, and I don't want to do anything to upset it . . . or them."

"Not all ghosts are in old houses," Claire told us. "One that I've heard about is on Victory Drive, a concrete block one from quite recent times. It was the home of a little old lady, who loved it, and died there. The next owner found that she was not alone.

"At night, she would be awakened by a knocking at her door, with no one there when she opened it. Still later, she would hear someone rocking in the next room. But there was no rocking chair in there! After a period of time, the second owner sold the house. It was all too much for her."

Claire added that there is another house on Victory Drive which has a charming and very sociable lady ghost. "She has been seen gliding down the steps in an old-fashioned gown. Several years ago, a startled news photographer caught her wavery image in a photo he took for the Savannah paper! What had happened was, he was sent out to get a picture of a host couple on the stairs, at a large social event.

"When it was printed, he was surprised to see a third party between the first two. He swore it was not a double exposure. So it's nice to know the lady is still attending parties."

I thought of a story which I had recently been told by another Savannah shopkeeper in Trustees' Garden about her family home in Columbus, Georgia. It had been planned by her father, a World War I veteran and architect. "On the night Daddy died," she told me, "I was alone in the house. Mother was with Daddy at the hospital. He wasn't supposed to be very sick, but a blood clot developed in his leg from the old war injury—of course, I didn't know that at the time.

"But I was walking through the hall, when I suddenly sensed someone walk by me. I could see no one, but I knew it was Daddy, and that he was gone.

"Later, the next owner of the house told a news reporter investigating such things that every night about ten o'clock, they could hear these unusual footsteps coming down the front hall toward the door, and then back about half way down the hall again, then toward the stairs.

"From the description, I knew they were Daddy's. He walked with a limp, from the game leg. Every night of his life, just before he went to bed, he would open the front door to check on the weather, and then go down the hall to adjust the thermostat, before going upstairs. Daddy really loved that house, because he had built it. I'm not surprised some reminder of his presence is still there."

"After my article on the ghosts of Savannah came out," commented Claire, "a middle-aged black woman contacted me with quite a touching story. Years ago, she said, she had a little sister who was standing in front of an open fireplace. Her dress caught fire, and she was burned so badly that she died. Afterward, the woman said that her mother would swear that she would sometimes look up, and see her little girl standing by the fire wearing the dress in which she had been buried, a pretty, ruffled white one.

"'At the time, we thought poor Mother was seeing things, and feared for her sanity,' the woman told me. 'What do you think?'

"'I think your mother was very likely reporting what she really saw,' I answered her. She thanked me, and seemed pleased to have her mother vindicated after all these years!"

Long-Distance Farewells:
Premonitions of Death

Of the many vivid incidents told me by average people in the past few years, it seemed the largest number and most touching involved sensing the death of a loved one before actual notice was received. In some cases, these took the form of unusual dreams; in others, voices or a glimpsed presence. One woman, shortly after the death of her mother, told of being enveloped for a minute in "a kind of glowing sense of total acceptance, peace, warmth, and love."

One of the most unusual was told to me by a middle-aged Savannah matron, widow of a prominent businessman, one morning under the hair dryers of our favorite Wilmington Island beauty shop. The owner had mentioned my research to her other customer, who told me she had a story which might interest me. It was an incident which had occurred to her as a child in Dublin, Georgia.

She had been the youngest of four girls, she said, with a father who was a strict Baptist minister. The oldest daughter, twenty-two, had rebeled against his stern discipline and gone to Savannah to work. This had displeased the parents, who were hoping she would come home.

"Mother was going to town," the woman recalled, "and I wanted to go, but she said I was too much trouble, and whined for everything in the stores. So I was left at home with the maid. Toward evening, feeling very bored, I was standing by the kitchen door, waiting for Mother to come home. I remember it was a Saturday evening, and the sun was just setting through the trees. There was kind of a golden glow over everything, that hazy look you get at sunset.

"The maid was standing by me at the work table, cutting up chickens for our Sunday dinner.

"Suddenly, kind of out of the sunset, I saw what looked like a long oblong box just come sailing up through the yard, up in the air a few feet above the ground. My older sister seemed to be lying in it.

"Well, just as it got by the door, she sat up, looked so sadly and reproachfully in my direction, at the house, lifted something to her lips, and laid down in the box. It kind of sailed on out under the trees, and vanished.

"I started to scream, and then the maid screamed at me, and Mother came home while all that was going on! She gave me a new box of crayons, and comforted me, told me it had to be my imagination. But there was no way I could forget what I had seen," the woman continued in obvious pain at the memory.

"Well, later that evening one of the neighbors came with bad news from Savannah. My sister had a fellow there, and she had taken his ring, then changed her mind. She gave it back, and told him she was coming home to Dublin. Then she came in and said to the landlady, 'I don't think life is worth living.' The landlady just tried to cheer her up, and told her she ought to go home for a weekend.

"Instead, she went to the drugstore and got some poison. She had to sign for it, but she told the pharmacist that she wanted to take some pimples off her back. Then she went back to the boarding house, and drank it in the bathroom, just at the time I saw her. She died before anyone could save her."

A BROKEN CHAIN

A native Savannahian, who was close to both his parents, told me that for him the death of each of them was marked by an unusual event. When his father died, he had been in New Orleans, and the father in Pennsylvania. "I had a dream one night," he recalled, "in which I was back home in Scranton, Pennsylvania. I was running down the stairs, and my father was at the bottom, in the hall. As I went by, he lightly put his hand on my arm and said, 'Oh, wait, Jackie, I want to tell you something.'

"It was so real, I woke up and looked at the clock. Then I tried to go back to sleep, but could not. I got up and made some hot tea, and I was still awake when the telephone rang. It was my family. Dad had died very unexpectedly of a heart attack, just at the time I woke up from my dream.

"When Mother died here in Savannah a few years ago, I was in the shower, getting ready to go to the nursing home to see her," he continued. "Suddenly, the religious medal which she had given me, fell to the shower floor. The chain had broken, though it was quite new. I was on my hands and knees, all soapy and helpless without my glasses, fumbling around for it when the telephone rang. It was my sister, telling me Mother had just died."

"I'M CHOKING TO DEATH!"

One member of a well-known Savannah family told me that she had a strange premonition of her brother's death during World War II, although it occurred half a world away. He had just been home to Savannah on leave, she recalled. "Somehow I felt uneasy about his health, although he looked as well as ever. He was on his way to service in the Pacific.

"One night, a few weeks later," she continued, "I woke up with this terrible sensation of, 'Oh, my God, I can't breathe, I'm choking to death!' I woke my husband, thrashing around. He tried to comfort me, but I felt that something dreadful had happened. The next day I felt emotionally dragged-out, very low, for some reason.

"Then we had word that my brother had been playing baseball one very hot afternoon on this little Pacific island where he was stationed. All at once he went into a seizure, couldn't get his breath, and died. No one knew he was a diabetic. Allowing for the time difference, I had somehow picked up on what must have been his last thoughts, at the time of his death."

THE NEW BLUE DRESS

A Savannah journalist told me that her husband was taking an afternoon nap in one room and their infant daughter in the next, on a quiet Sunday. When the telephone rang, the husband stopped to close the baby's door so she would not be awakened, on his way to answer the call. He was surprised to see his mother standing there at the crib, wearing a long blue robe he had never seen before, lovingly gazing at the baby.

Then he answered the telephone, and received the message that his mother had just died after a long illness. Shaken, he opened the nursery door, but there was no sign of a presence. He told his wife the story, remarking again about the unusually pretty long blue gown. It was different from anything he had ever seen his mother wear, he added.

He realized its significance the next day at the funeral home, as his sister showed him the dress in which she wanted her mother to be buried. It was soft and blue, in their mother's favorite color—the one he had already seen in the nursery.

THE MOTIONLESS SHIP

Conrad Aiken, the Pulitzer Prize-winning poet, was born at

Magnolia Hall on Whitaker Street in Savannah, and later moved as a child to a Marshall Row townhouse on Oglethorpe Avenue overlooking Colonial Cemetery. It was in that house that his physician father shot his mother and committed suicide, and the boy was sent to New England at age eleven. He and his wife, the artist Mary Hoover Aiken, returned to Savannah, which he called "the most magical of cities," for his last years at Marshall Row next door to his old home, from 1962 until his death in 1973.

In *The Selected Letters of Conrad Aiken*, edited by Professor Joseph J. Killorin of Armstrong State College, with the assistance of Mrs. Aiken, the poet wrote of an unusual dream which occurred the night his close friend author T. S. Eliot died in 1965:

"I think I can tell you," he confided to Valerie Eliot, the late poet's wife, "something extraordinary that happened to me on the day that Tom died. I don't know whether you believe in ESP and all that, and I don't know whether I do, but anyway I had that morning a very odd nightmare, in which I was on a ship at sea, and feeling ill. But as the ship was entirely motionless—I rationalized in the dream—it can't be seasickness, it must be something else.

". . . Allowing for the time difference, it puts my dream very close to the time when Tom actually died, and I can't help feeling that somehow I knew what was happening. . . it's very strange."

"I SAW HIS PICTURE IN THE PAPER"

"I definitely believe in ESP and premonition, because it happened to me," an attractive Savannah matron intrigued me by saying one day as someone mentioned my interest in the subject. "I was a child, and it concerned my older brother, here in Savannah, whom I adored.

"I dreamed that it was an early Sunday morning, and I had gone out to get the newspaper off the porch. When I opened it up, there was his picture, the class one he had just had taken. It was very clear on the page, but I couldn't read the headlines. It seemed a little strange, but I dream a lot, so I didn't think much of it.

"Six months after that, my brother was killed in a boating accident. It was a Saturday. The next morning, when I walked out to get the paper, and opened it to see what it said about him, it all came back to me. His picture, the placement on the page, was just as I remembered it. . . . I still couldn't read the headlines, because I was crying.

"After that," she went on, "I would see him sometimes here in the house, when we were alone. I got so I liked to be left when everyone else went out, so I could be with him. But my mother thought it was unhealthy for me to be alone that much, so I couldn't do it very often. After awhile, I didn't see him any more."

"A GIFT FROM GOD"

"Those fortunate enough to sense or see a loved one for the last time should cherish the experience," Lorraine Warren said when we discussed the phenomenon. "It is a gift from God, to say that they have survived in spirit."

A Wilmington Island woman told me of such an experience with a friend with whom she had been in nurses' training in Texas. Later, the friend, Bobbye, had married, had a family, and enjoyed vacations with her husband in their small private plane.

"One night in Savannah, a Friday, I was brushing my teeth when Bobbye was just 'there,'" the woman recalled. "I could see her so clearly in my mind's eye! I thought of her almost continuously that weekend, and told my husband I was going to call her in Texas. But just then I got a call from Bobbye's son-in-law, with the news I somehow already knew. Bobbye and her husband had been killed in the family plane during a skiing trip to Colorado.

"It was a trip some of the family members had begged them not to take, because of the possibility of bad weather, but they had gone anyway. They had bounced on the ice, and the plane had exploded. Bobbye was thrown clear; the only one of the four aboard whose body survived intact.

"After a period of mourning, my thoughts of Bobbye gradually faded. Then one day I saw her so clearly in my mind's eye," the woman continued. "She was wearing a beige pants suit I had never seen before, yet instinctively I knew it was what she had worn that last day. She was turned to one side, looking at me. The message I got so clearly was, 'It's all right. . . . Be well, be happy, and keep up to date.'

"Well, I understood the first part, but the 'keep up to date' part puzzled me. After all, I hardly considered myself 'pokey!' But I felt better about the rest of it.

"Just a few months ago," she ended the story, "I decided to take the brush-up course for nurses, and get back to part-time work. The first day at Memorial Medical Center, it all came back to me, training days, Bobbye. . .and then I had to smile. In going back to my work, perhaps I was doing what she had wanted when she said, 'Keep up to date!'"

THE FLASH OF LIGHTNING

As we discussed premonition, the woman telling the story said that there had been one other case in her family, involving her grandfather in Texas. His brother, then in his early twenties had gone to Oklahoma when the narrator's grandfather was only a teenager. They had never corresponded, though the boy in Texas of course did not forget the brother, and often wondered what had happened to him. The Texan married. One night when he was about forty, he woke his wife with a terrible nightmare. She asked him what was the matter, but he declined to discuss the dream, and went back to sleep. The same thing happened again.

"The third time," said the woman, "Grandmother insisted that he tell her what the dream was all about! He said he had just seen his brother out in a field, plowing, when he was killed by a bolt of lightning. After telling his dream, he was able to sleep, hoping it was only a nightmare.

"The next morning, a woman who introduced herself over the telephone as his sister-in-law, called from Oklahoma. She told him his brother had been in the field, hurrying to finish the chores before the rain came. He was killed, just as the dream had told him, by a sudden bolt of lightning attracted to the metal plow. Grandfather told her he wanted to come to the funeral.

"Then he went to his desk, and wrote something on a piece of paper, which he folded and put in his pocket before he went to the train station. Later, when he showed it to his brother's widow, she nearly fainted. He had described from his dreams exactly what his brother was wearing on the day he died. Yet, until he talked to the sister-in-law on the telephone, he had not even known that the man was a farmer."

A PUNCTUAL PHONE CALL

"We all feel an anxiety about death, and it helps if we have an experience which reassures us," the young chaplain of a Savannah hospital told me. "I think it is very important, when people have such experiences to report, that we allow them to share, that we pay attention. . . . It damages the validity of the experience for them, if they cannot comfortably do this."

In his work with the terminally ill and their families, he hears many such stories. And he listens with special compassion, because one such loving last communication happened to him.

"It involved a young man I was counseling," he recalled. "He was only nineteen, wealthy family, his life before him...and he was dying. I went with him through all the emotional stages, denial, anger, acceptance...and in the process, I became much closer to him than I normally do in my work, than perhaps I should for my own sake....But he was a very special person to us all.

"He spent his last days, when nothing more could be done, at his family's home west of here. It was in another time zone, so when he called at eleven, after the rates went down, it would be midnight our time. He called me every Wednesday night; he knew I worked late on that night. Then he died, and I attended his funeral with his family.

"As his mother and I walked slowly back up the long driveway of their home after the funeral, a strange thing happened. The sun had been shining, but a sudden cloud went over, and the sky became very dark. Then, in the garage, we heard the sound of his sports car racing...the Ferrari which he loved. No one else was near the garage, and the door was closed. Yet we heard that motor! I took his mother's hand, and knew he was somehow trying to say 'goodbye.'

"For the next two weeks in Savannah, on Wednesday, just at midnight, the telephone would ring! When I would pick it up, there would be no one there. Of course, I went through the process of crying, 'Who is this,' and so forth into the receiver, thinking of a wrong number or some other hopefully normal explanation.

"The third week, I was ready. When it rang, I picked it up and said softly, 'What is it you want to tell me?' There was no answer, and it never rang again. But I believe he just wanted me to know that he had survived, as we had both hoped that he would."

A CONVERSATION WITH THE DEAD

Although rarer than dreams, incidents of conversing with departed loved ones by telephone have been reported. One case of which I recently heard involved a middle-aged Savannah woman, a devout Southern Baptist with no previous history of, or interest in, supernatural experience, and her daughter, a bright, attractive young woman who was dying of cancer in a Savannah hospital. On the day the call occurred, the young woman had been in a coma for several days, and her death was expected momentarily.

The mother had called the hospital room, not to speak with the daughter, but with another member of the family, as they rotated a death watch at the bedside. She was astonished when the daughter answered, in a rather weak but pleasant voice. "Oh, I didn't expect you to answer!" the astonished older woman said happily. "How are you?"

"Oh, I'm fine," said the daughter. "I wanted to tell you that I'm all right...I feel better than I have for a long time." After a moment or two of more personal messages, she added, "Well, I've got to go now."

A few minutes later, while the mother was still overcome with emotions of mingled surprise and pleasure, another call came. Her daughter, as she was told, had died only moments before the woman had called the hospital. The reason no other member of the family was in the hospital room to receive the first call, was that they had left the room for a few minutes while the girl's body was being removed, and then come back to place the call to the home.

"It would have been so like her to want to reassure me one last time," said the mother, "and I feel that she did."

A similar message, but in a different manner, was received by a Beaufort, South Carolina librarian. "I had gone to sleep thinking about my son's teacher, who was dying of cancer," she recalled. "Suddenly, in a dream, I saw her. She looked so healthy, so radiant. She assured me that she was fine, that everything was all right. She smiled as she told me she was finally without pain. I wakened up and looked at the clock. Then I went back to sleep.

"The next morning, I woke up to the telephone ringing. It was from a friend at the school to tell me that this woman had gone...had died just about the time I saw her looking so well and rested."

"HE NEVER CAME UP!"

Sometimes only part of a message of premonition in a dream is received, and recalled later by an unusual scene or phrase. This happened to an Isle of Hope matron, who told Stephen and I of a dream she had experienced about a neighbor.

"I dreamed I was walking along the road near the river here, and he came by and offered me a ride," she began. "Just then, the car went out of control and into the water! I got out, but there was no sign of him. Then I saw another neighbor of ours standing there, and asked about our friend.

"He never came up," he replied, tears running down his face. 'He drowned...drowned...' at that point, I woke up.

"I almost forgot the dream," she continued, "but not long after that, my neighbor had a heart attack, and was in the hospital. He had a relapse, and something went wrong in the recovery room. I got the news from the friend I had seen in my dream. His words were in the same choked voice I had heard, 'He never came up...he drowned...drowned in his own fluids.'"

"SHE'S PROBABLY DEAD BY NOW"

Such premonitions do not always involve close friends or family. A Savannah woman told me of one concerning a kindly older woman she had seen only twice, one at an art show and once at her home in Gordonston. Both were pleasant events, but the two were not in contact afterwards. Six years passed.

"One night," said the narrator, "I woke up and found myself thinking so strongly of this woman. I was wondering how she was. Then I said to myself, 'I haven't heard for so long, she's probably dead by now,' and I went back to sleep.

"The next day, a mutual friend called me to say this lady had just died in her sleep...and at approximately the time I must have been thinking of her."

Flowers from the Dead

In one of the more ironic rites of our society, one often takes flowers to the dead. What is more rare is the opposite, which happened recently in Savannah to a middle-aged widow who lives in an apartment complex on the south side of town. This woman is an extremely practical sort, with no experiences in the supernatural except her own Catholic faith in life after death. She told me that she had gone to mass early one morning, distraught over the illness of a friend and feeling depressed about her own health.

When she emerged from the church a kindly-looking woman was waiting with a small but attractive bunch of hand-picked flowers.

"You don't know me," she said as she held the bouquet out, "but my little granddaughter wanted you to have these." What made the story she proceeded to tell unusual, was the fact that the child had then been dead for several weeks. As she talked, the woman receiving the flowers recalled the story, which had been in the paper, of a little girl, three years old, who had died in a freak choking accident.

"She loved flowers so much," the grandmother explained. "She liked to work with me in the yard, and help me take flowers to different people we knew. Well, she's still doing it—please don't think I'm crazy! Sometimes she comes and begs me to pick flowers for a certain person. Then she stays right with me until I do it! Today, she told me where to find you. At first this used to make me feel foolish, but the people are so happy, and they always say it was just right for them at that time."

"It was for me," said my friend, who went home smiling for the first time that day. Later she had the good news that her friend was expected to recover, and felt her spirits lifted by the strange encounter.

In a less dramatic fashion, several people have told me of sensing the presence of a loved one at least once after their death.

One mother spoke of losing a seven-year-old daughter. "The first vacation we were going to take after that," she told me, "I was packing in my room, with very mixed emotions about the trip.

"Suddenly the presence of both my daughter and my late mother were with me in the room, and stayed about half an hour. . . . I was very comforted; it was as though they were telling me it was all right, and they were together."

In separate interviews in different counties, two young women told almost identical stories about sensing the presence of a grandmother after death. "She used to come to me when I was just getting ready to go bed, about once a month," said one twenty-three-year-old girl. "Sometimes she was hazy, sometimes it was just her voice. But I knew she was there."

A young teacher told me that the presence of her grandmother had appeared to her very strongly one night just as she was drifting off to sleep. "She was a very strong-minded woman. . . . It was like she had come back to tell me things she wanted me to do, like you'd say last-minute things if you were going on a trip," she recalled.

A young mother told me of her four-year-old son, whose paternal grandmother had died before he was born. One hot day he came into the house and asked for "a glass of water for the nice woman outside with the funny sparkly glasses." His mother hurried out, but could see no such person in sight in the fenced yard where he said she had been.

"Then," she said, "I realized he was describing a woman he had never seen. Her most distinctive characteristic was her Harlequin blue glasses, with the frames decorated with little rhinestones. I think she just wanted to see him one time. Knowing her, my only question is, what took her so long!"

My friend Lu Waters of the Theosophical Society told me that she sensed the presence of her late father-in-law in the hospital room with her when she was very ill, just after childbirth. "He was wearing the brown suit he was buried in, and he looked so nice," she recalled. "I was so ill, I didn't think it was strange to see him . . . then he just disappeared."

Another young Savannah woman told me that her husband, who was older than she, had died not long after the birth of their only child. As the little girl grew, she would often hear her laugh and chortle in her crib. "What a good-natured baby!" she would think to herself.

When the child was three years old, the mother was unpacking papers and old pictures she had put away as too painful to have out after her husband died. The child picked up a large framed portrait

This is a drawing of The Castle on Craven Street by Roger Kammerer.

and exclaimed, "Why, here's Daddy!" She had never been shown his picture before, since they did not live close to any of their families.

"That was unusual enough," said the mother, "but a few times when my daughter was supposedly alone, I would hear her call out, 'Mother, make Daddy stop tickling me!'"

SCENTS AT "THE CASTLE"

"The scent of roses is really overpowering," Stephen remarked as we entered the grounds of the 1856 Beaufort, South Carolina landmark dubbed "The Castle" because of its massive medieval look. "I can also sense a Victorian woman tending them."

The idea surprised me, as few flowers were in evidence in the fenced yard shadowed by large oak and palmetto. He investigated a small brick building which held gardening tools at the rear of the mansion, but quickly emerged, rather pale. "A meat house," he murmured, "spoiled meat. . . a terrible, lingering odor. Nauseous."

Later, a current resident told us that the yard had indeed once had landscaped rose gardens, the pride of a past mistress. "This was a Yankee hospital during The War," she added. "Sometimes at night we've heard the sound of horses, men in boots, and then found nothing. The brick building was the morgue for the hospital."

263

To Lay a Ghost

Unfortunately, not all spectral visits are happy ones. A Savannah woman told me of an incident which gave her nightmares for years. It involved her late grandmother, who had died when the girl was only twelve years old, in South Carolina.

"I suppose she loved me, but I was terrified of her," my friend Betty recalled. "She was a terrible, overbearing, sharp-voiced woman who gave my mother no peace. I was an only child. On the first anniversary of her death, I was asleep, and I had a terrible dream. In it, Mother and I were outside, and a big storm was coming. Dark clouds rolled across the sky, the winds blew harder and harder, and we were running toward the house.

"Then I was in bed, but I could hear my grandmother coming up the stairs . . . tap . . . tap . . . tap, with her cane. Then, it wasn't a dream any longer! I was awake, and she was really by the bed! She put her hand out, and oh, it was cold! I'll never forget it. I could smell a lavender perfume she always wore, see the black silk dress she had been buried in. . . .

"I screamed, and she went out the door. My mother came running, but I could still hear her, tap . . . tap . . . all the way down the stairs. I nearly had hysterics; it was weeks before I wanted to sleep alone again."

Just as Betty reached that point in the story, the buzzer around her neck sounded. It was a signal to call the office, and she hurried off to use the Oglethorpe Club telephone. In a few minutes she was back, looking puzzled.

"The office did not buzz me," she said as she sat down. "That has not happened since I've had the buzzer. I don't understand it."

"Unless it's Grandmother," said Stephen.

Another friend told me of how she dreaded the task of clearing out her mother's home, after her death. It was made more difficult by the fact that they had never been close, though she had been an only child. "I felt like an intruder in Mother's things," she said, "but someone had to do it.

"One funny thing. I was always determined to be out of that house by 4:30 in the afternoon. Don't ask me why that time was in my mind. It was just a feeling. No way I would have stayed later than that! I thought I was just trying to get out every day before it started to get dark.

"Then my mother's best friend said to me, 'The worst time for me is around 4:30. That's when I really miss your mother.'

"'Why then, especially?' I asked, just trying to get out the door.

"Well, you wouldn't know this, but we had a little ritual. No matter what she was doing, at 4:30 she'd be in that chair, with her drink. I'd come over, and we'd have our little social time together every night."

"DON'T ANSWER! DON'T ANSWER!"

A black woman who works at a house museum in Savannah told a poignant story of seeing the ghost of her dead sister, who had died in childbirth. She had taken the little girl to raise after that.

"Sometimes I would see her, all dressed in white," she recalled, "leaning over the crib. I'd run in and say, 'Get away from that child!' because I knew if she touched the baby, it would die. Then she'd go away, but sometimes she'd come back.

"As the baby got bigger, sometimes I'd hear her voice, faint and far away, calling it," she went on. "The little child would look up, like 'Who's that calling me?' and I'd say, 'Don't answer; don't answer!' See, if the baby had started to answer her, it would have died too. After a few years, the voice went away."

But she added that the sister's ghost had returned one more time, for a good reason. The niece had grown, and was living in Statesboro. One morning the aunt woke up, too ill to even call for help. After she had lain there half-conscious most of the morning, she was surprised and happy to hear a familiar step outside, and her niece's key in the lock.

The niece explained that the same morning, a figure in white had been standing by her bed when she awoke. She had the feeling that it wanted to communicate with her, but could not do so. Her first thought was for her aunt, whom she had not heard from all week, and she had decided to surprise her with a visit.

TOO MANY WOMEN

Another Savannah maid reported that her neighbor across the street on Savannah's west side, had been bothered with the ghost of his late wife. "They stopped the funeral procession at the house after the service at the funeral home on the way to the cemetery," she explained, "and that's how it all started. That let the spirit of the woman get back to her home."

After that, she went on, the poor man couldn't do anything without the presence being there. "One night just before dark, I was standing talking to him in the yard. I saw the light go on in his kitchen. 'You've got company,' I said.

"He said that it was just his wife, that she was always doing stunts like turning on lights, just to let him know she was still there. 'I sit down in the living room at night, and the light comes on over her chair, things like that,' he told me. Another time I was talking to him and he said, 'There she is, leaning against the car in the carport with a cigarette!' but I couldn't see anything.

"He told me the problem was, he was seein' another woman, and he figured that was her way of makin' him feel guilty."

A few weeks later, the same woman was asked how her neighbor was getting along. "She's still there, but it's all right," she replied. "You see, now his wife is gone, there are two or three women in the neighborhood after him at once.

"But he tells them all he can't have them comin' to his house 'cause of this ghost woman being there, so they have to wait until he wants to go see them. If it wasn't for havin' that ghost, I tell you, that poor man would never get any rest at all!"

"DON'T LOOK DOWN! DON'T LOOK BACK!"

If you have an unwelcome ghost around your house, it is easy to get rid of, the same woman believes. All you need to know is who it was in life, and where that person is buried.

She explained that her son-in-law, a widower with four little boys, had lived with his father on a little farm near Sylvania. Then the grandfather, who had been especially close to the youngest child, died.

"Well, after that, they saw the old man once or twice," she said. "They'd wake up at night, feeling that someone had shaken them awake. The covers would be thrown on the floor; the little boy was terrified, for he had seen his grandfather by his bed. But the father had heard of such things from his family, and knew what to do. "You need to go to the graveyard where that person is buried, and find the grave. You start at the gate, and you keep walking, until you reach the grave. Then you turn around, and you walk right over the grave, backwards, and step over the marker at the head. Then you stop, and you step back over the marker facing frontwards, and you walk down again right across the middle of the grave. You walk staight out of the graveyard, and go home. Don't look down and don't look back; now, that's the whole secret. That puts the ghost right back in the cemetery, and keeps them there, every time."

Reincarnation: The Second Chance?

"It is not more surprising to be born twice, than once," the French philosopher Voltaire believed. "Everything in nature is resurrection."

One common belief among the psychic personalities whom I have interviewed in the past few years has been one in reincarnation, or what Hans Holzer has called "the law of just retribution." The Warrens saw it as a progression from one astral plane to another, with each life offering new opportunities for personal development. The "old souls," the wise and gifted and philosophical of our time, are those with the most positive experiences in past lives on our planet.

"I would prefer to believe in reincarnation rather than to think Mozart just happened to be able to compose opera by the time he was five years old," said Stephen the first time we discussed the subject. "Old knowledge can easily be relearned, and we go on from there. I believe it is not ordinarily given to us to remember our past lives, but sometimes we have flashes of recognition."

To those who believe, this accounts for such things as the sense of deja vu, of having been in a place before, as well as for the intuitive like or dislike we feel for a person or place at first meeting, if this is a strong feeling with no other logical explanation. I asked Stephen to describe some of his experiences which he believes are from past lives.

"Well, as Claire has told you, I feel drawn to Tudor England," he began. "Once, going through a doorway in Savannah, it was like I was going through another doorway, one at the end of a long, dark tunnel with this room at the other end of it.

"I seemed to know instinctively I was in England. It was a small room, with a fireplace, windows with little panes, a green chest, a jeweled urn on a tray...then I was back in Savannah. Much later, and for the first time, I saw a picture of that room. It was an audition chamber in the Tower of London. I believe I was a musician at the court of Queen Elizabeth I. Not a member of the nobility, but someone who was accepted and liked.

"I really have an affinity to England," he went on, "although I've never been there. . . . I know about the gorse on the heath, and the cliffs dropping down to the sea. . . . I have had one recurring dream over the years which is like the opening chapter of a historic novel. I always see the same young woman, fair-haired, with her thick hair braided down her back. She is being held in a castle by a dark, brutal man who wants to give her to the invading Normans to cement his own alliance with them.

"I feel her sense of revulsion, and I know this is going to happen. Then I see her outside the castle, standing sadly on a little stone bridge, looking down at the water below. It is not very deep, she is thinking, not deep enough to jump into. . . . I see her going over the bridge and down a little hill, looking back at the castle as though she wants to get away, but knows that she can't, that even then she is being watched.

"It is not a story-book castle; it is a dark, massive, ugly stone fortress. I feel her sense of wanting to escape from whatever is there. . . . Then, I always wake up."

I knew that in reincarnation, there seems to often be memories of having lived as both sexes. Stephen described another intuitive flash he had experienced concerning an English monk.

"It happened as I was singing with the choir one Sunday morning," he explained. "I was coming in with the recessional, singing along in a normal way, when suddenly it all changed and instead I was in a very rude chapel in eleventh century England. I was a monk, in a heavy, coarse, long brown robe, tied at the waist. I was walking along in a processional with my fellow monks.

"It lasted for only a moment, but in that time I could clearly see all the details, the stone floor, the dark chapel with the candles, the rough, plain wood of the pews. Only the cross at the head of the procession was the same; maybe seeing it triggered the experience. Then I was back with the choir, marching and somewhat shaken, but still singing."

I remarked that I had read another theory for supposed reincarnation memories which says that there is some sort of a vast oversoul of universal knowledge. What seems to us to be flashes from our own past, are in reality recollections of things which have happened to others. By some process still unknown, we at times can pick these up with such great clarity, that they seem to be happening to us.

Others have theorized that one is simply remembering a stored forgotten memory triggered by a like event, such as visiting an old house similar to one in our past, or one we have seen in a movie or read about. However, many to whom such experiences happen, deny this as an answer.

"What I am talking about is a really clear feeling," said Stephen. "There is a sense that it happened to me personally. I also feel a deep affinity for people born about 1900, for 1920s clothing. I especially hate the sound of airplanes flying over; it absolutely terrifies me! This is such a strong emotion, I wonder if I am remembering a life cut short by the bombings of World War II."

By coincidence, Stephen's mother Etolia has remarked about a recurring dream in which she is trying to rescue a pilot in a World War II flying suit from a small wrecked plane.

"Maybe we're not supposed to know about these past lives because we need to go on, and not fall into old patterns," added Stephen. "When we do remember, it may be that we do not have a perfect erasure of that memory. Sometimes these subconscious residual memories may come out in dreams."

I thought of a young man in Savannah who told me he had experienced one such vivid dream, as a boy of twelve visiting in Ohio. It happened on a night when he was very tired, having just completed a long flight with his service parents from Panama to Columbus. By coincidence, though he did not know it at the time, he was spending the night in a brick home which had once belonged to a distant cousin of General Sherman's.

"I could see this woman, a young, pretty blonde woman, with two small children, babies, in her arms," he said. "First I would see her face, and then the children became clearer, first one and then the other. . . blonde little things, just like her. Twins. I was in a blue Civil War uniform, and I was saying goodbye. I knew they were my babies, and I would never see them again, and I awoke with an absolute desolate feeling of loss.

"In the dream, I was going out the door, and I don't remember coming back.

"Years later, here in Savannah, they were filming the Civil War movie The Lincoln Conspiracy out at Fort Pulaski," he went on. "I was in it as an extra; I just felt it was something that I had to do. I can't tell you how happy, how right, it felt to put on that uniform, even just to walk around on the movie set and march with the other soldiers. Those few days were among the happiest in my life."

"Sometimes I think this is why I like to work with antiques," said Stephen. "It's like I'm trying to get back to what I almost remember."

"Perhaps," I said, "people like to visit museums, and buy period furniture, for the same reason."

"Could be. There is also, you know, a theory about the peace movement, that the young people who were killed in the first two World Wars, and never got a chance to live their lives out, have come back. They are determined to see that it does not happen again."

"I was told by one psychic person that she believed I had been a Roman Christian girl who was killed by the lions," said Claire. "I do know my faith is very important to me, for whatever reason, in this life."

"I think that one reason I love the Savannah area so much," said Margaret Lee Dixon, "is that I feel I've been here before. I think that I was once an Indian boy out on Skidaway Island, completely free and happy. Maybe that's why I'm so independent! But I also think I was killed out there; I never lived to grow up in that life.

"I am also completely happy around the Pirates' House area of Savannah," she continued. "There is an old town house on a square near there, that I first recall passing in 1967. Then it hit me that I knew where I was; I'd been there before. Suddenly I could see every detail of that house as it had been nearly 200 years ago. I could see the parlor, with a tea set out, and a little old lady in black taffeta, pouring tea.

"I was young and pretty, happy and excited about something. Oh, I could see myself, yet at the same time, I knew it was me. I had just come in from outside, and I was wearing a little black velvet hat, and my hair hung down behind in long ringlets. I was laughing, describing something to her, and she was looking so fondly at me.

"When I saw that house, I felt as though I could describe everything that had been in its parlor. I don't know what it's like now, of course. I've never been inside. But I wish I had the courage to ring the bell, and look in!"

A young Savannah man told me that he had a recurring dream which seemed to involve the bayou country of Louisianna. "In the dream, I'm always walking up this long lane with the oaks and Spanish moss, and then I'm at this very old house. . .it's not much of a house now, it's really falling down, but it had been a fine one. . . always the same house.

"And there's always the same woman coming to meet me, young, pretty, very French-looking. . .Creole. In the dream, she always puts her arms around me and we go inside and. . .well, let's

271

just say I'd sure like to meet her in this life, and I'll know it, if I ever do."

A young Savannah woman named Anna told me that she was convinced that she had lived at least twice before, and probably more. In an earlier life, she believes that she was the daughter of an Indian chief whose entire tribe was killed by U.S. Cavalry in the prairie region in the 1870s. "My father from that experience is still with me at times as a spirit guide," she said.

"The second time, I was a woman in England, sometime after the turn of the century. I also know that when I lived in England a few years ago I felt totally at home there, and happier than I have ever been in my life.

"I had a most unusual experience a few years ago in the Holy Land," she went on. "I had gone there to work on an article on the fighting among the various groups. I was riding with a nurse and two soldiers in a jeep, alone out in the desert, near the front, when I heard a man's voice right at my ear. It did not belong to anyone I know now, but it said harshly and abruptly, 'Move!' Instinctively, I leaned over and turned to see who had spoken.

"At that moment, the woman beside me was killed by a sniper's bullet in her head. Had I not moved, it would have hit me first."

I thought of a Savannah midwife, who believes that her choice of a profession is hardly accidental. On her first case, supervised by a doctor in Charleston, she knew exactly what to do. After the delivery, he turned to her with, 'You didn't tell me you had done this before!' He could not believe, having witnessed her instinctive grasp of medical detail, that it was her first childbirth experience.

One Savannah woman who lives in a very historic house told me that she had an emotional affinity for everything having to do with the War between the States. Her favorite pin is a Maltese Cross, a design which she later learned has been the favorite of at least two other women, Sybil Leek and Mrs. Robert E. Lee.

I thought of my own love of the South, and of things suggestive of nineteenth century America: country antiques, small calico print patterns, shawls, blue china, patched quilts, high bedsteads, and old wash stands. There is a sense of looking for something I cannot name when I visit house museums. As the poet Dorothy Parker once asked, "What is it, what is it, I almost remember?"

ESP: A Bond Across Time and Space

"I don't know about ghosts, but I do believe in ESP. That has been proven in the laboratory," is a remark I have heard often in the past years. It is a tribute to the work of Dr. J. B. Rhine and others that what my Irish mother called "following your hunches" has become newly respectable.

"All persons have, to some degree, the ability to perceive things through ESP," Mary Ann Woodward of the Association for Research and Enlightenment at Virginia Beach told me once during a newspaper interview. "This is something that can be developed. You have to be open to such messages; you have to be aware."

My own belief in a communication capability we are only beginning to understand came out of a dramatic incident several years ago. It involved a college classmate, Laura. We had always said there was a special bond between us. We were such good friends; we understood each other so completely without a great deal of explanation.

Now move forward fourteen years from graduation, flipping the calendar pages as they do in the movies to denote the passage of time. I was sweeping the walk in front of our navy quarters on the Monterey Peninsula, when I suddenly thought of Laura. We had not spoken for nearly three years by telephone, and I had not heard from her since a hurried note on her Christmas card from the Washington, D.C., area.

Suddenly the impulse to call her, to hear her voice, was undeniable. I threw down the broom, hurried into the house, and got out my old Christmas card list for her address. Then I called information for her telephone number. How surprised she would be to hear my voice! Impatiently, I heard the telephone ringing a continent away.

I knew her throaty voice at once, though it somehow sounded blurred and weak. I would get a bad connection, I thought. She

273

seemed pleased to hear me, and was asking, "How are you?" I plunged into a recital of my recent life's adventures and why I had suddenly felt like calling her. Finally, stopping for breath, I waited for her reply.

Instead, in the telephone, I could hear the soft sound of sobbing. "You know I always thought of you as a sister," she was saying. "You were the best friend I ever had...." The voice trailed away as though she were no longer on the telephone.

Wild with anxiety, I kept calling into the receiver, "Laura, are you there?" There was no reply. I hung up, dialed again. The line was busy; then there was no answer. I had no idea what to do except to keep calling the number.

A few days later a note arrived, written while Laura was convalescing from the illness and depression which had almost taken her life. On the Sunday I had called her, she had felt too discouraged to go on. Telling her husband she was going to take a long nap, she went to the bedroom and closed the door. She got out a handful of sleeping pills, some aspirin, and a tumbler of vodka from a bottle she had hidden earlier. Then she lay down, just as the telephone rang.

She had tried to talk to me, and went to sleep with the receiver in her hand. In a few minutes, her husband looked in to see why the telephone was off the hook. He saw the pills and the bottle, and rushed her to Bethesda Naval Hospital. From the crisis, she wrote, some personal problems were resolved. This year they celebrated their silver wedding anniversary, and Laura is a happy and respected member of her profession. The two children have done well.

"This is all the proof I shall ever want," she wrote me, "that there are at times bonds of love and friendship that deny time and space, if the need is there."

OTHER CASES OF ESP

Of the several somewhat less dramatic cases told me recently, one involved a woman with an aching back in Texas when her sister went into early labor in North Carolina. The same woman told of an impulse to call the sister just before she was flying from Texas to see her family in Beaufort, S.C. The woman telling me the story denied the impulse, because she would be seeing the sister soon. The sister died in her sleep that night, her luggage packed for the flight.

A friend in Savannah told of having a wonderful time on the excursion train through the north Georgia mountains during "leaf season," when she was suddenly seized with such a feeling of apprehension that she insisted her husband call home from the next stop on the schedule. The family member answering the phone told them that a son had been badly injured in a motorcycle accident, and they had been frantically trying to think how to contact the train.

Later, when the boy went into surgery, my friend reported that her own arm became numb in sympathy; she was also taken to the hospital for observation, by friends who were sure she was having a stroke.

AVOIDING ACCIDENTS

Such discussions inevitably lead to the subject of precognitive experiences. Several which I have been told recently involve automobiles, not an unusual fact in our commuter society. One woman told me that while living in Texas, she loved to drive, had a new car, and went home to see her parents, a 250-mile trip, once a month. But one Friday she was scheduled to leave right after work, the Wilmington Island resident went on. She had felt so nervous and apprehensive that she had called and cancelled the visit.

"Since the weekend was shot anyway, I decided to take my car in the next day for a routine check at the garage," she recalled. "The attendant, a friend of mine, opened the hood and whistled. 'It's a good thing you didn't have this thing out on the highway!' he exclaimed. As he lightly touched the driveshaft, it fell into two pieces. 'This thing was hanging by a thread,' he pointed out. 'If that had happened in traffic, your steering would have been gone.'"

Two others spoke of being detained for a few minutes in unusual ways just short of the sites of potential accidents. Vicky Blitz recalled a trip when she had been driving, and her husband was in the other front seat. "Suddenly," she said, "as we pulled away from our lunch stop, the long hill ahead seemed very familiar and I didn't like it, though consciously I had not been there before. Seeing me hesitate, my husband asked if I wanted him to drive. I agreed, and as we changed sides, it seemed to me I had seen the whole scene before, in a dream.

"Those few minutes were quite timely, as further down the road, a car pulled out from under a tree, and crossed the road right in front of us. Of course he might not have hit us, but the sense of dread I had earlier, makes me remember the incident."

A Savannah man spoke of leaving his drug store one night, when his key refused to turn the lock. After several more tries, he had gone back for a spare key, and tried that with the same frustrating results. Inexplicably, his own key then turned the lock, and he went to his car.

"Just a few miles further," he recalled, "a little red sports car that had passed me while I was cursing at my lock, was in the road, totally destroyed by a tractor-trailer rig, and several other cars had lesser damage. I'm convinced it would have been me instead of the sports car if my lock had worked as it normally does. Strangely enough, it never gave me any trouble after that."

"WATCH THAT CAR!"

An Oatland Island mother told of being out in the car with her daughter, sixteen, who had a learner's permit, and was at the wheel. "We were doing the legal speed limit, and had just turned from Route 80 onto what they used to call Toll 80 toward Savannah. It was a beautiful day, and everything was fine. Suddenly, I noticied an old white Volkswagen in front of us, on which we were gaining. There was an older woman, white-haired, alone in it.

"I surprised and rather embarrassed myself by screaming, without stopping to think, 'Watch that car! Slow down! She doesn't know what she's doing!'

"'Honestly, Mother, your nerves are going,' my daughter said, somewhat exasperated, as she is really a good driver. But she did slow down a little, and watched the car. Suddenly it stopped, turned off the road, and made a U-turn, back toward Route 80.

"I'm not saying we would have hit her, but given my daughter's inexperience, and the fact that the other driver neither looked in our direction nor signalled, and the element of surprise, who knows?" she concluded. "But it was nice to have a little warning."

"THERE'S SOMETHING THERE"

"I have had three distinct cases of what I would term ESP in my life," said a Savannah writer on Tattnall Street. "They may sound trivial, but each case is clear in my mind because my premonition was so quickly fulfilled. They are enough to convince me that there is 'something there.'

"In the first," she went on, "I was working in the yard in north Georgia, building a patio with a pile of rock in the back yard. As I turned over one, the thought popped into my mind, 'This would be an ideal place for black widow spiders.'

"I very cautiously turned over the next rock, and sure enough, two spiders were on it and a whole colony underneath, where I had nearly placed my bare hand."

"Another time," she continued, "when my son was a baby, I

276

was preparing dinner for ourselves and a bachelor friend of my husband's. Suddenly the thought popped in my mind, 'He's going to buy Johnny a panda bear!'

"I smiled at the absurdity of it, our very dignified friend who did not even very much like children or toys, with a stuffed animal under his arm. But the mental picture had been there.

"After a while, the doorbell rang. I could hardly believe my eyes! There he stood, with his briefcase and a small toy panda bear! 'I just saw them in a shop window, and thought I'd get one,' he said, rather embarrassed. 'It was just an impulse; I hope he doesn't already have one.' As near as I could tell, he was buying the bear at the moment the thought of it came to me."

"The last case of that type I recall," she concluded, "happened several years ago with our daughter when she was about ten, and spending the night with a friend nearby. I was perfectly content to let her go, but then I awakened at two in the morning with the sudden thought, 'Now why did I let her do that? If she gets sick, Mary's mother is so lazy and selfish she won't get up to see about her.'

"But then a second, comforting thought came to me, 'Oh, but Larry (Mary's father) will.' And I went back to sleep. A little while later, the doorbell rang. There stood Larry, and our Jean.

"Sure enough, Jean had awakened during the night with an upset stomach, and wanted to go home. Mary's mother had called in for them to be quiet, and gone back to sleep. But the father had gotten up, determined the child was really ill, and brought her home to us—just as I somehow knew he would."

"Such Stuff As Dreams Are Made Of"

"We are such stuff
As dreams are made of,
And our little life
Is rounded with a sleep."
—William Shakespeare, "The Tempest," IV.i.

From earliest times, the experience of dreaming has caught the imagination of humanity. The Irish once believed that on St. John's Eve, June 23, souls visited the place where they would meet death. In some cultures, people have been afraid to sleep in a house where someone had recently died, because of a fear of being tempted away by the soul of the deceased. In ancient Greece, nightmares were considered supernatural visits which could be eased by some bread and rue under the pillow.

As Homer remarks in his *Odyssey*, there seem to be two kinds of dreams, "glimmering illusion, fantasies," and those which may "be borne out, if mortals only knew them."

For persons with whom I spoke while working on this book, the dreams recounted ranged from precognitive to those in which the subconscious mind seemed to continue working out a problem which had been on the dreamer's mind at the time of sleep. Some of the former concerned animals.

A Savannah photographer, Helen Converse, told me of a sad experience when she agreed to take care of her son's dog while the son went to England. "The very first night," she said, "I was busy, and someone let the dog out the door. He was hit by a car, and killed. I dreaded telling my son, but I didn't have to. About the time this happened, my son was asleep on a plane over the Atlantic. In his dream, he saw his dog being hit by a car. As soon as he landed, he called me, and I had to confirm it. In a way, he's never gotten over it."

On a more optimistic note, a Savannah woman told me she had

once had a persistent dream which literally helped to lay a ghost in her life. It involved a young man whom she had been desperately in love, a bright and charming fellow who had died tragically in an automobile accident. The girl had been miserable at home at this time, and the lover had been the only happy thing in her life.

"After a while," she told me, "I discovered that I could dream about him almost at will. I could go to sleep, and soon be back with him, going to parties, walking the beach, all the wonderful things we used to do. I knew it was unhealthy, but I couldn't seem to help myself.

"Then one night I dreamed we were outside of a friend's home, on the front porch, as though going to a party. I could see the happy people inside, hear the music and the laughter. But instead of going in the door, my friend just stood there and held me in the shadows.

"'Listen, you know you shouldn't be doing this, calling me back,' he said very gently. 'It isn't right. I have to go on, and you do, too. Now go in there, darling, and have a good time for both of us.' With that, he turned and walked off the porch without looking back. I awoke feeling stronger and more comforted than I had been at any time since his death. It had been so like him, telling me to go on! Years later, I dreamed of him one more time.

It was after she had married and raised a family, she explained. "In that dream, I was going out of our home here, and down the street. Suddenly I saw a fifty-year-old man, just a nice middle-aged fellow with a newspaper, coming toward me along the street. Somehow, I knew that it was that boy, as he would have looked now. He wasn't even as good looking as my husband! We met, spoke pleasantly, talked a few minutes, and then went on in different directions.

"Once again, it was something I needed—to be reminded how he would have looked if he had lived. I saw how unrealistic the mental picture I had of him in the back of my mind, where he was always twenty years old, was for my life, now. The strange thing is, I know that is really how he would have looked, had he lived."

During the period of working on this book, I had several dreams which struck me with their clarity. One seemed symbolic of my affection for the city of Savannah.

"In my dream," I told Stephen, "I was on a street that I instinctively knew was the historic section here. I was in a townhouse, and the people whom I knew, and now see about town, were with me, though their identities were indistinct when I woke up. In that one house, we were all in modern dress. But we could walk across the street, and then were in another, a period townhouse

279

of the 1860s, and we were all wearing clothing of that period. It was so clear to me that the same people were in both periods, like a play or a movie, but it was so real.

"One time, when I was in the 1860s house, I looked around and said, 'Well, who's going to be Sherman?' No one else was amused, and I felt very foolish."

"Maybe the dream was saying that you had been here before," said Stephen. "Would you recognize the street if you saw it again?"

"Well, it was a little like Jones Street. There were brick and stucco townhouses on each side, and shrubbery and trees. It was all kind of dim and shady."

Stephen smiled. "You have just described about half of the blocks in downtown Savannah."

In my second, more frightening dream, I had been out for an evening with friends. Then I was back at the home of a relative whom I had known, as though I were spending the night. My hostess sleepily got up from her bed as I came in, drowsily kissed me goodnight, and then lay down again.

As she touched me I drew back, thinking how cold she was. She seemed the same as I remembered, and yet different. Then I realized that she was wearing the same clothing, hair-do and makeup in which she had been buried. . . .

"Perhaps someone's trying to tell me something." I thought when I woke up. "Maybe I'm getting involved in something it would be better to leave alone," and I thought of the many stories concerning deceased persons which I had just heard. But then I realized that the same woman had taught me to finish whatever I started. At any rate, she has not been back.

My final dream occurred about the time I had finished writing this book. In it, I was going with Stephen late one afternoon to visit a house which we had heard was haunted, in the vicinity of Savannah's Victorian District just off Habersham Street. It seemed we had arrived at the large, old, unpainted two-story wooden house, and been invited inside. While Stephen was talking with the owner, I noticed a little white dog outside, wandering about as though lost. I left the house and pursued the dog for some time through the quiet streets, attempting to catch him. Then I realized that I was the one lost, and it was nearly dark.

After searching a while longer, there seemed to be nothing more to do but to go home. It seemed a symbolic end to our project, as though someone were telling me that part of our work was over, and so it was.

"Rapping" with the Spirits

During the latter half of the nineteenth century, one expression of the great interest in the subject of spiritualism was table tapping. In this exercise, the participants sat around the chosen piece of furniture, hands spread on its top, fingers touching to form "a magnetic circle." After contact with whatever forces were responsible for the subsequent activity was established, the tables would appear to move, tapping out answers to questions.

One of the best descriptions of this phenomenon is found in a book privately published by the late Savannah artist, Leonora Quarterman, in 1965. A descendant of an old Liberty County family, Miss Quarterman included in the book the memoirs of her father, Luther H. Quarterman, and of her mother, Elizabeth Walker Quarterman.

In the latter, the woman describes her life as a girl with the family of her brother, a young widower with three children. Because of his recent bereavement, they did not go out to parties or entertain when a young in-law whom he later married, Annie, came to visit. "We found what recreation we could among ourselves with books, music, and fun we could get out of the children," Elizabeth recalled.

"One of our amusements was, of all things, table rapping! This was a pastime considered very risque, closely allied to an intimacy with his Satanic majesty, not understood in the least as a demonstration of the fact that everything received into the human brain is indelibly recorded; there to emerge and declare itself on occasion; and probably also a demonstration of the control of mind over matter.

"Father never forbade our indulging in this pastime. He did very much to discourage it, as not being very wholesome because of the air of mystery involved. Weird things were sometimes brought to light. We found this medium a great help in locating lost articles.

"Once I mislaid a quite elaborate piece of embroidery I was

working on, and search as I might, I couldn't find it. On inquiring of the table, I was told to look on the bookshelf, find the sixth book from the left on the third shelf, and turn to page 261. There lay the neatly folded piece of work where I had placed it in some moment of abstraction, with my subconscious mind taking note of the action.

"But I am still baffled by what happened one night. We sat on the porch after supper in the dim moonlight, and amused ourselves as usual with this subject of inquiry and that. Annie suddenly exclaimed, 'Let's ask it where Florence's pin is!'

The pin, Elizabeth goes on to explain, was important because a friend had given it to Annie as a symbol of friendship while the same girl wore Annie's ring, a common sentimental Victorian custom. Now the young woman had misplaced the brooch, and was afraid to go home and face the friend without it. Hence the appeal to the table.

"The table began gently tapping on the floor. 'Are you ready?' asked Reade, the brother.

"One rap, 'Yes.'

"'Can you tell us where to find Florence's pin?'

"One rap, 'Yes.'

"'Well, please tell us, then.' For a few minutes, the table was silent.

"'Look under the dresser,' it spelled.

"'I've already looked there,' said Annie. 'It isn't there.'

"The table was motionless. No further questions induced any movement. Finally, after a space of time, it slowly spelled out, 'Look under the dresser.'

"With some impatience, Annie went inside, pulled the dresser out from the wall, and made a thorough search. With great irritation, she came back saying, 'It isn't there!'

"Then she was instructed, 'Look behind the wash stand.'

"The identical performance was repeated. On her return from this second fruitless search, Annie remarked disgustedly, 'It doesn't know anything! Let's ask it something else.' As soon as she put her hands back on the table to join ours, the table began hopping violently, as though to express anger.

"'What's the matter?' asked Reade. 'Do you want to tell us something?'

"One rap, 'Yes.'

"'Spell it, then.'

"Very slowly came the taps, spelling out, 'Take your hands off while I go and find that pin.'

"'How long do you want?'

"Slowly, almost meditatively, ten was rapped out on the floor.

"'Ten minutes?'

"'Yes.'

"So, we sat back in our chairs and talked of other things until ten minutes had been ticked off on Reade's pocket watch.

"'All right,' said he. 'Let's see what the thing knows now.'

"'It doesn't know a thing more now than it did before,' said Annie. 'It's a fraud.'

"We were placing our hands as she spoke. On the instant, without waiting to set up what we called the magnetic circuit, the table began moving.

"'Well, what have you to say now?'

"Briskly it tapped out, 'The washerwoman will bring it on Thursday.'

"'Now I know you are a fraud,' Annie cried in exasperation. 'The washerwoman doesn't bring the clothes, we go after them in the buggy, and we always go on Friday! Let's just forget the whole thing.'

"Angrily the table bounced for some seconds, then settled to immobility. No amount of coaxing could draw another rap for the whole evening! The strange thing was what followed.

"On Thursday, the washerwoman came walking in with the basket of clean laundry deftly balanced on her head. 'I been have to go off a piece tomorrow,' she announced. 'So, I bring de clothes myself.' She was paid, and took her departure.

"Annie stalked to the basket saying, 'Now, we'll prove that table is a falsifier!'

"With that, she drew off the covering cloth. There, on the very top of the pile, fastened into one of her shirtwaists just as she had left it, was Florence's pin!"

The late Sheriff J. E. McTeer of Beaufort wrote in his memoirs, *Fifty Years As A Low Country Witch Doctor*, about the psychic powers of his grandmother, Louisa Guerard Heyward, descendant of some of the leading families in South Carolina.

"Grandmother was a frail woman, but I have seen her join hands with a group of people around a table, and I have seen the table creak and groan as if it were trying to escape. Also, with no apparent effort on Grandmother's part, a Ouija board would seem filled with life."

Two Savannahians told me that they remembered the practice as children around the turn of the century. In both cases they were later forbidden by relatives to pursue the activity.

"We used to use an end table," said one. "I tell you, when we got going, we could make that table walk! This was in the dining room of a house on Henry Street. One night Dad was standing in the doorway, laughing at us, when he swore something brushed his shoulder. He made us put it away, and would never speak of it again."

"Oh, we used to do it in the house we grew up in on East Duffy Street," another elderly woman told me. "One night Uncle was coming down the stairs in the half-dark to see what was going on, and he swears something passed him. He would never let us do it again."

A Spectral Jest

"The preternatural has an enduring fascination for us all," John Laffiteau Sutlive, the late distinguished editor of the *Savannah Evening Press*, wrote in an article in the newspaper in 1965. "Ghosts interest or frighten us, the concern with seeing them or keeping out of their way being ageless. They weave their way through ancient literature, dominate many modern tales, and real or fancied, command an attentive audience. This is being currently demonstrated in Savannah through the reported antics of wraiths that walk aged stairways, and with the revival of tales of Low Country ghosts, who seem to be everlastingly restless.

"Men of science probe into the reports, seeking to determine the facts of the strange goings-on. Less scientific folk either believe in or scoff at the alleged apparitions, but among both the very mention of 'ghosts' has long whetted the inquisitive appetite of Savannahians."

Sutlive had been inspired to write of spectres, he went on, because he had just been reading in the scrapbook of his grandfather, John W. Sutlive. The elder Sutlive, also a noted journalist, had died during the terrible Savannah yellow fever epidemic of 1876. Earlier that same year, he had written a Savannah ghost story, which his grandson then preceded to reprint.

The story was headed "A Remarkable Phenomenon! Is it Electricity, Photography, or Spiritualism?" in an old-fashioned single-column headline, with the byline of Blackwell, the pen name of Sutlive. It told the strange story of a prominent jeweler of the town, who allegedly glanced through the front window of his shop one day to find a well-dressed, middle-aged stranger looking through the glass. After a few minutes the merchant became curious, as the man seemed to be staring into the store itself rather than at the merchandise.

"Not appreciating such steady surveillance of his premises by an entire stranger," the story stated, "he went to the door for a closer

285

observation of the party. Judge of his surprise, when upon looking out into the street, no one was to be seen! This performance was repeated several times, and each time with the same result. The form was seen gazing in at the window when the proprietor was inside the store, but all efforts to find a corresponding form on the outside were unavailing.

"The form left the window about 2:30 p.m., withdrawing apparently like any other casual observer. On the following day the same thing was repeated, the form appearing about 11:30 a.m., and retiring at the same hour as before."

At that point, it went on, the merchant called in two of his businessmen friends for a committee of observation. Again the next day at the same time, the phenomenon was repeated. After three hours, the man appeared to turn and leave his post, but nothing could be seen from the outside.

The next day a "photographic expert and a celebrated scientific gentleman" were invited to the store. They gravely pronounced after several hours that they knew of no photographic or scientific law which would account for the sightings.

The mystery deepened when a retired Colonel, a descendant of one of Savannah's earliest families, happened in the store while the earnest, aristocratic-looking stranger was visible through the window. In surprise, he recognized "the exact likeness of Le Comte Poisson d'Avril, a French nobleman. Driven from France on account of his zealous advocacy of religious tolerance about 1728, he had fled to England for safety, and joined Oglethorpe in his colonial expedition to America, being one of his most trusted friends and advisors."

In fact, he added, he even had a picture at home of the gentleman, except that he was dressed in the clothing of the eighteenth century. The story ended with the promise to contact "one of our most learned professors, who has devoted much time to researches into electricity and electro-magnetism in connection with their effects under certain atmospheric conditions." A full report of his findings was to be made in a later edition of the paper.

Intrigued by the story, but puzzled at finding no further references to this "tale of tales about Savannah ghosts," John Sutlive turned his attention to the matter in the best tradition of investigative reporting. There was no mention of such a count in the early Georgia history books on his shelf. He determined to write the French Embassy in Washington.

"I had no sooner typed out the word 'Poisson' then I smelled something," he wrote. "I have very little French except my middle name, but I have read menus. That word, I said to myself, means

286

'fish.' Reaching for the *Dictionary of Foreign Terms*, I turned to the listings. There is was, under 'p,'—*poisson d'avril*, lit., fish of April; mackrel; April-fool joke.

"If my grandfather's ghost is among those reputedly still in touch with Savannah," he concluded good-naturedly," he must have had a good chuckle over his grandson swallowing in 1965 the bait of the 'remarkable phenomenon' story, which was published, as I know now, in the *Savannah Morning News* on Saturday, April First, 1876."

"John all hippl'd up,
John all crippl'd up,
Give John a dime and
Raise John's spirit up.
Anybody want John, call
John back."
—Fish hawker's cry, Savannah, early 1900s.

When The Savannah Police Played "Ghost"

Along with its many other municipal "firsts," as recited by the local Chamber of Commerce, Savannah may be the first and only city in the country where an attempt to force a confession from a murder suspect was made by a police officer dressed as a ghost. This was more than seventy years ago, long before the recent Supreme Court rulings on the information rights of the accused. But it didn't work.

One thing about growing up with real ghosts; you can spot an imitation every time.

The incident occurred after one of Savannah's most bloody and brutal crimes, a triple murder at a rooming house on the southwest corner of Montgomery and Perry Streets. Found dead on a raw and unpleasant December 10, 1909 day, were Mrs. Elizabeth Gribble, the elderly, hard-of-hearing landlady, and her daughter, "Miss Carrie," a Mrs. Ohlander. So badly injured that she died the next day, murmuring her estranged husband's name, was Mrs. Maggie Hunter, a thirty-five-year-old seamstress. An axe and knife, perhaps a hammer, were thought to be the missing murder weapons.

Emotional crowds thronged around the house that night, and in the nearby square. Many were armed, and one suspect was threatened with mob violence. Blood hounds were unsuccessfully brought out. A reward of $1,000 was offered for the apprehension of the killer.

Suspicion soon centered around a recently-hired black handyman, "Shorty" Cooper, who had disappeared immediately after the crime was discovered. Found six weeks later and grilled intensively, he surprised the detectives by having adequate alibis for his defense.

Then the county police produced Bingham Bryant, who had

288

been arrested four days after the murder for stealing a carpenter's plane. He was said to be wearing blood stained clothing when arraigned, and to have blood stains under his finger nails. Desperate for a confession, the detectives placed three life-sized figures from a local clothing store in the house, reenacting the murder scene. A large quantity of red ink was used for realism.

As Bryant was brought into the house under heavy guard, an officer dressed as a ghost stepped forward. He confronted the suspect with the terrible crime, and accused him of murdering the three innocent women. The accused cooly looked at his disguise, and told him he was mistaken.

After that the case against Bryant, too, seemed to fall apart. One woman accused him of stealing her turkey, which might have accounted for the blood on his clothing. He went back to jail for theft, but the murder charge was dropped.

Then one of the patrolmen remembered that J. C. Hunter, sixty-six, the husband of one of the victims, had been arrested on the Ogeechee Road a few months earlier for chasing his wife with an axe handle. Others testified that he had said in the past that he would like to see her dead. One recalled that he had been standing before the Gribble house the day of the murders, in the crowd, and had remarked, "Somebody's gone to Hell today."

Although he had been working nearby on a house on Oglethorpe Avenue on the fatal day, Hunter protested his innocence. The five bricklayers on the job with him were ready to corroborate his story. However, one was his son-in-law, and all were, like him, from Effingham County.

On May 28, after a twenty-six-minute deliberation, the jury came back with a murder verdict on the dramatic stroke of midnight. Hunter was sentenced to be hanged, but was later given life imprisonment. In failing health, he was later moved to a rest home, where he died.

For years afterward, the house at Montgomery and Perry Streets was reported to be haunted. From time to time, no matter how often it was repainted, blood stains were said to appear on the walls of the rooms where the crime took place. The old house was eventually torn down, and a commercial building is now on the site of Savannah's triple tragedy.

The Man Who Cursed Savannah

After the heady optimism of the trans-Atlantic voyage of the S. S. *Savannah* and the building of some of the region's most famous mansions, the city on the river fell on very hard times. First there was the national depression of 1819, which affected shipping, followed by the great fire of 1820 and the yellow fever epidemic later the same year, which caused much of the population to leave town.

Even the brilliant young architect William Jay, who had been the designer of Savannah's finest buildings, was so disillusioned that he went to Charleston with the comment; "Savannah had become a Niobe of cities, a chaos of ruins. Who can trace the void without remembering her former greatness? She was rising a model; she has fallen as a monument."

Another youthful resident, the physician and publisher Dr. John M. Harney, was equally disgruntled. Two years before, he had started a weekly newspaper, *The Georgian*. Embittered by its local reception and other problems, he sold it in 1820 to I. K. Tefft, a businessman later famous for his autograph collection, and Harry James Finn, an actor with the troupe which had opened the Savannah Theater.

In his last issue, Harney published a long, rambling, vitriolic poem which he called, "A Farewell to Savannah, or, Curse on Savannah," which began:

Farewell, oh, Savannah, forever farewell,
Thou hotbed of rogues, thou threshold of hell.

A later physician and author, Dr. Richard Arnold, called Harney "an erratic son of genius...a brilliant Bohemian, and he exhausted the patience and purses of his friends, which were both on a liberal scale." Some say he was especially angry because the city officials would not allow his black house servants to have a party at his home, near what is now the Broughton Street business district.

For Harney, his Savannah problems are the latest in a dramatic, nomadic life which had begun in Delaware in 1789. He studied medicine, and served in the army as a surgeon. After the death of his first wife in Tennessee he sought solace in travel, and toured England, France, Italy, and India. Later he went to South America, and served for a short time in the Brazilian navy.

Then he came to Savannah, and married Eliza Cooper Rowen, daughter of Judge John Rowen, in 1814. While in Savannah he wrote for several literary journals, and gained a reputation as a poet. One of his best-known poems, "Dream Fever," was probably written about his bout with yellow fever.

After leaving Savannah, Harney took his wife and young daughter to Bardstown, Kentucky, where he died at age thirty-six in 1825. His newspaper in Savannah later merged with another weekly, the *Journal and Courier*, and then both disappeared.

Harney and *The Georgian* are remembered now mostly for the poem which complained:

> But the soil of Savannah new vigor imparts
> To vices transplanted from all foreign parts.
> Cursed be the winds that blew me to your strand,
> Your houses are board, and your alleys are sand!

After cataloging evils which ranged from slavery to mercenary merchants and fickle women, it dramatically ended:

> Now to finish my curses upon your ill city,
> And express in few words all the sum of my ditty,
> I leave you, Savannah, a curse that is far
> The worst of all curses—to remain as you are!

Just a story, of course. Yet, over 160 years after Harney's departure, the houses of his time are lovingly restored and refurbished in the fashions of an era he deplored. The Davenport, Hampton Lillibridge, Wayne-Gordon, and Jay's own Owens-Thomas, Telfair, and Scarbrough houses are still beautifully maintained. Regency decor is the most fashionable in the historic area, even inspiring the theme of a restaurant, museum gift shop, and the new Hyatt Hotel on River Street. The house colors, wallpaper, and furniture of Harney's time have been cataloged and duplicated, and are now widely available in replicas.

Meanwhile, the city he slandered has survived fires, earthquakes,

291

epidemics, and hurricanes. Even the punishing torch of General Sherman's infamous march stopped just at its gates, and then turned to the destruction of South Carolina a few weeks later. Savannah's flourishing restoration movement has not only won national acclaim, but it has brought the doctor's curse of an unchanging city, set in time, closer to reality than he could ever have imagined.

Its ghosts could not be happier.

Spectres: In Conclusion

We live today in a time of greater interest in the supernatural and occult. Some fundamentalist Christians, remembering the Biblical warnings against sorcery and witchcraft, view such inquiry with horror. They fear the Demonic, pacts with Lucifer, Satanic cults of fallen angels, the darker possibilities of strange rites under the full moon.

Others scoff at what they see as a step backward from the light of scientific knowledge toward the darkness of witch hunts and superstition.

Some have likened the new interest in spiritualistic topics to the popularity of the subject around the turn of the century, when such disparate men as Carl Jung, Luther Burbank, Julian Huxley and Sir Arthur Conan Doyle were fascinated by the theories then expounded. Thomas Edison is said to have worked on a telephone with which he hoped to communicate with the dead. Philosopher William James helped found the American Society for Psychical Research in 1895. Sigmund Freud is quoted as saying on his deathbed that he wished he had specialized in psychic rather than psychiatric studies.

This interest manifested itself more popularly in parlor games such as table tapping and Ouija boards, sometimes with unfortunate results. Tragically, it was also employed by unscrupulous persons who rigged seance rooms with all sorts of devices to mislead the credulous, preying on grief and emotional instability in their professed ability to reach the deceased. The resulting disillusionment has since clouded the entire subject.

It has also been said that today's new awareness of the supernatural is another manifestation of the same search for something in which to believe which has caused the decline of rationalistic religious groups, and the growth of fundamentalist, charismatic ones. Some see it as simply escapism, a more chic form of Victorian table tapping.

293

At the time when part of the public feels that modern science has created an almost inhabitable world, others are questioning the primary assumptions on which that world seemed so firmly based only a few years ago, such as the nature of time and matter, and our own perceptions of reality.

Meanwhile, much of the religious establishment, both liberal and fundamental, view psychic research as suspect, a kind of philosophical red-headed step-child. Others think it is strange that the two institutions most concerned with the subject of informed life in this world and the next, have avoided a subject in which so many have claimed experience. Some point out that you cannot eradicate belief in a thing simply by stating that it does not exist.

To be sure, parapsychology has made some notable advances in the last fifty years, such as the studies in ESP and other phenomenon which Dr. J. B. Rhine and others conducted at Duke University, and those suggestive of reincarnation which have been carried on by Professor Ian Stevenson and others at the University of Virginia.

Membership was granted by the American Association for the Advancement of Science to the Parapsychological Association, an international group, in 1969 as the result of anthropologist Margaret Mead's speech to the Association. In it she said, "The whole history of scientific advance is full of scientists investigating phenomena that the establishment did not believe was there."

"ESP research," Dr. Rhine said of his work, "is at about the stage where general psychology was about a hundred years ago."

Studying available material on the subject, one might wish for a less prejudicial vocabulary. The very words paranormal, supernatural, and parapsychology hint that we are talking about subjects beyond the realm of science and everyday experience, as though the rest of our knowledge had already been neatly filed and cataloged. Those having unusual experiences in their homes, during an illness, or waking in the middle of the night to the heavy and accurate knowledge of a family tragedy before the telephone rings in the darkness on the bedside table, are thus somehow outside the accepted limits of human activity.

There is no lonelier person than the individual who takes such an experience to his religious advisor, physician, or another family member, only to be told it is only one's imagination, a hallucination, or even a Satanic overture. However, according to one study conducted by the University of Chicago's National Opinion Research Center several years ago, 36 percent of those interviewed reported feelings of contact at some point in their lives with "a superior force which seemed to lift them out of themselves," according to the

Reverend Andrew Greeley, a priest and sociologist at the center. Sixty-one percent told of deja vu feelings of having seen or done something before, when in reality one has not. Thirty-four percent reported having experienced the sensation of contact with dead relatives or friends.

Some, including my friend Stephen, believe that we may be on the verge of a breakthrough in which new proof of life after death will merge with fresh scientific knowledge about the nature of life and death as a continuous process. There may even be an explanation for such things which both the theologian and the scientist can accept.

"The person of science," says Lorraine Warren, "tries to prove what the person of faith already knows."

"I feel it is given to the average person to have only one or two of these experiences in a lifetime," Stephen concluded of some of the stories here. "Perhaps it is to tell us there is more to this life than what we can see, smell, and touch. . . . For most of us, once or twice a lifetime is enough!"

This research has been rewarding for me in that it has made me more personally aware of the central theme with which many of the stories dwell, however indirectly, the survival of the human personality beyond death. Rather than being enticed by demons, the result has been an enrichment of my own faith, as well as an appreciation of the infinite wonders of existence.